Education, Conflict and Development

Education, Conflict and Development

Edited by
Julia Paulson

Oxford Studies in Comparative Education
Series Editor: David Phillips

SYMPOSIUM
BOOKS

Symposium Books Ltd
PO Box 204, Didcot, Oxford OX11 9ZQ, United Kingdom
www.symposium-books.co.uk

Published in the United Kingdom, 2011

ISBN 978-1-873927-46-5

This publication is also available on a subscription basis
as Volume 20 Number 2 of *Oxford Studies in Comparative Education*
(ISSN 0961-2149)

Printed and bound in the United Kingdom by Hobbs the Printers, Southampton
www.hobbs.uk.com

Contents

INTRODUCTION

Education, Conflict and Development

JULIA PAULSON

In recent years education in emergencies has become 'a key priority for the international community' (United Nations General Assembly, 2010). From the early advocacy of those who saw first hand the lack of adequate educational services available to communities displaced by armed conflict (Sommers, 1999; Crisp et al, 2001; Sinclair, 2001, 2002), to the effective work of the Inter-Agency Network for Education in Emergencies (INEE), who have, among other things, created minimum standards for education preparedness, response and recovery (2010), to the commitment of major international donors and organizations, the need for quality education in and after disasters and violent conflict is well recognized. With approximately half of the world's out-of-school children living in countries affected by conflict, the reasons for this growing international priority are clear (Save the Children, 2008).

This volume aims to investigate the changing contours of international work around this clearly acknowledged need. The book centres upon the investigation of three processes – education, conflict and development – and the relationships between them. Some of these relationships have been well established, while others are under-researched and little understood. The interactions of the three together, the ways in which conflict might confuse connections between education and development, for instance, are still largely unclear.

The interactions between the first two processes – conflict and education – are, at least in one direction, relatively well understood. That is, the multitude of ways in which conflict can involve, limit, damage and destroy education are now widely acknowledged and have been evidenced in many countries and communities. Resources are often directed away from education in times of conflict, sometimes to the degree of complete neglect for education services from central governments. Communities of teachers and learners are disrupted, threatened and displaced – schools can be become sites for attack, abduction and recruitment or can be abandoned entirely. The content and delivery of education itself can also feed into conflict dynamics, perpetuating particular versions of history, teaching stereotypes and hatred and excluding the perspectives of particular communities. Access (or lack thereof) to education can reflect and maintain social inequality and poverty. Despite these 'negative faces' of education, its importance is maintained by the international actors outlined above, at least in part, because communities affected by conflict continue to prioritize and seek it out. In post-war Sierra Leone, education for their children was the first priority for families after securing basic needs like health care and shelter (Graybill & Lanegran, 2004).

Like the ways that conflict can affect education, the ways that education can prevent and transform, and assist in the recovery from conflict are well articulated. With the international commitment to education for those affected by conflict come a number of promises – protection for children; psychosocial care; a returned sense of normalcy; a tangible service incentive to maintain peace; access to skills, jobs and future livelihoods; values and knowledge for human rights, citizenship and peace; a democratizing effect; reconstruction; reconciliation; economic growth; a lasting peace. The priority around education in emergencies has emerged at the international level, based, at least in part, on the presumed ability of education to lead to, or at least to contribute towards, this long list of positive outcomes. However, while ample evidence – well-researched and anecdotal – exists to demonstrate the ways that conflict affects education (see for example, Bush & Saltarelli, 2000; O'Malley, 2010), these promises rely more on the normative power of education than they do on evidence of education's contribution in conflict-affected communities. It is in order to better understand the ways that education might affect and transform conflict and post-conflict situations that the third central process – development – becomes critical.

Education has long been a key part of various development agendas. Those that strive for the recognition of universal human rights around the world see education as an enabling right, critical to achieving other fundamental rights (Annan, 1999). Education is also important for those who find the key to development in economic growth, with evidence that higher levels of education lead to higher individual earning and, within a society, to macroeconomic growth (World Bank, 2009). For proponents of development through democratization, education is also an important component, with research linking higher levels of enrolment and literacy with stronger democratic institutions and strong social cohesion (World Bank, 2009). The relationship between education and development is tight, well researched and multifaceted. As development actors increasingly cooperate and align their priorities, around, for instance, the Millennium Development Goals (MDGs) and the harmonization of aid delivery, education is a broad priority that they can all agree upon. Education has been shown to be a key area for the broader rapprochement between social or rights based approaches to development and those more oriented towards economic growth, since it offers normative promises as a foundation for both (Mundy, 2006).

Within this broad consensus about the importance of education, education in emergencies occupies a firm place on the agendas of development actors. The aspirations for education in emergencies have moved beyond the early campaign to make education a 'fourth pillar of humanitarian response' (Nicolai & Triplehorn, 2003) towards more developmental concerns and outcomes. Those working towards meeting Education for All (EFA) and Millennium Development Goals (MDGs) acknowledge the challenges that conflict poses to goals for universal primary education and gender parity alike. Conflict will be the focus of the 2011 EFA Global Monitoring Report, which charts progress towards and challenges facing the achievement of the EFA goals. Conflict will also orient the 2011 World Development Report, authored by the World Bank, which remains one of the largest contributors towards educational initiatives around the world. The knowledge of the ways that education can be 'complicit' (Buckland, 2005) in conflict does not limit the degree to which education's potential is heralded and promised in post-conflict situations.

This volume seeks to provide more evidence as to whether and how education meets the promises its advocates make for it in post-conflict societies. Contributors seek to explore the potential contradictions between education and development in situations where the legacies of conflict and education's role within it loom large – to discover how and in what ways particular educational policies and initiatives might erase education's negative faces and open space for its promises to be enacted. Contributors also ask questions about and trace the ways in which education in emergencies operates within, among and alongside development agendas and aspirations. This means that contributors analyse the politics, language and actions behind education in emergencies as an international priority, as well the effects of its interventions in discrete contexts around the world. The first part of the book, in particular, focuses on these conceptual elements, teasing out the historical, political and discursive influences that have helped to configure the present commitment towards education and emergencies and that continue to affect the possibilities for education to meet its promises, both humanitarian and developmental. The second part explores the relationships between education, conflict and development through a series of international case studies – highlighting the diverse and complex ways in which education is expected to and can contribute towards development in the post-conflict context. The third part of the book takes Northern Uganda as its focus. Here contributors explore the legacies of conflict in classrooms and on learners and teachers, collectively highlighting the need to better understand peacebuilding processes and education's role therein in order to best see education contributing to development in post-conflict Northern Uganda.

Part 1: Concepts, Relationships and Assumptions

In this first section contributors adopt various approaches towards understanding the processes at the core of the book, the relationships between them and the assumptions that underpin them. In the opening chapter, Colin Brock reflects on what he calls the 'fundamental relationship' between education and conflict, detailing a much longer and more entwined relationship than current international discourse around education in emergencies suggests. The 'education as a humanitarian response' that Brock proposes is much different from that which early on drove the development of education in emergencies as a priority, and is rooted in education's potentials to deliver justice and equality in the face of conflicts not just violent, but environmental, economic and global.

Stephanie E.L. Bengtsson's chapter usefully draws the reader's attention to the language of education in emergencies. In exploring what is meant by the term 'fragility' – a 'buzz phrase' that has guided the educational work of many international actors in conflict contexts – Bengtsson highlights the lack of conceptual clarity behind an agenda that has spurred considerable work around the world. Bengtsson shows how lack of clarity and consensus does not necessarily limit action, but does limit the kinds of solutions that can be imagined and, importantly, the effect that those solutions can have on educational realities in situations affected by conflict.

Jeremy Rappleye's reflections on the education, conflict and development relationship in Nepal closes the first section. Rappleye's chapter insightfully shows how the assumptions that various actors carry about development and progress shape the ways in which they envision education's contribution towards transforming conflict. Rappleye shows how the promises of development are premised on assumptions in much the same way as those around education are. Rappleye argues against presumed causal relationships between conflict, education and development that cover over this uncertainty and highlights the limitations of the prescriptions for peace that emerge based upon them.

Part 2: Understanding Relationships: country case studies

Language, politics and assumptions continue to prove important in the case studies offered in this second section. Here contributors turn their attention to conflict, education and development in a diverse set of case studies. Christine Pagen's chapter explores the ways in which adults in southern Sudan learn about concepts of human rights and democracy. This kind of learning is thought to be central to the internationally sponsored development process in southern Sudan, in which democratization takes centre stage and international norms shape reconstruction. In Pagen's work international agencies themselves emerge as important sources of learning about these concepts, with interesting implications for the promotion of formal, informal and non-formal education in post-conflict contexts.

In the next chapter Mitsuko Matsumoto engages young people in Sierra Leone in assessing the contribution that education has made towards development in the years since the civil war. Matsumoto argues that for education to make any meaningful contribution towards peacebuilding and development in Sierra Leone, the relationship between education and state and society must be transformed from the pre-war relationship that played into the conditions of conflict. From the perspectives of the young people that Matsumoto works with, this change has not occurred, in part because of the presumption on the part of the international community that education can operate independently from the society in which it is embedded.

Tomoe Otsuki's fascinating exploration of the development of a joint textbook initiative between Japan, China and South Korea closes this section. Otsuki's chapter is important in reminding readers of the long and disparate legacies of conflict within societies and of the need to reconcile conflict experience across borders and generations. Like earlier contributors, Otsuki's work broadens the theoretical and temporal considerations of the book beyond the normal confines of education in emergencies while highlighting concerns that will resonate with scholars and practitioners who locate their work squarely within it.

Part 3: Education, Conflict and Development in Northern Uganda

The final part of this book takes the post-conflict situation in Northern Uganda as its focus and offers three pieces of recent research there. All illuminate the challenges facing children, young people and educators and call upon education to respond specifically and preferentially to these needs in order to best contribute towards building peace and fostering development in the region. Maureen Murphy, Lindsay Stark, Michael Wessells, Neil Boothby & Alastair Ager open the section by presenting important results from their research into sexual violence and educational opportunities for girls in the region. The authors found that all girls in the study, whether survivors of sexual violence or not, faced barriers to accessing and remaining in education – those girls that were survivors of sexual violence were therefore 'doubly disadvantaged' as these experiences compounded the other barriers to schooling that they already faced. The findings from the study call for education that is responsive to eliminating the barriers that face vulnerable groups, including girls in general and survivors of sexual violence in particular.

Next, Betty Akullu Ezati, Cornelius Ssempala & Peter Ssenkusu offer important findings from their study into the effects of conflict experiences on teachers and learners' classroom experiences in Northern Uganda. These researchers expand understandings of the ways that experiences of violence and displacement affect young people and educators and their possibilities for teaching and learning. The authors show how poor learning outcomes and low educational quality are not only symptomatic of the post-conflict context but can result from and be maintained by it when the specific and conflict-related emotional, psychosocial, physical and economic needs of students and teachers are not met. Education still serves important purposes – like offering a sense of acceptance, providing something to do, etc. – to these young people, but like the evidence from the previous chapter suggests, its more development-related promises hinge on meeting learners' specific and conflict-related needs.

Jeremy Cunningham's chapter also looks at what schools are and are not doing for children in Northern Uganda by assessing their contributions towards peacebuilding through school practice. Cunningham offers a framework through which knowledge, values and actions for skills learned at school might be considered as 'peacebuilding education' and finds some early evidence of this kind of education in practice in Northern Uganda. By deepening opportunities for this kind of education within the formal curriculum, extra-curricular activities and school culture, Cunningham makes recommendations to enhance the peacebuilding potential of educational practice.

Conclusions and New Directions

The chapters in this book come from varying perspectives and draw on evidence from a diverse set of case-study countries and from the international-level practice of education in emergencies. They do not all reach a common set of conclusions. Indeed, they sometimes differ not just in their assessment of the contributions of particular post-conflict educational initiatives towards broader social and economic development, but also in their overall understandings of the potential for those working in education in emergencies to contribute towards development. For Christine Pagen, there may be potential in understanding international organizations like USAID as educators themselves, spreading international norms as much through their presence and practice as through their intentionally educative activities. For Jeremy Rappleye, this spread of democratizing norms on the part of USAID and other international agencies is part and parcel of that which must be analysed and questioned in order to reveal the opaqueness and complexity at the centre of the relationships in question in this volume. Rappleye and others in the volume insist on pulling the discourse and practice of education in emergencies and its various actors into the analysis of the relationship between conflict, education and development.

This expanding of the frame of reference for research around education in emergencies is an important contribution from the authors of this volume. Stephanie E.L. Bengtsson usefully brings the language of education in emergencies to bear on the possibilities that it can open and close for educational change around the world. Tomoe Otsuki shows how issues such as curriculum development, which are important to those working in short and medium term educational response to conflict, continue to divide communities more than 65 years since the termination of the Second World

War. Colin Brock shows how conflicts beyond the violent are also relevant to understanding and harnessing the promises of education, drawing attention to environmental issues and to persistent inequalities around the world.

Along with expanding the scope of research and analysis within and about education in emergencies, however, contributors also remind researchers of some fundamentally important elements of educational research in general that must continue to be fundamental to research in education in emergencies. Mitsuko Matsumoto usefully insists that the relationship between education and the society in which it operates must be of interest not only to researchers but also to those who design and implement educational initiatives. Programmes that assume that education can function independently from society will succeed in transforming neither education nor broader society and its development. Likewise, Matsumoto and the contributors to the third part of the book who ground their research in the experiences of young people, remind us of a critical point. Their work firmly demonstrates that, in addition to seeking to understand what education does discursively, at the international level, or in combination with particular assumptions and political underpinnings, we must also, crucially, seek to understand what it does for children and young people. Perhaps in seeking to transform education at this level, to ensure that it meets the specific needs of girls and boys affected by conflict, the complex influences of these other international-level phenomena on educational outcomes will become less significant.

References

Annan, K. (1999) Foreword, in C. Belamy (Ed.) *The State of the World's Children 1999*. New York: UNICEF.

Buckland, P. (2005) *Reshaping the Future: education and postconflict reconstruction*. Washington, DC: World Bank.

Bush, K. & Saltarelli, D. (2000) *The Two Faces of Education in Ethnic Conflict: towards a peacebuilding education for children*. Florence: UNICEF.

Crisp, J., Talbot, C. & Cipollone, D. (Eds) (2001) *Learning for a Future: refugee education in developing countries*. Geneva: United Nations High Commission for Refugees.

Graybill, L. & Lanegran, K. (2004) Truth, Justice and Reconciliation in Africa: issues and cases, *African Studies Quarterly*, 8(1), 1-10.

Inter-Agency Network for Education in Emergencies (INEE) (2010) *Minimum Standards for Education: preparedness, response, recovery*, 2nd edn. New York: INEE.

Mundy, K. (2006) Education for All and the New Development Compact, *Review of Education*, 52, 23-48.

Nicolai, S. & Triplehorn, C. (2003) The Role of Education in Protecting Children in Conflict, Humanitarian Practice Network. HPN Paper 42. London: Overseas Development Institute.

O'Malley, B. (2010), *Education under Attack*. Paris: UNESCO.

Save the Children (2008) Children in Conflict-Affected Countries Short-Changed in Education Funding. News release. http://www.savethechildren.net/alliance/media/newsdesk/2008-06-03.html

Sinclair, M. (2001) Education in Emergencies, in J. Crisp, C. Talbot & D. Cipollone (Eds) *Learning for a Future: refugee education in developing countries*. Geneva: United Nations High Commission for Refugees.

Sinclair, M. (2002) *Planning Education in and after Emergencies*. Paris: International Institute for Educational Planning.

Sommers, M. (1999) *Emergency Education for Children*. Cambridge, MA: Mellon Foundation/MIT.

United Nations General Assembly (2010) The Right to Education in Emergency Situations. A/64/L.58. http://www.ineesite.org/uploads/documents/store/UN_Resolution_Education_in_Emergencies.pdf (accessed 22 July 2010).

World Bank (2009) Education and the World Bank. http://web.worldbank.org/WBSITE/EXTERNAL/TOPICS/EXTEDUCATION/0,,menuPK:282391~pagePK:149018~piPK:149093~theSitePK:282386,00.html

PART 1

Concepts, Relationships and Assumptions

CHAPTER 1

Education and Conflict: a fundamental relationship

COLIN BROCK

SUMMARY This chapter considers the relationship between education and conflict in a wider context than has become customary in the contemporary literature on 'education in emergencies'. It does so in both geographical and historical terms with the aim of showing that the relationship is a fundamental one operating at many levels and scales. After a definition of terms, conflict within education is considered through such contexts as policy making and decisions about medium of instruction. These can have both intended and unforeseen outcomes, ranging from deliberate acts of aggression, oppression and neglect to naive miscalculation of the implications of decisions. The role of organised religion in the formation and operation of education systems is considered and is an element of both political and cultural dimensions. Education within conflict is then discussed in dimensions ranging from the local, such as in Northern Ireland, to civil war to global conflict. Finally, education is considered in relation to socio-cultural conflict, environmental conflict and violent conflict, though in reality these are often intertwined.

Preamble

This is a discussion about a profound relationship. It is deliberately not limited to the consideration of the relatively recent and contemporary field of educational study conventionally defined as 'education in conflict and post-conflict situations' (Smith & Vaux, 2003), which in turn is related to the emergent field of 'education in emergencies'. Within that field, conflict and post-conflict considerations have been the focus of the majority of the literature to date, and with good reason. Recent global publications such as the 2010 EFA Global Monitoring Report, the 2010 edition of Brendan O'Malley's *Education under Attack*, and the volume put together by Mark Richmond for UNESCO (2010), *Protecting Education from Attack: a state of the art review*, all bear witness to the severity of the problem of education in conflict and post-conflict situations. The decision to focus the 2011 EFA Global Monitoring Report on progress towards meeting the Millennium Development Goals on the issue of conflict is a further indication of the level of contemporary concern on the part of UNESCO, the governments of its members and other agencies.

The purpose of this discussion is not to gainsay any of this, but to place it in the context of a fundamental relationship between education and conflict with implications far beyond, as well as within, the situation of violent conflict. It is unfortunate, to say the least, that the *Oxford Dictionary* refers to 'education' specifically in terms of systemic learning, thereby failing to convey the reality of the acquisition of knowledge in whatever form it comes. This discussion will therefore open with a definition of terms, for 'conflict' is similarly flexible in relation to interpretations to which it is susceptible.

In response to the thesis encapsulated in the title of this chapter, the narrative will then move on to consider 'conflict within education', and 'education within conflict'. Two other significant contextual situations will then be discussed, namely 'education and socio-economic conflict' and 'education and environmental conflict'. They are, of course, not unrelated to the conventional paradigm, but extend beyond it and help to explain it. Some discussion of 'education and violent conflict' then follows, ranging from education and war, through more localised scenarios such as civil war, specific attacks on facilities and personnel, and discrimination to the point of neglect, and exclusion with the threat of violence. The final component of the discussion considers 'education as a humanitarian response' as a necessary reaction to various forms of conflict, and also a mitigating factor affecting the development of future conflictual situations. Throughout the discussion the significance of issues of scale, both temporal and spatial, provide an underlying contextual continuum.

Definition of Terms

As indicated above, the phenomenon of education is not limited to the formal mode, which comprises what goes on in a systemic provision. Such a system normally comprises a compulsory phase, or schooling, required by law on a national scale, and post-compulsory sectors of further and/or higher education. The existence of compulsion with regard to schooling is particularly relevant in the context of a discussion about conflict: first its enforcement, and second its curriculum, normally also controlled by political authority.

Education is in reality about learning and teaching, leading to the acquisition of knowledge and skills. For a Taliban militant in Afghanistan, learning how to manufacture an improvised explosive device (IED) is an educational experience. He may well acquire this skill from a colleague, or simply by observing a colleague. Both parties may well be illiterate in the conventional sense, but we are all learners and teachers. The majority of what we learn comes through the other two forms of education, non-formal and informal. Both are life-long, unlike formal education, which for the majority of the world's population is cursory, but whereas non-formal education assumes some degree of organisation, informal education is involuntary.

Overall, education is culturally embedded, but as far as formal and much of non-formal education are concerned, politically delivered. In societies where there is strict control of the media, much of informal education may also be politically delivered.

So the first example of the wide-ranging relationship between education and conflict is that between education and politics, the political being by far the most influential of the range of factors that determine educational experience. This leads directly to the issue of scale, as it is not immediately evident as to why the political dimension of a society is not so deeply embedded in the culture. Culture is normally much more localised in scale than are political systems, which became much more organised with the rise of the European nation-state. As Dodgshon (1987) puts it, 'With the formation and territorialisation of state systems, we enter a phase in which the political definition of space transcends community at all levels' (p. 136).

Through European colonialism this trend dispersed to many parts of the world, though not uniformly. For example, the French policy of so-called 'direct rule' contrasted strongly with the British 'indirect rule'. Some of the most severe examples of recent violent conflict involving education are in former colonies such as Sierra Leone, Rwanda and Timor-Leste. Such former colonies are now mostly independent with some degree of systems of formal education, but these are often severely dysfunctional due to underfunding, corruption, maladministratin and a multiplicity of local languages. There is often devolution by default to local communities, and in any case the key decisions concerning access to schooling are taken at the level of the family. Hence the section on education and socio-cultural conflict below.

In the more developed former colonies of Britain, such as Australia and Canada, federal systems of education developed, necessarily introducing the potential for conflict over education between provincial and federal governments. In the USA a much more local scale obtained, as indicated by McPartland (1979). This, he explains, was due to the small scale of colonial survival settlements, their strong internal governance, and an initially hostile situation of conflict with the indigenous populations. The culture of small school districts has survived, especially in the east. As McPartland puts it: 'Spatial and ecological forces may have prompted the emergence of these features; contemporary economic, sociological or political arguments have ensured their survival' (p. 130). In some cases highly localised governance of schooling relates positively to local cultural scale, but such small compartments of systems, especially in large urban areas, can lead to ghettoisation and conflict.

Just as 'education' is susceptible of a variety of definitions, so is 'conflict'. The *Oxford Dictionary* variously describes the term as: 'a state of opposition or hostilities'; 'a fight or a struggle'; 'the clashing of opposed principles'; 'to clash'; 'to be incompatible'; 'contradictory'; 'conflicting'; 'in conflict; and 'conflictual'. *Chambers Dictionary* also includes: 'a mental conflict' and 'to contend'. Clearly this range of interpretation takes us well beyond what, in contemporary academia, characterises the emergent field of education and conflict. In his attempts to promote integrated curricula in the heady days of the 1970s, Professor David Jenkins of the then New University of Ulster used to refer to subjects as 'groups of people'. Tony Becher put the same idea more conflictually in his book *Academic Tribes and Territories* (Becher & Trowler, 2001). Academics are prone to bandwaggoning as well as tribalism and internecine warfare. Consequently, it is a prime purpose of this chapter to explore the relationships between conflict and education in more fundamental and yet extensive terms.

Conflict within Education

Largely because of the political control of formal and non-formal education, conflict is endemic and inherent in policy making and implementation in this field. This is evident at various scales from macro to micro and across the centuries. Examples range from the use of the German vernacular in the schools of the Lutheran Reformation of the sixteenth century, presenting a direct challenge to the medium of Latin in the more selective Catholic schools, to the imposition of Afrikaans as the medium of instruction in apartheid South Africa in the twentieth century. The issue of medium of instruction has been one of conflict over many centuries and in numerous locations from Amazonian Peru through the Indian state of Orissa to post-colonial Malaysia.

Beyond the fundamental cultural issue of language, conflict arises over the competition for places in schools, both where provision for all is a reality as well as where it is not. Access to schooling is not just geographical. It has also to do with the fundamental issue of selection, which in turn has to do with control (Hopper, 1968; Broadfoot, 1984). To act as a political and social control mechanism is one of the prime functions of education systems. This remains the case even when ostensible marketisation of schooling exists in the form of so-called school choice mechanisms. Related devices such as league tables – local, national and international – add fuel to conflict and may invoke both reward and penalty. At least sport has managed to ritualise conflict (Morris, 1981). Education has not.

A particularly concerning aspect of conflict within education is that connected with its relationship to economy. While it is self-evident that, in modern terms, a highly literate and numerate society can promote and support economic development while an illiterate and innumerate society cannot, a number of questions are still left begging. Fundamental among these is how to reach sustainability. This is because correspondence between curriculum and economy is extremely difficult to achieve. They are in a conflictual relationship. In the context of a 'developed' or industrialised society, normally highly urbanised as well, 'curriculum' means that obtained in compulsory schooling. Curricula do not change rapidly. National economies do. For most people in such societies their *rite de passage* through the controlled curriculum takes about 10 years. If they are fortunate they will receive a liberal education; that is to say a learning experience balanced as between those elements that support technical and material skills and those that do not. Increasingly, however, the pull of international tests of mostly technical skills in the early teens is narrowing the knowledge base. Even worse, such schemes, especially the Programme for International Student Assessment (PISA), purport to show a causal and predictable link between high technical scores in early adolescence and the economic advance of a country's economy decades later. This takes no account of the potential subsequent influence of on-the-job learning, a massively under-researched area of non-formal education. And so the dislocation between curriculum and economy continues, with all that is implied for sustainability.

In the context of the majority of the world's communities, the rural poor of Latin America, Asia, sub-Saharan Africa and many of the small nations of the tropical world, the challenge of sustainability is much more basic. It relies on the generation of social, economic and environmental capital at the local level. Because of the weakness of formal education, relative to the informal, correspondence between curriculum and economy is more likely to be achieved. This is enhanced where there is also an appropriate contribution from non-governmental organisations (NGOs) such as ActionAid, Practical Action – the modern version of Schumacher's 'Intermediate Technology' – and Oxfam. Although such NGOs can reach only a minority of the rural poor, there are many local NGOs buying into this approach. In such contexts there is more interconnection between formal, non-formal and informal education. This means potentially less conflict within education.

Another potential conflict area within education is that between public and private sectors of provision. This need not be fatal, so long as it is not too institutionally correlated with social class and privilege. If it is so correlated then it can be very divisive, as is the case in England. Here the minority with private schooling occupy a disproportionate number of places in prestigious universities, and then the majority of positions of power in government, the military, business and civil society. Current policies of involving private capital in the operation of so-called maintained schooling promise to make the situation even more divisive. This is clearly a situation of conflict. It would appear that the public/private relationship may be somewhat less invidious in some developing countries, where encouraging things are happening (Srivastava and Walford, 2007). The factors behind such developments range from devolution to community funding by default in some sub-Saharan systems, to a strong tradition of secular and religious philanthropy in India. In Sierra Leone, in general a land-owning peasantry, there has long been a tradition of tribal chiefs supporting schools in their communities. There, and in many other sub-Saharan African countries, Christian denominations and their missions contribute a significant proportion, sometimes the majority, of schools in the national system. Are they private? Whatever, the blurring of the public/private divide helps to diminish potential conflict. And what of the status of Islamic contributions to the stock of schooling in sub-Saharan Africa? In itself this need not be divisive, but religion, like language, is a key identifier of culture and can be a source of conflict. The periodic mutual destruction of schools, as between Christians and Muslims in the 'shatter zone' of central Nigeria, is a case in point, as is the suppression of Islamic schooling in Mindanao by the majority Christian regime in the Philippines (Milligan, 2005). Whether this is conflict within education or education within conflict is a moot point.

Education within Conflict

This is concerned with the contribution of education to conflict, a contribution well demonstrated by Davies (2004). It has to do with certain of the definitions of conflict mentioned above, especially 'to be in opposition', a 'state of opposition', 'contradictory' and 'the clashing of opposed principles'. An obvious and much publicised case is that of Northern Ireland, with its school system still largely segregated along denominational fault lines. Despite considerable effort the conciliatory integrated schools movement has progressed at snail's pace (McGonigle, 2002). What is taught in certain subjects can fuel conflict, and has. It does not have to be knowingly false. Partiality is enough. During the Cold War from the 1950s to the 1980s, the partiality of information about the USA and USSR in their respective school systems was tantamount to miseducation. Indeed on both sides it descended into the realms of propaganda. Such is part and parcel of the armament of real violent conflict, in war or civil war. During the Cold War, in the schools of the West, hardly a mention was made of the fact that the then USSR had suffered more fatalities and casualties than all other combatants combined in both European and Asia-Pacific theatres of the 1939-45 war. That post-war era was marked by technological competition between the two superpowers. When in 1957 the USSR was the first to put a satellite (Sputnik) in space, and in 1961, a man (Yuri Gagarin), in the USA blame was heaped on the public schools. The same happened in France after defeat in the Franco-Prussian War of 1870-71 and in England after defeat in the Second Boer War of 1899-1902. This is of course ludicrous, but is the downside of the tendency to see education as a panacea for success in national competition, including violent conflict.

Cold conflict, such as that between the post-1945 USA and USSR, exists not only between nations, but also within. For example, at the time of writing (July 2010), a major conflict is raging in Iran over the control of the country's massive Azad Islamic University with its 1.5 million students and staff (*The Guardian*, 2 July 2010). The current president of Iran, Mahmoud Ahmadinejad, is accusing former president, Ayatollah Ali Akbar Hashemi Rafsanjani, of using his influence as head of the Assembly of Experts to pack the university management team with his allies and opponents of the current regime. This is no ordinary university, reportedly having 'hundreds of campuses across Iran and assets worth tens of billions of dollars'. So the stakes are high.

Universities, and the intellectual class in general, are always a focus of government unease across the world. This is due to their unrivalled ability to undertake research and disseminate their findings on a global scale. Dictatorial regimes, such as that in contemporary Iran, have always sought to persecute professors, teachers and students. Modern examples include Nazi Germany and the Chile of Augusto Pinochet. These and other cases have resulted in the exodus of highly educated and skilled human capital to the benefit of other countries.

At a more mundane but nonetheless significant level is the tendency of governments in more democratic situations to seek to control the research of universities that could be critical of their policies. This can be done by influencing publicly funded research bodies by ensuring that 'placemen' populate their committees. If important research funded by independent trusts and foundations turns out to be critical of government policy, the findings are immediately castigated and 'binned' by government. Such was the fate of the exemplary *Cambridge Primary Review* in England in 2009, which was, in effect, stillborn. Inevitably, it seems, universities and academics, ideally seekers after truth, are in a situation of conflict with political authority and politicians whose stock in trade is to be economical with the truth. This is also due to the capacity of most intellectuals to consider different points of view to explain or predict. For many politicians the only *raison d'être* is to acquire power and retain it. Qualities of leadership, rather than collegiality, are what counts. This places conviction above consideration.

A form of information, and therefore education, that has a direct relationship within conflict is 'intelligence'. This can range from various examples within civil society, through politics to the military. It can be found in combat and non-combat situations alike, but always in the context of competition, and may well have commercial value. At the tiniest of scales, but still in operation, we have the payment, in money or in kind, for access to the answers in school homework from another pupil who has the necessary 'intelligence' and is willing to trade it.

Much more serious in the university context was the finding of Brock and Cammish (1997) in Cameroon of sexual exploitation of female anglophone students by francophone males in return for coping with the francophone programme in the university in that sector. This arose as a result of the francophone national political authority denying a university facility in the anglophone sector of the country, a situation that has since been rectified. However, another outcome of this internal conflict was for many female students to go instead to universities in neighbouring Nigeria, and then remain there.

Education and Socio-Cultural Conflict

The most profound and significant area of conflict in socio-cultural terms is that between the genders. Maternal authority in less developed, especially rural, societies is central to decisions as to whether or not individual children attend school, if and when it is available. A relatively stronger maternal authority can challenge patriarchal convention. Many such societies are a long way from reaching the Millennium Development Goal of basic education for all (EFA). Successive EFA Global Monitoring Reports since 2002 have indicated significant improvements in enrolment in basic education in many developing countries, but they mask less impressive figures for attendance and wastage. Just as with issues of school choice in more developed societies, the key decisions as to enrolment and attendance in school in poor rural communities are made at the level of the family. In this context they are most strongly influenced by issues of kinship and economy. Both are areas of gender and conflict and were found by Brock and Cammish (1997) to be the two most influential of 11 factors affecting female participation in primary education in a range of developing countries. Kinship systems vary in detail but broadly divide as between patrilineal and matrilinial. With the authority dimension added they become patriarchal and matriarchal. In some cases no significant issue is made of the gender dimension of kinship, in which case the situation is referred to as bilateral (Todd, 1987). Nonetheless, the majority of kinship systems are patriarchal, and even in matriarchal situations it does not necessarily mean that authority figures, such as tribal chiefs, will be female. Senior females may designate one of their sons for such a position.

In the situation of predominant patriarchy in actual or near subsistence economies, females are mindful of the age–sex hierarchy. That is to say, through informal education, females gain a perspective of the balance to be struck between degrees of personal independence and influence and overall family well-being. This is not to deny the existence of gender conflict, but conflict is not necessarily violent and resolutions can be peaceful. The aim is to maximise maternal authority, among other things in the interest of influencing decisions about the education of children. According to Todd (1987), maternal authority is closely related to the age of females at marriage and the duration of the learning process between birth and marriage. Todd's general hypothesis is that 'cultural take-off is related to family', and that more specifically:

> the educational power of a family system may well be determined by the strength of maternal authority. The strength of maternal authority is itself a function of two different anthropological factors: the overall strength of parental authority, and the relative status of women in the family system being considered. (p. 17)

The key issue in Todd's discourse is 'cultural take-off', as this is an essential condition for the achievement of sustainability of human survival on planet Earth. Sustainability does not mean maintaining the status quo, indeed quite the opposite since that status quo in both so-called developed and underdeveloped countries and their communities is unsustainable. Sustainability means managing a cultural adjustment to the environment in which we find ourselves, whether it be in poor rural economies in Africa or burgeoning urban industrial economies in large parts of China.

Fundamental cultural turns are necessary everywhere because of the most potentially destructive conflict yet created; a conflict that has been largely created by education, yet depends on a fundamental revision of education for its resolution. That is 'education and environmental conflict'.

Education and Environmental Conflict

Human communities are in conflict with the environment in which they live. In this regard, education has a great deal to answer for. At the simplest, people live in a threefold integrated environment comprising the natural environment, the human environment and the built environment. None of these are sealed. They integrate with, and affect, each other. People are in conflict with all three and that conflict is getting more difficult due to the effects of fragmented education. As David Orr (1994) has observed:

> In thinking about the kinds of knowledge and the kinds of research that we will need to build a sustainable society, a distinction needs to be made between intelligence and cleverness. True intelligence is long range and aims towards wholeness. Cleverness is mostly short range and tends to break reality into bits and pieces. Cleverness is personified by the functionally rational technician armed with know-how and methods but without a clue about the higher ends technique should serve. The goal of education should be to connect intelligence with an emphasis on whole systems and the long range with cleverness, which involves being smart about details. (p. 11)

What Todd referred to as 'cultural lift-off' is a cultural turn that will enable the approach advocated by Orr to be understood and taken up. This is not the same cultural turn for everyone, and can only begin at the local level. The cultural capital that needs to be employed in order to enhance cultural capacity will be different from place to place, and can only be generated locally and through a profound rethink about education. We need to invoke the kind of thinking found in the informal education of indigenous societies, which in all cases placed respect for the environment at the centre of things. A range of examples can be found in the King & Schielman/UNESCO volume on *The Challenge of Indigenous Education.* In place of respect for the environment, so-called advanced societies, deceived by the cleverness of their compartmentalised education, have substituted 'management of the planet'. This is an approach born of monumental stupidity and arrogance that renders the epithet '*sapiens*' hopelessly inappropriate. It has much to do with formal education systems being nation-bound, and fortunately there are some international bodies that take a broader view. For example the *3rd UN Global Bio-Diversity Outlook* published in May 2010 (UNESCO, 2010), known as GBO-3, warned of the approach of imminent 'tipping points' regarding the oceans and forests of the world which, if disregarded, will send the global environment 'spiralling towards collapse'. This can only be avoided by appropriate action being taken in every community and location, building towards an aggregate whole as argued in *Education as a Global Concern* (Brock, 2011).

This is real conflict on a grand scale born of miseducation, and capable of resolution only by fundamental educational reform. Where can we turn to help us embark on this urgent task? Certainly not to national curricula, but to the United Nations again. The 2009 Global Assessment Report on Disaster Risk Reduction is particularly helpful in bringing together the natural, human and built environments in its advocacy of steps that can be taken in different contexts to reduce the occurrence of disasters and mitigate their effects. UNESCO's distinctive 2003 publication on *Planetary Sustainability in the Age of the Information and Knowledge Society* is likewise an outstanding interdisciplinary contribution to the UN Decade for Education and Sustainable Development (2005-15). The fundamental issue of scale is its first consideration with regard to planetary sustainability: 'How to understand is as dynamic, perfectible and adaptable to the setting of each community, country and continent' (p. 7). It then proceeds to pose the question: 'how to understand education in this context?' Among the responses offered by UNESCO to this question are:

> From this standpoint, we must encourage education based on life, on the overwhelming desire for radical transformation and moral change in the character of society. We must then be concerned about promoting collective wisdom and human understanding, unveiling the new truths that have been concealed for various reasons and represent elements of scientific rationality and folklore that have built up and enriched generation after generation. (p. 43)

> This approach to education, involving all its forms, is crucial to facilitate and orient these changes. The great challenge is that, on the basis of this notion, we will be obliged to almost reinvent education on every continent. It will not be simple modifications or adjustments that will give education this new brilliance and excellence that we need from it, nor simple experimental projects or remediation of competencies. (p. 43)

These observations show just how much education has been in conflict with the vital goal of planetary sustainability and the realisation that this can only be achieved primarily at the local scale. While it is difficult to say anything positive about disasters, the majority of which are due to human conflict, they do – whether natural or 'man made' – present an opportunity to adopt a fundamentally new approach to education. This opportunity is hardly ever taken due to political authority, the control of which over much of all forms of education has been a major contributor to conflict.

Violent Conflict and Education

As indicated at the outset of this chapter, it is not its concern to focus on conflict and post-conflict in the sense of 'education and emergencies'. Other chapters deal with that in some detail. However, a brief contextual discussion may be helpful to provide a broader perspective on this type of conflict and relationships to education.

The issue of scale has run through this narrative, and here one will be concerned more with war, and to some degree civil war, than with more localised violent conflicts. Wars go back through the millennia and have always had some relationship to, and effects on, education in its various forms. The first issue to mention is that wars have often included within themselves and also as an aftermath, changes in political geography. This means national boundary changes and/or complete takeover of territory previously under the authority of another power. This will inevitably result in a new educational system and sometimes a new language. Central, southern and eastern Europe have seen countless such changes, the most recent resulting from the 1939-45 war and the Balkan conflict of the 1990s. At the end of the 1939-45 war in Europe, the four victorious powers occupied sectors of Germany. Attempts to influence education in the USA, United Kingdom and French sectors of occupation were short-lived, but in the USSR sector the new territory of the German Democratic Republic (GDR) acquired a Soviet style all-through school strongly influenced by the Russian polytechnical model. The dismantling of this model as part of the re-unification of Germany in 1990 involved further conflict within education, both with regard to the former teaching staff and the decisions of new *lande* as to whether or not to return to the old tripartite schooling system.

Yugoslavia, born out of the earlier 1914-18 conflict, was kept out of the Soviet orbit by Marshall Tito, but in the 1990s imploded and gave birth, and rebirth, to a number of new countries. Somewhat curiously, Yugoslavia had achieved a degree of success in such areas of the curriculum as citizenship and student participation in school governance. Re-Balkanisation seems to have put paid to that.

Wars can enhance educational opportunity in various ways. Increased opportunities for women, through skills acquisition in relation to occupations previously occupied or dominated by men, was a feature of both world wars in Europe. As a result of the American Civil War of the 1860s two important outcomes were: a significant expansion of higher education in general, and of new educational opportunities for Black Americans, albeit still affected by degrees of segregation, especially in the 'South'.

Major educational reforms are associated with large-scale violent conflict, and as already mentioned above, may arise from defeat. In England and Wales the 1939-45 war saw a major reform legislated well before the end of hostilities (Gosden, 1976), in effect taking on board the principles of the Spens Report of 1938. The implementation of the recommendations of the 1944 McNair Report on teacher training, especially the establishment of territorial Institutes of Education in all universities to oversee and validate teacher training, meant that massively enhanced opportunities for 'emergency training' of demobilised service personnel were able to respond to the significant demand for teachers in the enhanced secondary sector as well as the expansion of primary schools due to the post-war 'baby boom'.

Global violent conflicts can also be catalysts for high-level research, especially in the spheres of technology and applied science. Clear beneficiaries of the 1939-45 global conflict were computer science, all forms of engineering, and medicine. Within all branches of the military, a wide range of skills were enhanced and also experienced by a larger proportion of the population, albeit mainly males, than was previously the case. This enhances the quantity and quality of the human capital available to a country.

There are significant downsides for education of course, as a result of major violent conflict. Among these are the degradation of the human and physical environment, including destruction of schools, colleges and universities (O'Malley, 2010). This was a major feature of the 1990s civil war in Sierra Leone, which, following several decades of corruption, reduced what had been the 'jewel in the crown' of sub-Saharan African education literally to rubble. In the horn of Africa, across several countries conflicts have enhanced desertification, which inevitably increases competition for grazing and cultivable land, and related challenges for education of all kinds. Nomadic communities, of which there are several in this area, are especially likely to experience this type of conflict. Such communities are found in many parts of the world, and for them acceding to statutory formal schooling can be a double-edged sword. While it, especially the acquisition of literacy, can help them confront inappropriate demands from political authority, at the same time schooling challenges the highly localised family-scale informal education that serves their economic survival. In the case of the major travelling culture in Europe, the Roma, political authority in some countries has sanctioned the destruction of both settled and traveller communities.

The potential for education to exacerbate the endemic cultural conflict that is inherent in the human species comes to the fore in and through violent conflict. As has been mentioned already, information provided in textbooks and other teaching materials can contribute to conflict, as can the influence of powerful informal educational channels, ranging from family attitudes to children's comics to influential media images such as television and film. In England, subjects from the 1939-45 war still fuel such conflict. At the time of writing (July 2010) the football World Cup is going on, including a match between England and Germany. Some primary school pupils, when interviewed and asked why they would support England, gave the 1939-45 war as a reason, even using terms such a 'Nazi' and 'Hitler'. At a time when, as indicated in the previous section on education and environmental conflict, we need much greater cooperation and coordination between nations to address the challenges posed by the global financial crisis and the ecological imbalance of the planet's natural environment, education in all its forms is not helping. It is not only those who suffer disasters leading to emergencies that need humanitarian assistance, education included. It is education itself that needs to be reconceived overall as a humanitarian response.

Conclusion: education as a humanitarian response

Education isn't working. There are a number of reasons for this, among which is its mutual relationship with conflict in many different contexts. Most fundamental is the conflict between its three forms, informal, non-formal and formal. Together, for everyone, they constitute what education is, as a whole, over the lifespan of each individual. But they rarely provide the holistic education that is necessary to meet the interconnected challenge of human and environmental survival. A key problem is the notion that formal education constitutes 'education', and through the formative association of education systems with the nation-state it has become controlled by the political factor. Consequently, de facto, the prime functions of formal systems of schooling are: (a) to be part of the political and social control mechanism of the state, and (b) to enable the acquisition of knowledge and skills thought to be conducive to the economic development of the state. Clearly the unit of scale is the nation-state, and competition between states is being played out in part through international tests of a narrow range of mainly technical subjects. Except in poor communities in less developed countries there is little connection between formal education and its non-formal and informal counterparts, and even then, mainly by default.

Nonetheless, because there is a degree of interconnection in such situations, there is the possibility of the generation of cultural capital to effect what Todd (1987) termed 'cultural lift-off'. This means the maximisation of all forms of education to address the human and environmental challenges. As indicated above, the United Nations and bodies associated with it, report regularly on the imminence of these challenges, and periodic conferences such as that held in Copenhagen in 2009 achieve little because they are beset by national-scale concerns of self-interest.

Just as situations of poor rural communities, because of their direct contact with the environment in terms of survival, provide opportunities for sustainable development to be attained with the help of holistic education, so do circumstances of emergency due to disaster, natural or man-made, where formal education has been dislocated. In both contexts, NGOs rather than government play a key role. However, such NGOs are only present with the permission of the government of the country concerned and are under pressure to reconstruct the *status quo ante* rather than to redevelop along more sustainable lines with the integration of the three forms of education maximising its potential contribution. Such an approach, as a humanitarian response, is also needed through a reconceptualisation of education in all countries and communities in the world. It would reduce, if not remove, the fundamental relationship between education and conflict. Conflict is dangerous. As the aphorism goes, 'a little bit of knowledge is a dangerous thing'. That 'little bit' is the compartmentalised and dislocated formal dimension, fuelling the 'cleverness' of which David Orr (1994) rightly despairs. A more holistic approach would enable the technical skills of cleverness to be informed and applied in association with the knowledge he seeks to promote. Together they could approach the wisdom of the indigenous communities who used to live in harmony with their environments by respecting them.

While the United Nations and its agencies can point the way at a global scale, individual nations are unlikely to cooperate and in any case there are about 200 of them. A coordinated approach based on UNESCO's regional offices might be a way forward, as this is proving promising in respect of that agency's efforts to provide guidelines for the rationalisation of higher education standards. Indeed, higher education institutions with their global networks and high levels of information and communications technology are the element of education best placed to help resolve the most urgent issue of conflict, that of achieving human and environmental sustainability on planet Earth.

References

Becher, T. & Trowler, P.R. (2001) *Academic Tribes and Territories*, 2nd edn. Milton Keynes: Society for Research into Higher Education and Open University Press.

Broadfoot, P. (Ed.) (1984) *Selection, Certification and Control: social issues in educational assessment.* Lewes: Falmer Press.

Brock, C. (2011) *Education as a Global Concern.* London: Continuum.

Brock, C. & Cammish, N.K. (1997) *Factors Affecting Female Participation in Seven Developing Countries.* London: Department for International Development.

Davies, L. (2004) *Conflict and Education: complexity and chaos.* London: Routledge.

Dodgshon, R.A. (1987) *The European Past: social evolution and spatial order.* Basingstoke: Macmillan.

EFA Global Monitoring Report (2010). Reaching the Marginalized. http://unesdoc.unesco.org/images/0018/001866/186606E.pdf

Gosden, P.H.G.H. (1976) *Education in the Second World War.* London: Methuen.

Hopper, E.I. (1968) A Typology for the Classification of Education Systems, *Sociology*, 2, 29-46.

King, L. & Schielmann, S. (Eds) (2004) *The Challenge of Indigenous Education.* Paris: UNESCO.

McGonigle, J. (2002) Integrating Secondary Schools in Northern Ireland, in R. Griffin (Ed.) *Education in Transition: international perspectives on the politics and processes of change*, 151-168. Oxford: Symposium Books.

McPartland, M.F. (1979) The Emergence of an Educational System: a geographical Perspective, *Compare*, 9(2), 119-131.

Milligan, J.A. (2005) *Islamic Identity, Post-coloniality and Educational Policy: schooling and ethno-religious conflict in the Southern Philippines.* New York: Palgrave Macmillan.

Morris, D. (1981) *The Soccer Tribe.* London: Jonathan Cape.

O'Malley, B. (2010) *Education under Attack.* Paris: UNESCO.

Orr, D.W. (1994) *Earth in Mind: on education, environment and the human prospect.* Washington, DC: The Island Press.

Smith, A. & Vaux, T. (2003) *Education, Conflict and International Development.* London: Department for International Development.

Srivastava, P. & Walford, G. (Eds) (2007) *Private Schooling in Less Economically Developed Countries.* Oxford: Symposium Books.

Todd, E. (1987) *The Causes of Progress: culture, authority and change.* Oxford: Basil Blackwell.

United Nations (2009) *Risk and Poverty in a Changing Climate: invest today for a safer tomorrow.* 2009 Global Assessment Report on Disaster Risk Reduction. New York: United Nations.

UNESCO (2003) *Planetary Sustainability in the Age of the Information and Knowledge Society for a Sustainable World and Future: working towards 2015.* Paris: UNESCO.

UNESCO (2010) *Protecting Education from Attack: a state of the art review.* Paris: UNESCO.

CHAPTER 2

Fragile States, Fragile Concepts: a critical reflection on the terminology of fragility in the field of education in emergencies

STEPHANIE E.L. BENGTSSON

SUMMARY 'Fragile states' is one of the latest buzz-phrases to emerge within the aid sphere, and is thus of increasing importance to those working with education, conflict and development today. Whether positive or negative, buzz-phrases and buzzwords play a central role in aid policy because they help frame solutions to problems by suggesting that problems can be clearly defined and categorised, and thus tackled in a systematic manner. This chapter presents preliminary findings from a larger study, which aims to examine how the terms 'fragile states' and 'fragility' are defined, conceptualised and used by education aid professionals at the global policy level. The chapter critically analyses the policy of a small but influential group of international individuals from different organisations involved in shaping global policy related to education and fragility: the Inter-Agency Network for Education in Emergencies (INEE) Working Group on Education and Fragility. By focusing on how and why certain words are used within the aid realm, and investigating the emergence and current usage of these terms, the author aims to encourage self-reflexivity among aid practitioners, and to contribute to a clear, shared and useful understanding of the concept(s) these terms are meant to denote.

Introduction

If the tower of Babel was a language disaster,
disaster itself has a language. (Gunn, 2003, p. 35)

> Modern English, especially written English, is full of bad habits which spread by imitation and which can be avoided if one is willing to take the necessary trouble. If one gets rid of these habits one can think more clearly, and to think clearly is a necessary first step toward political regeneration: so that the fight against bad English is not frivolous and is not the exclusive concern of professional writers. (Orwell, 1946, p. 156)

'Fragile states' is one of the latest buzz-phrases to emerge within the aid sphere, and is thus of increasing importance to those working with education, conflict and development today. Amongst the plethora of buzzwords and buzz-phrases in aid today, there are some, such as 'participation' and 'poverty reduction', that have positive connotations, and others, such as 'fragility' and 'difficult partnerships', with negative ones. Whether positive or negative, buzzwords play a central role in aid policy because they help frame solutions to problems by suggesting a 'governable, controllable world' (Cornwall & Brock, 2005, p. iii). Positive buzzwords accomplish this by lending actions an optimistic sense of purpose; negative ones by naming or identifying problems, the first step in classic problem-solving strategies (Nickerson & Zenger, 2004; Cornwall & Brock, 2005).

As a buzz-phrase, the term 'fragile states' appears to have come about to fill a conceptual gap in the aid literature, connected to the perceived blurring of the traditionally separate spheres of development and humanitarian assistance that has occurred since the end of the Cold War (Stepputat et al, 2007; Uvin, 2008). The term opens the possibility of conceptualising mechanisms to provide aid to countries that do not seem to be in a direct emergency, which would qualify them for humanitarian aid, or ready for economic growth, which would qualify them for development assistance (Brorsen et al, 2005).[1] The term 'fragile states' has spread quickly through the aid sphere, largely due to the impact of United States national security doctrine post-9/11 on the global community, with many aid players adopting some form of fragile states strategy or discussing the problem of 'fragility' in their policy documents (Woodward, 2004). Thus, unsurprisingly, many of those working within education aid have started adopting fragile states terminology to garner financial and political support, particularly at the global policy level. A case in point is the formation of the Inter-Agency Network for Education in Emergencies (INEE) Working Group on Education and Fragility, which was founded in early 2008 and is made up of representatives from 20 different institutions, including donors, non-governmental organisations (NGOs), United Nations (UN) agencies, inter-governmental organisations (IGOs), think tanks and universities.

In this chapter, I argue that the phrases 'fragile states' and 'fragility' only give an illusion of a 'governable, controllable world' because they suggest that a unique problem – that of fragility – has been identified, and can therefore now begin to be solved through appropriate strategies. In fact, there is no consensus on what that problem is or on what the terms 'fragility' and 'fragile states' encompass and exclude. As Cammack et al (2006) point out: 'In most cases, these labels do not have a meaning that is clearly understood far beyond the author who has used them' (p. 16). As these terms become a regular part of aid vocabulary without a concerted effort to understand their roots, they obscure the original meanings they were intended to convey, compounding the number of possible problems covered by these buzzwords and rendering attempts at developing solutions difficult, if not impossible.

I am motivated by what I see as the untapped potential for linguistic change to bring about meaningful change in aid practice. Despite an increase in 'politically correct' [2] language in aid in the last decade, linguistic changes to date have at best been superficial, and have not led to any real change in practice.[3] Linguistic changes are generally made when enough people express discomfort with an existing term. However, that term is more often than not simply exchanged for a related, more politically neutral term, an exchange that often obscures elements of the original concept the term was intended to describe. This is one reason that aid discourse shifted from using the term 'failed states' to 'fragile states' in the first place. As important as politically correct terms may be for diplomacy, there are elements that the term 'failed states' captured that 'fragile states' fails to describe, and vice versa (Doornbos, 2006; Governance and Social Development Resource Centre [GSDRC], 2006). Thus, with every superficial linguistic change, the concept to be described becomes increasingly nebulous. Nonetheless, the existence of a concept in need of description is never questioned, and the conditions of existence of that concept in need of description remain unexamined. By introducing the concept of stereotyping – a phenomenon I argue is more pervasive with increasing conceptual blurriness – I will demonstrate that the continued unanalysed usage of the buzz-phrases 'fragile states' and 'fragility' can be detrimental to the very places education aid is meant to assist.

This chapter opens with a brief introduction to fragile states in the literature. It attempts to understand which problem(s) the term is meant to denote, including a discussion of the relationship of the term 'fragile states' to other terms in the aid literature such as 'failed states' and 'collapsed states'. This section will also consider what differences, if any, there are between 'fragile states' and 'fragility' as terms, focusing in particular on the role played by concepts of the 'state' in defining these terms. Subsequently, I will examine the conceptual roots of the fragility/fragile states terminology by briefly examining the history of aid work and presenting some ideas about the emergence of the concepts of the 'relief-to-development gap' and of the 'relief-to-development continuum'.[4] The final section of this chapter is devoted to an exploration of the possible dangers of using a term without a shared understanding. Here I discuss how the term 'fragile state' can function as a stereotype, potentially leading to negative consequences for those places described as such. This chapter primarily consists of a review of both academic literature and what is often termed grey literature (the literature of aid agencies such as project reports, often unpublished, often available online), and, where relevant, this review is supplemented by some of the findings from a series of interviews conducted with members of the INEE Working Group on Education and Fragility during 2009. It should be noted that I am not offering an alternative to the term 'fragile states', rather I am suggesting that education practitioners and other stakeholders need to revisit the original concept(s) or problem(s) they wish to describe when they use the term 'fragile states'. Once that problem – or set of problems – has been isolated, stakeholders can then 'let the meaning choose the word, and not the other way about' (Orwell, 1946, p. 169).

The 'Fragile States' Problem

So, what problem(s) is the term 'fragile states' meant to denote? According to the aid literature, fragile states are 'characterized by weak policies, institutions, and governance', weaknesses caused by a lack of political will, capacity, or both (Carvalho, 2006; Rose & Greeley, 2006). This commonly used definition is extremely vague at best. In fact, depending on which agency you ask, the percentage of the world's population living in fragile states ranges from 14% (Department for International Development [DFID]) to 30% (United States Agency for International Development [USAID]), a difference of nearly one billion people (Kirk, 2007). While many agencies use similar language to define fragile states in their policy documents, for one estimate to be twice another suggests the actual understanding of what constitutes a fragile state is anything but shared. The divergence in estimates probably results from the fact that these agencies came to the term via different agendas (Cammack et al, 2006). In fact, when agencies define fragile states, they often begin with a disclaimer that there is no internationally agreed-upon meaning for the term or list of 'fragile' countries (GSDRC, 2006).[5] Yet, work on fragile states continues unabated, without a serious attempt to determine what the term entails, or how many people's lives are encompassed by it. How is any education aid to be delivered effectively to those living in what might be termed 'fragile states' if the size of the population to be assisted cannot even be reasonably estimated?

If we examine the literature more closely, we see just how imprecise the terminology accompanying state fragility is, because it is so often used interchangeably with related terms such as 'state failure', 'collapse', 'conflict' and 'post-conflict', or, is defined in a similarly vague fashion (Woodward, 2004; Inter-Agency Task Team – Fragile States – Fast Track Initiative [IATT-FS-FTI], 2005; Brinkerhoff, 2007). This is perhaps a result of the fact that literature on the relationship between development and conflict is 'often of the grey kind' (Uvin, 2008, p. 161). As previously mentioned, most definitions given are a variation on the following: 'fragile states can be seen as those which lack either the capacity or the will to deliver on core state functions' (IATT-FS-FTI, 2005, p. 2). This echoes Gros's (1996) conceptualisation of a failed state, a buzz-phrase in its own right, that has 'in its essence the inability or unwillingness of public authorities "to carry out their end of what Hobbes long ago called the social contract" and to deliver public services on a wide range of issues related to welfare' (in Da Costa, 2008, p. 565). The World Bank uses the term 'low income countries under stress' (LICUS) almost interchangeably with 'fragile states' in many of its documents, a term that suggests that the problem of state fragility is somehow economic as well as political in nature and has to do with an inability to cope with (undefined) pressure or stress (Uvin, 2008). Bradley's (2007) observation that many fragile states are so-called 'newly independent countries' (NICs) or 'nascent states' (p. 91) emphasises the political dimension of the problem of fragility. The Save the Children Alliance take this notion a step further, applying a conflict lens through which to view the problem with the term 'conflict-affected fragile states' (CAFS) (Save the Children, 2008). It is clear from these examples that understandings of the problem(s) behind fragility are not shared among agencies.

A term related to conflict and post-conflict situations that has been in popular usage, particularly in the academic literature, longer than 'fragile states' is the term 'collapsed state'. State collapse 'means that the basic functions of the state are no longer performed, as analysed in various theories of the state' (Zartman, 1995, p. 5). Defined as such, the term seems to be indicating the same vague general concept/phenomenon that the 'fragile states' term is suggesting. And herein lies the problem. If the term 'collapsed state' already existed to describe a state that is not performing its basic functions and responsibilities, why has the term 'fragile state' emerged? I suggest there is a general inclination to move away from the notion of finality that is suggested by the word 'collapsed'. Rather than continuing to use the term 'collapse' but defining it as a slow process rather than an endpoint as historians suggest (Yoffee, 1988; Eisenstadt, 1988), it seems that many today prefer the concept of fragility as it conveys a sense of impending trouble that can potentially be prevented, rather than a sense of something broken in need of rebuilding and repair. Where state collapse suggests having to put Humpty Dumpty together again after a nasty fall, state fragility allows for the possibility of preventing Humpty's fall (or at least providing him with padding!) However, according to the GSDRC (2006), many still use the term 'collapsed state' 'mistakenly' to refer to any weak or fragile state, suggesting that confusion reigns about these concepts.

Fragile States versus Fragility

It is clear from these emerging definitions and themes that a common trend among agencies working with fragility has been to view the state as the unit of analysis. According to Stepputat and colleagues (2007):

> [t]o make sense of the discussion of state fragility, weakness, or outright failure and collapse, one must begin with the normative ontology of the sovereign, territorial state which dominate [*sic*] theories of international politics and which have [*sic*] developed alongside the actual formation of modern states. (p. 6)

The authors point out that, particularly in the West, states (as defined by Weber in Weber et al, 1991) have come to be regarded as 'something natural' (Stepputat et al, 2007, p. 6), with their sovereignty as a central distinguishing feature according to most political scientists (Dawisha & Zartman, 1988). Along with that sovereignty comes the state's '"responsibility" to seek the welfare of its citizens' (Weiss, 1995, p. 157) by protecting them from violence, oppression and terror, and by meeting their basic needs and fulfilling their human rights (Brinkerhoff, 2007). It is the failure to meet this responsibility that the terms 'fragility' and 'fragile states' are meant to define. According to Chomsky (2006), 'among the most salient properties of failed states is that they do not protect their citizens from violence – and perhaps even destruction – or that decision makers regard such concerns as lower in priority than the short-term power and wealth of the state's dominant sectors' (p. 38). Violence, it seems, can be both a cause and an effect of the state's failure to meet its responsibility to its citizens (Deng, 1995). The above terms are therefore often associated with pre-conflict, conflict and post-conflict situations.

INEE Working Group members are distancing themselves from such state-centric analysis, arguing that it often obscures the complexity of the actual picture on the ground. This behaviour is consistent with that of other aid practitioners who, according to the GSDRC (2006) have recognised 'the empirical and normative shortcomings of the term "fragile states" ... [and] are now increasingly favouring the much broader terminology of "fragility" or "situations of fragility"'. In fact, when the INEE Working Group was initially created in 2008, a decision was made to name the group the 'INEE Working Group on Education and Fragility', rather than 'on Education and Fragile States'. The primary reason for this decision revolved around the idea that fragility might not affect an entire country.

The term 'fragile state' implies that both the problem and the solution are located within the state structure; therefore using the term 'fragile states' can be a potentially detrimental label – politically and economically – for a country (Interview, 9 November 2009). However, despite the fact that most members of the Working Group interviewed preferred the term 'fragility' to 'fragile states', many were unable to define 'fragility' without using the concept of the state. This further illustrates the problem alluded to earlier, where a superficial linguistic change is made because a significant number of stakeholders have expressed discomfort with an existing term. Instead of responding to the perceived inadequacy of the existing term with a concerted effort to understand the problem that term is meant to denote and clarifying its parameters, the term is simply thrown out and replaced with a less politically-charged one. In order to understand why the terms 'fragile states' and now 'fragility' have become so pervasive in the aid literature today, we must attempt to understand the historical context in which these terms emerged.

Conceptual Roots of Fragile States in Aid History

According to some scholars, the term 'fragile states' has not emerged to describe a new phenomenon. Rather, it is one of the latest and more 'fashionable' trends in a string of words and phrases attempting to categorise the vast number of countries that do not fit neatly into traditional aid categories (Woodward, 2004, p. 2; Brinkerhoff, 2007).[6] The domain of international aid is often conceptualised as being made up of two kinds of assistance – development [7], which dates back to the mid 1940s and addresses long-term socio-economic goals, and humanitarian [8], which dates back even earlier to the late nineteenth century and addresses immediate relief issues (McMichael, 1996; Norberg, 2000; Macrae, 2004). Prior to the Cold War, these two types of assistance were for the most part separately compartmentalised within aid work (Raisin & Ramsbotham, 2001; Bowden, 2004).

Education emerged on the development agenda during the 1950s and 1960s when development practitioners recognised a positive link between education and economic growth, through modernisation theory and human capital theory (Schultz, 1971; Inkeles & Smith, 1974). According to Bray et al (1986): 'The education system may ... be compared to a vehicle which carries people from one place to another' (p. 30). Largely ignoring the idea that '[t]he direction in which the educational vehicle takes society depends firstly on the intentions of the government and other members of society, and secondly on the resources available', more and more development professionals saw education as a means for countries to drive towards economic (and later social and political) development (Bray et al, 1986, p. 30; Fagerlind & Saha, 1989). In fact, the amount of overseas development aid (ODA) set aside for education increased significantly in the late 1990s and early 2000s (UNESCO, 2005). With the recognition of education as a key tool for development by members of the international community, universal education became an international goal, known as 'Education for All' (EFA) (Jansen, 2005).[9]

Professionals working in the humanitarian sphere have long seen education as a key part of refugee camp activity, whereby children can be kept occupied and learn basic life skills (Kagawa, 2005). However, during the greater part of the twentieth century, education provision varied widely from context to context, and was not always recognised as a formal activity during humanitarian action and thus not always contemplated in assistance budgets. Things began to change with the publication of Machel's (1996) milestone report, *Impact of Armed Conflict on Children*, in which the importance of education in conflict situations was officially acknowledged, and the recognition after the Cold War by aid scholars of a gap between relief and development that needed to be filled as it was preventing people from having their rights met (Crisp, 2001). Around this time, there was a shrinking of the 'intellectual and operational gap' between development and security, largely because post 9/11 donor governments (particularly the United States) began to recognise a link between development in the so-called Third World and global security (Uvin, 2008, p. 161; Stepputat, et al, 2007). This shrinking process compounded the blurring of boundaries – both conscious and unconscious – between the traditionally separate spheres of humanitarianism and development, as stakeholders began to recognise that in order to undertake development activities in countries perceived to be a risk to global security, humanitarian activities would have to take place as well and vice versa. There has been significant overlap in the activities of humanitarian and development agencies in recent years.

In fact, within education, the second World Conference on Education For All in the year 2000 saw the expansion of the EFA goals to formally include work within humanitarian aid beyond refugee education, and thus a corresponding increase in funding towards education in emergencies, chronic crises and reconstruction. As a result of the conference, INEE was formed to ensure the right to education in crisis situations (INEE, 2005). Thus, for many scholars, education became a symbol of the blurring between humanitarianism and development. Pigozzi (1999), for example, advocates a developmental approach to emergency education within humanitarian response. In other words, education is increasingly understood as able to provide short-term relief *and* lay the foundation for long-term development goals. In line with this thinking, a key recommendation in an EFA assessment report was that education 'be seen, and planned from Day One, as part of the development process and not solely as a "relief" effort' (UNESCO, 2001, p. 7). This suggests that education can act as a bridge between humanitarian aid and development, allowing nations to move more smoothly across the gap from a state of crisis to a state of stability, or, if we return to our vehicle metaphor for a moment, education allows nations to drive out of crisis, towards stability, and then keep going along the road to development. Though overly simplistic and problematic in its envisioning of a linear transition between relief and development, the EFA recommendation does demonstrate that education is now considered by many to be a core component of crisis mitigation and consequently is no longer confined to only those so-called developing countries considered 'stable'.[10] The problematic nature of this linear model of transition as a way to conceptualise aid activities has been highlighted by many and will be discussed in more detail below.

The Relief-to-Development Continuum and Fragile States

As has been previously mentioned, during the Cold War, funding and implementation of aid agencies' programmes were largely based on a supposed division between relief and development (Raisin & Ramsbotham, 2001). This division remained in place conceptually after the Cold War, with the inception of Resolution 46/182 [11] by the UN in 1992. '[T]he prevailing view was of a linear progression from relief-to-development with humanitarian and reconstruction assistance being separately compartmentalised' (Bowden, 2004, p. ix). However, the increase in number and duration of conflicts and the changing nature of conflict from predominately international to predominately intra-national in the post Cold War climate, as well as the 'failure of pure humanitarianism' in Rwanda in 1994 [12], led to 'growing conceptual and operational links between relief, rehabilitation and long-term development' and the creation of the relief–development continuum model in the 1990s (Sollis, 1994; Raisin & Ramsbotham, 2001, pp. 152, p. 143).[13] This model emerged to fill the 'institutional, financial and conceptual' gaps (known collectively as the 'relief-to-development gap') between the work of development and humanitarian agencies (Crisp, 2001, p. 168). It included the recognition that humanitarian assistance can make eventual development more difficult if driven by a completely different logic and organisational culture (Raisin & Ramsbotham, 2001). According to Ryscavage (2003), the relief–development continuum is a linear model that progresses from relief (humanitarian assistance) to rehabilitation (a 'midwife stage' between relief and development) to development (in the form of economic growth, assisted by aid). The model aims to provide a conceptual framework for aid, where relief is provided to countries which are affected by crisis, and assistance continues to be provided in the form of rehabilitation until the country has moved to the other side of the continuum and can begin working towards economic growth, which is supported by development aid. For several years, this continuum was seen as 'the mother of all solutions. We attempted to rationalise a situation into a logical process that, step by step, would bring a crisis from emergency to relief, then to immediate reconstruction of the basic social fabric, and finally to long-term development' (Ambrosi, 2004, p. 45).

The term 'fragile states' appears to have emerged to describe countries in which traditional aid modalities will not work, either because these countries are not perceived to be in need of relief, or because they are not perceived to be 'ready' for development. In other words, from the perspective of the widely-used linear model, fragile states can denote countries in the 'midwife stage' between relief and development: they require rehabilitation assistance. Brorsen and colleagues (2005) distinguish between developmental, fragile and conflict-affected states through distinctive development patterns, as illustrated in Figure 1.

For the authors, '[a]ll states lie somewhere on a stability continuum'. This appears to correspond with the relief–development continuum:

developmental states are at the more stable end of the continuum and are recipients of development aid, the conflict-affected states at the less stable end and are recipients of relief (p. 7). In this simplified model, it would seem that 'fragile states' describes what is in between.

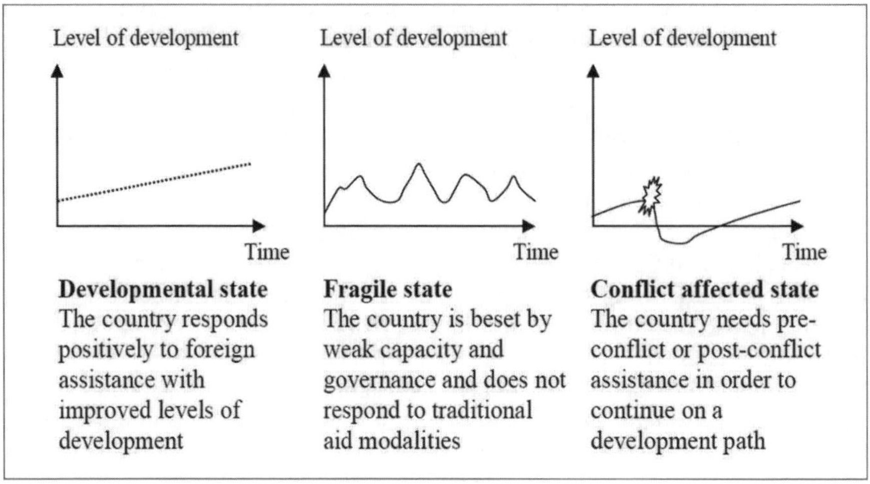

Figure 1. Differences between a developmental state,
fragile state and conflict-affected state (Brorsen et al, 2005, p. 3).

From this perspective, the term appears to have some use value. As a think tank representative on the INEE Working Group puts it:

> I think the thing that is useful about the fragile states concept, is breaking down the humanitarian and the development divide. So, it's a shift in conceptual thinking. It's not that places or countries are in war or peace, humanitarian or development. I mean ... there's the in-between – transition ... emergency–transition–development. (Interview, 22 October 2009)

For this informant, the use of the term has helped people to stop thinking about the world in binary terms, and has brought about a conceptual shift, as it has allowed them to label the 'in-between-ness'. This was echoed by another member, an academic, who, when asked about the utility of the term 'fragile states' said:

> Well, I do think it's useful ... as a more abstract and therefore more transcending concept. And therefore it forces people out of their silos a little bit, to think beyond simple need-and-response. For example, I think it does to some extent encourage people in disaster relief, humanitarian assistance to think beyond the short-term engagement that they have in the situation. (Interview, 3 April 2009)

In other words, if we think back to the idea of education as a bridge between relief and development, the concept of fragile states could potentially help to describe those places where that bridge needs to be built.

However, both informants recognised that the term's utility is quite limited and were quick to point out those limits. Informants agreed that the buzzword 'fragile states' brings people together who might not otherwise interact (for example, academics and international governmental organisations, etc.), and to some extent helps to break down unproductive dichotomies. However, they felt that the term itself is ambiguous and the actual situation 'on the ground' is not as simple as the relief–development continuum implies. As Ryscavage (2003) argues, the linear continuum is only one way to think about social problems; in the real world events do not follow this pure continuum. This suggests that fragile states as an in-between stage would be difficult if not impossible to identify in practice – leading, perhaps, to the fact that the labelling of fragile states differs so radically between different agencies.

Indeed, the continuum has not proven to be the solution to bridging the gap between relief and development. According to Ferris (2008), since the mid 1980s, when the international community first began to recognise the relief-to-development gap, there have been numerous attempts in the form of papers, conferences, and recommendations to find better ways to move from relief to development, but these attempts have so far proven unsuccessful. Framing the problem and subsequent solution in linear terms has proved to be problematic.

While the conceptualisation of relief and development as the ends of a linear continuum provides a simplified theory of the aid process, it does not clarify on-the-ground complexity and therefore provides an inadequate theoretical framework for understanding the aid process as a whole. Slim (1997) refers to this as a 'crisis of theory', and suggests calling this debate the 'relief–development conundrum' (p. 9). The problem with the linear model is that it does not give an accurate representation of the in-country situations, where 'humanitarian activities, reconstruction and even development activities may take place concurrently' (Bowden, 2004, p. ix). This concurrence phenomenon has also been recognised in the fragility literature. Brorsen and colleagues (2005) argue that states can move between the patterns of 'developmental state', 'fragile state' and 'conflict-affected state', and two regions within one country can experience different patterns at the same time. Among informants, this was referred to as the 'pockets of fragility' phenomenon. It stands to reason, therefore, that simply inserting fragile states into the existing relief-to-development continuum model as a label for the in-betweenness and expecting it to fill the conceptual role of the subject for crisis prevention or for reconstruction and rehabilitation will do little to clarify and thus improve aid mechanisms.

The idea of a continuum has become quite important to a number of scholars working with this in-betweenness. For Francois & Sud (2006), while the words 'weak', 'fragile', 'failing', 'failed' and 'collapsed' tend to be used 'interchangeably', in practice these terms are related and connecting, but different, themselves forming parts of a continuum, with fragile states at one end and failed/collapsed states at the other (p. 143). This resonates with Gros's (1996) call to develop a taxonomy of state failure, which would ascribe different terms to different stages of state failure. Here is present a linguistic problem, in addition to the problem of an oversimplified linear continuum model: while a minority of scholars have pointed out that these terms all have very different yet related meanings, the majority of scholars (and aid practitioners) continue to use these terms interchangeably, apply similar vague definitions to them, and fail to examine the exact, underlying issue(s) that the terms attempt to encompass. The terminology around state failure and indeed state fragility 'is like a destructive idea machine that turns individually clear concepts into an aggregate unclear concept' (Easterly & Freschi, 2010).

The lack of shared understanding would probably be less problematic if the current aid era was not one of inter-agency collaboration, as set out in the Monterrey Consensus of the International Conference on Financing for Development (2002) [14] and the Paris Declaration on Aid Effectiveness (2005).[15] Within education aid, the collaboration phenomenon is evidenced by the creation of two entities: the Inter-Agency Network for Education in Emergencies (INEE) established in 2000 as a global network of education stakeholders, including UN agencies, donors, NGOs and individual practitioners [16]; and the Fast Track Initiative (FTI) established in 2002 as a multi-agency initiative spearheaded by the World Bank, intended to ensure that all countries achieve universal primary education by 2015.[17] The logic behind these types of collaboration involving a large number of stakeholders is that education aid can be more effective and more far-reaching with the increased harmonisation and alignment of policies and pooling of resources. However, without a consensus on the meaning of key terms such as 'fragile states', harmonisation and alignment become more difficult, and the potential benefits of involving more actors in improving access to and quality of education for children around the world may never be realised. As Gunn (2003) argues: 'a certain understanding of the technical, administrative and operational terminology of the many disciplines involved becomes paramount if the inherent difficulties of the disaster are not to be compounded by an overlay of communicational disaster' (p. 35). The current communicational disaster around fragile states is particularly problematic because it is a silent one. That is, while agencies collaborating on education do not share an understanding of what the term 'fragile states' means, they continue to operate as if they did. They discuss how to 'solve the problem' of fragile states and draft education strategies based on these discussions without fully defining the problem. Indeed, they engage in discussions about the relationship between education and fragility, and how education can be delivered effectively in fragile states, without a consensus of what is meant by 'fragile state'.

The 'Emergency Alibi'

Given the intangibility of that in-betweenness, it is perhaps hardly surprising that when asked for their personal understandings of the term 'fragile states', members of the INEE Working Group provided a wide range of definitions. In fact, one common thread through most informants' personal definitions is that the term 'fragile state' is seen as nebulous. An International Non-Governmental Organisation (INGO) representative stated that while she would not directly refer to the term as 'fluid', the INEE Working Group had settled on the Organisation for Economic Cooperation and Development-Development Assistance Committee (OECD-DAC) definition [18] 'for want of a better definition' (Interview, 24 March 2009). An academic from the Working Group echoed this: 'There is no agreed-upon ... definition of the term, but it's taken to mean, as Rose and Greeley point out, a lack of willingness or capacity on the part of the state to deliver basic needs, basic services to its people' (Interview, 25 March 2009). Finally, a donor representative stated that his understanding of the term encompassed a 'much broader definition' than current agency lists of fragile states would suggest (Interview, 21 April 2009). Despite this recognition of the nebulousness of the concept, only a few of the members of the INEE Working Group favoured doing away with the term altogether. Most see the terms 'fragile states' and 'fragility' as flawed, but nonetheless see them as the best terms currently available and therefore think it important to keep using them, particularly as they view their work around these issues as urgent. I would argue however, that this is an extension of the 'emergency alibi', in which '[i]nterventions are increasingly temporary and makeshift, and emergencies are seen as events that require swift action, rather than opportunities for critical reflection' (Martone & Neighbour, 2004, p. 11). Interventions, particularly those undertaken by inter-agency groups, should be based on a shared understanding among aid practitioners of the parameters of the problem those interventions are meant to address, in order to maximise efficiency and effectiveness. The building of such a shared understanding requires time, and while I am not suggesting that immediate responses should cease in the meantime, I do think that setting aside a substantial amount of time for collaborative critical reflection would have a positive impact on the outcomes of future initiatives.

The Dangers of Conceptual Nebulousness

Today, while several members of the INEE Working Group on Education and Fragility recognise that the term 'fragile states' is problematic and not very useful, they argue that 'fragility as a concept, and not a label, still has merit' (INEE Secretariat, 2009). However, these same practitioners do not have a shared concept in mind when using the descriptor 'fragility'. This causes problems when constructing inter-agency agendas and strategies, through what Smith (2001) calls a 'method of blob-ontology' where 'for every discursive object named, there is assumed to be a something out there of which we can speak without worrying about how it exists' (p. 166). Rather than assuming that we have misnamed the concept(s), and that work on education should continue until 'better' terms are found, I argue that it is necessary to revisit the original concept(s), and explore which problem(s) practitioners actually wish to describe with the terms 'fragile states' and 'fragility'. Once that problem is isolated, it may be possible to establish whether 'fragile states' and 'fragility' are the most appropriate descriptive terms or to propose more suitable alternatives. Simply allowing these buzzwords to persist in the literature is not constructive. As with the term 'nation-building', which came to use in the international community to emphasise the importance of the nation-state, repetition of the term 'fragile states' 'has not clarified the term's meaning. People have several things in mind' (Goldsmith, 2007, p. 26). In fact, the 'ontological ground of whatever is represented in these nominalisations is left wholly indeterminate', as is illustrated by Figure 2 (Smith, 2001, p. 167).

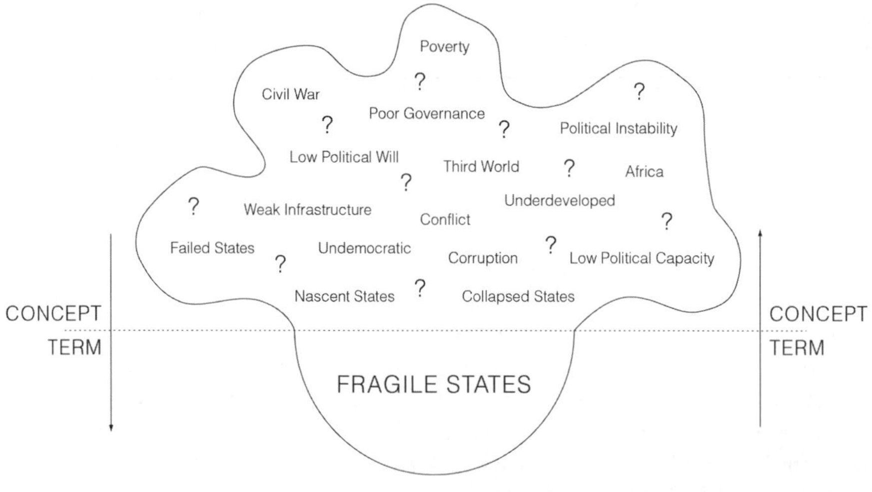

Figure 2. The problem of incoherence between the term and concept.[19]

As can be seen in Figure 2, a solid, clear signifier exists (the term 'fragile states'), which is widely used, yet the concept it is meant to signify is left indeterminate. In fact, the signifier 'fragile states' gives the illusion of being a 'solid-looking concept', thanks to the number of times it is used by official, international sources (such as the World Bank, USAID, DFID). Yet, on closer examination, that solid-looking concept begins to 'dissolve', perhaps leading to the discovery that 'there isn't any such thing' (Cowgill, 1988, p. 246).

One could argue that this is an example of the aid discourse serving a 'maieutic [naming] function' through which fragile states are brought into being through the repetition of the term in authoritative documents (Wolin, 1991, p. 184, in Erickson, 2004, p. 124). For Vavrus & Seghers (2010), 'policies are, by definition, texts imbued with authority' (p. 77). Thus, the inclusion of 'fragile states' in aid policies gives the illusion that this term is a technical, scientific term, and sets up a power imbalance where the possessors of this 'technical knowledge' exert power on those countries labelled 'fragile', often without either party recognising that this is happening (Apthorpe, 1986; Erickson, 2004). Through the maieutic function, the aid discourse creates 'the individual [in the developing country] who perceives himself as being poor, lacking, and part of an inferior culture' which is in direct opposition to the self-sufficiency that development claims to bring to the so-called Third World (Du Bois, 1991, p. 25). This is particularly problematic for the leadership of fragile countries and for other individuals who participate in the construction of aid discourse. As the President of Burundi, the leader of a country often labelled as fragile, puts it:

> We heard the terminology around 'fragile states'. We wish to underline the importance of being cautious in using this term. It is labelling countries in a negative way, where we are trying to develop and become stronger and prouder nations. (Nkurunziza, 2008)

Many of the INEE Working Group members are aware that the terms 'fragile states' and 'fragility' serve a maieutic function, recognising that they are 'donor constructs'.[20] In their discussion of the problems associated with donor concepts such as 'early recovery', Bailey & Pavanello (2009) ask their readers to consider 'when, why and for whom it is useful'(p. 3). We also have to ask when, why and for whom such terms are potentially harmful. Not only can the maieutic function within the aid sphere lead to negative self and national perception for recipient countries, it can also occasionally lead to stereotyping. According to Quasthoff (1989), stereotypical thinking arises out of the desire 'the human mind has to simplify to a certain degree in categorising and forming expectations about the world' (p. 184). Through an extensive review of the literature, she determines that stereotypes are 'categories which over-generalise and oversimplify', are 'emotionally evaluative', and often 'are contrary to the facts or do not contain more than a "kernel of truth"' (p. 182). Indeed, the definition of fragile states as those 'lacking political will and/or capacity' is nothing if not an oversimplification, and the fact that 'there is no agreed list of fragile states' among aid professionals suggests that there are no solid criteria for determining whether or not a country is a fragile state (IATT-FS-FTI, 2005, p. 5). Brannelly et al (2009) provide readers with four agency lists of fragile states, and supplement those with one of their own making. The lists range in length from 28 to 39 countries, and only 17 countries appear on all five, demonstrating quite clearly that there are 'not tight enough parameters to produce a homogeneous enough group', as one donor representative from the INEE Working Group pointed out (Interview, 12 October 2009). Thus the process of calling a country a fragile state becomes nothing more than what Sornig (1989) refers to as '*name-giving*', where the name that is given takes on the nature of a nickname which 'need not be justified', cannot 'be contradicted or disproved' and, above all, is difficult if not impossible for the country in question to rid itself of because it is bestowed by an official, international source (p. 100).

Nowhere is this problem more acute than on the African continent. A common thread running through much of the literature on poor economic performance, state collapse, state failure, conflict and state fragility is the claim that while these phenomena are found worldwide, their presence is most acute and most obvious in Africa (Hyden, 1992; Khadiagala, 1995; Gambari, 1995; Zartman, 1995; Brauch, 2008). Scholars cite mounting evidence of a so-called '"African" effect' which is blamed on African geography and/or African politics (Humphreys & Bates, 2005, p. 407). In her work on stereotyping, Quasthoff (1989) illustrates how opinion that appears in print influences public opinion and charges her readers with the task of remaining watchful as the 'publishing of stereotypes will be used as a resource of power to gradually establish collectivity of stereotypical thinking as a means for preserving power' (p. 193). An academic representative on the INEE Working Group explained his reluctance to use fragility terminology in a similar vein: 'I think that's another reason for my resistance to fragility because it does tend to ghettoise and overemphasise that fragility only exists in the "developing world" and the "low economies"' (Interview, 3 April 2009). Through stereotypical thinking, in this case around the term 'fragile states', African countries risk becoming further marginalised or ghettoised in the international community as terms such as 'fragile states' become more deeply entrenched in aid work. As Mbembe (2001) puts it, Africa is seen as a 'world par excellence of all that is incomplete, mutilated, and unfinished' (p. 1). Ironically, as previously mentioned, this marginalisation is directly opposite to the professed desired outcome of international aid.

Several members of the INEE Working Group are unhappy with the negative connotations of the term 'fragile state' – one informant referred to it as 'condescending' – and also claimed that much of its potential use value was lost because it was only being applied to the so-called Third World (Interview, 12 October 2009). An NGO representative felt very strongly that the term can only be useful if it is applied consistently:

> I honestly think that the term is useful if it goes all across the different states, and by that I mean developed and underdeveloped countries. If there is a set of criteria that could be developed whereby even the developed countries can undergo to

> determine whether they are in a fragile state or not – that would be helpful. But just to use it to describe a certain set of states that are underdeveloped ... as fragile states, I don't think this is very much relevant because some developed countries are fragile. (Interview, 5 May 2009)

This was echoed by a donor, who argued that an increase in violence in European and American schools in recent years demonstrates that fragility can occur everywhere, including the so-called developed world (Interview, 2 April 2009). In other words, there is a strong feeling among this small group of INEE members that while the terms 'fragile state' and 'fragility' have been useful in serving as a conceptual bridge between the traditionally separate spheres of aid and development, they are now becoming a wedge between so-called developing and developed countries, a sentiment that is echoed by others in the aid sphere beyond education.

Conclusion

In this chapter, I have argued that the buzz-phrases 'fragile states' and 'fragility' only give an illusion of a 'governable, controllable world'. They suggest that a unique problem – that of fragility – has been identified, when in actual fact the terms are used by different stakeholders to define different problems. The continued usage of 'fragile states' or 'fragility' in aid discourse without a concerted effort to try to understand the problem(s) these terms are attempting to signify, brings to mind US Justice Potter Stewart's famous attempt to explain what is 'obscene', by saying, 'I shall not today attempt further to define the kinds of material I understand to be embraced ... [b]ut I know it when I see it'.[21] The danger of this kind of definition is that it is entirely subjective, and it allows the person or agency with the most power in the situation to determine which definition (or lack thereof) will come out on top. Even when these persons or agencies have the best of intentions, the consequences can be detrimental for the very countries aid interventions are intended to help, as demonstrated during the discussion of the maieutic function and stereotyping.

Until now, studies on fragility and education have focused on contexts identified as fragile and on how stakeholders operate within those contexts, even though the criteria by which contexts are identified as fragile are often unclear, and, more importantly, not shared between members of the research and practitioner communities. In this chapter, I have taken a different approach, aiming to subject to micro-level analysis what is traditionally left unanalysed as the macro or global level, and through such an analysis revealed some of the many complexities of the global layer of aid policy, so often viewed as homogeneous. I hope that this will emphasise the importance of 'studying up' (Nader, 2002, p. 284), and encourage other scholars to do the same. While some might argue that in a field so driven by a sense of urgency, one cannot afford to get caught up in debates about language, I think it important to consider that 'one can probably bring about some improvement by starting at the verbal end' (Orwell, 1946, p. 170). After all, interventions informed by a clear conceptual framework are more likely to succeed than those that are rushed into without adequate preparation.

Notes

[1] The reality, however, is much less clear-cut, as will be demonstrated later in this chapter. Many countries that are considered direct emergencies, such as Afghanistan, Sudan and the Democratic Republic of Congo, and many countries that receive large amounts of development assistance, such as Uganda and Ethiopia, are often referred to as fragile states as well.

[2] I use 'politically correct' in the sense of 'conforming to a body of liberal or radical opinion, especially on social matters, usually characterized by the advocacy of approved causes or views, and often by the rejection of language, behaviour, etc., considered discriminatory or offensive' (*Oxford English Dictionary*, 2009).

[3] For an example of this problem, please refer to 'World Bank Development Policy: a SAP in SWAP's clothing' (Klees, 2001).

[4] As this chapter is particularly interested in fragility terminology in relation to education aid, this discussion will highlight education throughout.

[5] See, for example, World Bank (2007) and DFID (2005).

[6] In addition to the terms mentioned in the previous sections, others include weak states, failing states, difficult partnerships, etc.

[7] The development project began on a large scale with the Marshall Plan in 1947, and the Bretton-Woods agreement, where the American Government pledged money to assist war-torn Europe in reconstruction efforts (McMichael, 1996; Brautigam & Knack, 2004). At the end of 1961, the UN introduced the First Development Decade during which a number of newly founded organisations began development work with the goal (however idealistic and at times unsuccessful) of helping their fellow man (Lulat, 1988).

[8] The idea behind humanitarianism is a simple one, involving recognition of a neutral universal space (humanitarian space), where other actors can help victims as members of one humanity (Grossrieder, 2003; Smillie & Minear, 2004). Early humanitarian aid was based on a 'charity principle', involving the satisfaction of basic needs including food and water, shelter and health care (Etxeberrìa, 2001, p. 79).

[9] In 1990, representatives from 155 countries and from 150 international and local development agencies met in Jomtien, Thailand for the World Conference on Education for All (WCEFA), and committed to Education for All (EFA) by 2015. In 2000 at the second WCEFA held in Dakar, Senegal, this goal was reaffirmed as the second Millennium Development Goal (MDG) calling for universal primary education by 2015.

[10] It is important to note that there has been much work in recent years in the field of education in emergencies that recognises that education can also

contribute towards crisis, as it can serve as a catalyst for tension and conflict. For a detailed discussion of this, see Bush & Saltarelli (2000).

[11] Resolution 46/182 is 'Strengthening of the Coordination of Humanitarian Assistance of the United Nations'.

[12] According to the Office of the United Nations High Commissioner for Refugees (UNHCR) in their *State of the World's Refugees Report* (2000), between April and July 1994, 800,000 people were killed as Hutu extremists attacked the Tutsi population and Hutu moderates. 'Although a multinational UN peacekeeping force, the United Nations Assistance Mission to Rwanda (UNAMIR), had been deployed in Rwanda in October 1993 with a limited mandate to help the parties implement the Arusha Agreement, the bulk of this force withdrew soon after the outbreak of violence. This failure by the United Nations and the international community to protect the civilian population from genocide was examined and acknowledged in a UN report published in December 1999' (UNHCR, 2000, p. 245). The report goes on to describe how millions of Rwandans were displaced and many of those who found themselves in refugee and internally displaced people (IDP) camps fell victim to cholera epidemics and other disease outbreaks, or under the control of the Rwandan *génocidaires* (the perpetrators of the genocide). By year's end, over half of Rwanda's population had been affected in a major way by the events around the genocide.

[13] Sollis (1994) states that 'InterAction ... commissioned a working group of relief and development practitioners to prepare a paper entitled "The Relief-Development Continuum"' (p. 452).

[14] The Monterrey Consensus emerged out of the Monterrey Conference held in 2002, which was attended by numerous heads of state, and heads of organisations, including the World Bank, the World Trade Organisation and the International Monetary Fund. It aims to act as a framework for a new partnership for global development, with both so-called developing and developed countries taking responsibility for global poverty reduction.

[15] The Paris Declaration was endorsed on 2 March 2005 by more than a hundred ministers, organisation heads and other senior officials. It is an international agreement on increasing efforts in harmonisation, alignment and managing aid.

[16] INEE was formed in 2000 as a result of a strategy session during the World Education Forum in Dakar and a follow-up consultation in Geneva, in recognition of the fact that emergencies were a barrier to achieving education for all. Its current mission is 'to serve as an open global network of members working together within a humanitarian and development framework to ensure all persons the right to quality education and a safe learning environment in emergencies and post-crisis recovery' (INEE, 2008).

[17] The Education for All – Fast-Track Initiative (FTI) was launched in 2002, as an international partnering between donors and developing countries to accelerate progress towards the second Millennium Development Goal – universal primary education by 2015. According to the website, 'All low-income countries which demonstrate serious commitment to achieve universal primary completion can receive support from FTI' (EFA-FTI, 2007). FTI is

primarily concerned with financing, increasing aid efficiency, providing technical support for sector policies in education, and increasing accountability (EFA-FTI, 2004).

[18] The OECD-DAC definition reads: 'States are fragile when state structures lack political will and/or capacity to provide the basic functions needed for poverty reduction, development and to safeguard the security and human rights of their populations' (OECD-DAC, 2007).

[19] This diagram builds on Saussure's (1959) concept of the linguistic sign as being made up of a signifier and a signified (or, for my purposes, a term and a concept that term is meant to denote).

[20] This was mentioned a number of times during interviews and repeatedly at the INEE Global Consultation 2009: *Bridging the Gaps: risk reduction, relief and recovery*, which brought together more than 250 practitioners, researchers and policy makers from national and international NGOs, UN agencies, multilateral institutions, government agencies, ministries of education, teachers unions, academic institutions and youth groups to explore emerging developments in the field of education in emergencies, chronic crises and early recovery (see http://www.ineesite.org/index.php/post/global_consultation_2009).

[21] See *Jacobellis v. Ohio, 378 U.S. 184, 197* (1964).

References

Ambrosi, E. (2004) The Changing Nature of Humanitarian Crises, in Office for the Coordination of Humanitarian Affairs (OCHA) (Ed.) *The Humanitarian Decade: challenges for humanitarian assistance in the last decade and into the future.* Vol. 2. New York: United Nations.

Apthorpe, R. (1986) Development Policy Discourse, *Public Administration and Development*, 6, 377-389.

Bailey, S. & Pavanello, S. (2009) Untangling Early Recovery. Humanitarian Policy Brief 38. London: Overseas Development Institute.

Bowden, M. (2004) Foreword, in Office for the Coordination of Humanitarian Affairs (OCHA) (Ed.) *The Humanitarian Decade: challenges for humanitarian assistance in the last decade and into the future.* Vol. 2. New York: United Nations.

Bradley, M.T. (2007) Globalisation and Political Elite Institutional Choices: the impact on democratisation in Africa and the Middle East, *Journal of International and Area Studies*, 14(2), 91-102.

Brannelly, L., Ndaruhutse, S. & Rigaud, C. (2009) *Donors' Engagement: supporting education in fragile and conflict-affected states.* Paris: UNESCO, International Institute for Educational Planning and CfBT Education Trust.

Brauch, H.G. (2008) Introduction, in H.G. Brauch, U.O. Spring, C. Mesjasz, et al (Eds) *Globalisation and Environmental Challenges: reconceptualising security in the 21st century.* New York: Springer.

Brautigam, D.A. & Knack, S. (2004) Foreign Aid, Institutions, and Governance in Sub-Saharan Africa, *Journal of Economic Development and Cultural Change*, 13, 255-285.

Bray, M., Clarke, P.B. & Stephens, D. (1986) *Education and Society in Africa.* London: Edward Arnold.

Brinkerhoff, D.W. (2007) Introduction: Governance Challenges in Fragile States: re-establishing security, rebuilding effectiveness, and reconstituting legitimacy, in D.W. Brinkerhoff (Ed.) *Governance in Post-Conflict Societies: rebuilding fragile states.* London: Routledge.

Brorsen, P.W., Brett, J., Krogh, E. & Skadkaer Pedersen, F. (2005) *Improving Development Assistance to Fragile States.* Kongens Lyngby, Denmark: COWI Conflict and Development Network.

Bush, K. & Saltarelli, D. (2000) *The Two Faces of Education in Ethnic Conflict: towards a peacebuilding education for children.* Florence: UNICEF Innocenti Research Centre.

Cammack, D., McLeod, D., Menocal, A.R. & Christiansen, K. (2006) *Donors and the 'Fragile States' Agenda: a survey of current thinking and practice.* Report submitted to the Japan International Cooperation Agency. London: Overseas Development Institute; Japan International Cooperation Agency.

Carvalho, S. (2006) *Engaging with Fragile States: an IEG review of World Bank support to low-income countries under stress.* Herndon, VA: World Bank.

Chomsky, N. (2006) *Failed States: the abuse of power and the assault on democracy.* New York: Metropolitan Books.

Cornwall, A. & Brock, K. (2005) Beyond Buzzwords: 'poverty reduction', 'participation' and 'empowerment' in development policy. Overarching Concerns, Programme Paper Number 10. Geneva: United Nations Research Institute for Social Development.

Cowgill, G.L. (1988) Onward and Upward with Collapse, in N. Yoffee & G.L. Cowgill (Eds) *The Collapse of Ancient States and Civilisations.* Tucson: University of Arizona Press.

Crisp, J. (2001) Mind the Gap! UNHCR, Humanitarian Assistance and the Development Process, *International Migration Review*, 35(1), 168-191.

Da Costa, T.G. (2008) Political Security, an Uncertain Concept with Expanding Concerns, in H.G. Brauch, U.O. Spring, C. Mesjasz, et al (Eds) *Globalisation and Environmental Challenges: reconceptualising security in the 21st century.* New York: Springer.

Dawisha, A. & Zartman, I.W. (Eds) (1988) *Beyond Coercion: the durability of the Arab state.* London: Routledge, Kegan & Paul.

Deng, F.M. (1995) State Collapse: the humanitarian challenge to the United Nations, in I.W. Zartman (Ed.) *Collapsed States: the disintegration and restoration of legitimate authority.* Boulder: Lynne Rienner.

Department for International Development (DFID) (2005) Why We Need to Work More Effectively in Fragile States. London: DFID. http://www.dfid.gov.uk/Pubs/files/fragilestates-paper.pdf

Doornbos, M. (2006) Fragile States or Failing Models? Accounting for the Incidence of State Collapse, in M. Doornbox, S. Woodward & S. Roque *Failing States or Failed States? The Role of Development Models: collected works.* Working Paper.

Madrid: Fundación para las Relaciones Internacionales y el Diálogo Exterior (FRIDE).

Du Bois, M. (1991) The Governance of the Third World: a Foucauldian perspective on power relations in development, *Alternatives*, 16, 1-30.

Easterly, W. & Freschi, L. (2010) Top 5 Reasons Why 'Failed State' is a Failed Concept. http://aidwatchers.com/2010/01/top-5-reasons-why-%E2%80%9Cfailed-state%E2%80%9D-is-a-failed-concept/

Education for All – Fast Track Initiative (EFA-FTI) (2004) Education for All – Fast Track Initiative. Accelerating Progress towards Quality Universal Primary Education. Washington, DC: EFA-FTI.

Eisenstadt, S.N. (1988) Beyond Collapse, in N. Yoffee & G.L. Cowgill (Eds) *The Collapse of Ancient States and Civilisations*. Tucson: University of Arizona Press.

Erickson, F. (2004) *Talk and Social Theory: ecologies of speaking and listening in everyday life*. Cambridge: Polity Press.

Etxeberrìa, X. (2001) The Ethical Framework of Humanitarian Action, in The Humanitarian Studies Unit (Ed.) *Reflections on Humanitarian Action: principles, ethics and contradictions*. London: Pluto Press.

Fagerlind, I. & Saha, L.J. (1989) *Education and National Development: a comparative perspective*. 2nd edn. Oxford: Pergamon.

Ferris, E. (2008) Challenges in the Humanitarian Field: the big picture. Speech given to the Brookings Institute on April 29, 2008. http://www.brookings.edu/speeches/2008/0429_humanitarian_action_ferris.aspx

Francois, M. & Sud, I. (2006) Promoting Stability and Development in Fragile and Failed States, *Development Policy Review*, 24(2), 141-160.

Gambari, I.A. (1995) The Role of Foreign Intervention in African Reconstruction, in I.W. Zartman (Ed.) *Collapsed States: the disintegration and restoration of legitimate authority*. Boulder: Lynne Rienner.

Goldsmith, A.A. (2007) Does Nation Building Work? Reviewing the Record, in D.W. Brinkerhoff (Ed.) *Governance in Post-Conflict Societies: rebuilding fragile states*. London: Routledge.

Gros, J-G. (1996) Towards a Taxonomy of Failed States in the New World Order: decaying Somalia, Liberia, Rwanda and Haiti, *Third World Quarterly*, 17(3), 455-471.

Grossrieder, P. (2003) Humanitarian Action in the Twenty-First Century: the danger of a setback, in K.M. Cahill (Ed.) *Basics of International Humanitarian Missions*. New York: Fordham University Press & The Centre for International Health and Cooperation.

Governance and Social Development Resource Centre (GSDRC) (2006) Fragile States: terms and definitions. http://www.gsdrc.org/go/topic-guides/fragile-states/terms-and-definitions

Gunn, S. (2003) The Language of Disasters: a brief terminology of disaster management and humanitarian action, in K.M. Cahill (Ed.) *Basics of International Humanitarian Missions*. New York: Fordham University Press & The Centre for International Health and Cooperation.

Humphreys, M. & Bates, R. (2005) Political Institutions and Economic Policies: lessons from Africa, *British Journal of Political Science*, 35, 403-428.

Hyden, G. (1992) Governance and the Study of Politics, in G. Hyden & M. Bratton (Eds) *Governance and Politics in Africa*. Boulder: Lynne Rienner.

Inter-Agency Network for Education in Emergencies (INEE) (2005) *Minimum Standards for Education in Emergencies, Chronic Crises and Early Reconstruction*. Paris: INEE.

Inter-Agency Network for Education in Emergencies (INEE) (2008) *About INEE*. http://www.ineesite.org/index.php/post/about/'

Inter-Agency Network for Education in Emergencies Secretariat (2009) Terminology of Fragility: a note from the Working Group on Education and Fragility. Email message to INEE Listserv, dated Wednesday 3 June 2009.

Inter-Agency Task Team – Fragile States – Fast Track Initiative (IATT-FS-FTI) (2005) Exploring the Desirability and Feasibility of Expanding the EFA Fast Track Initiative (FTI) to Fragile States. Background Paper for the FTI Partnership, submitted by an inter-agency task team, November 2005. Washington, DC: FTI Partnership.

Inkeles, A. & Smith, D.H. (1974) *Becoming Modern*. Cambridge, MA: Harvard University Press.

Jansen, J. (2005) Targeting Education: the politics of performance and the prospects of 'Education for All', *International Journal of Educational Development*, 25, 368-380.

Kagawa, F. (2005) Emergency Education: a critical review of the field, *Comparative Education*, 41(4), 487-503.

Khadiagala, G.M. (1995) State Collapse and Reconstruction in Uganda, in I.W. Zartman (Ed.) *Collapsed States: the disintegration and restoration of legitimate authority*. Boulder: Lynne Rienner.

Kirk, J. (2007) Education and Fragile States, *Globalisation, Societies and Education*, 5(2), 181-200.

Klees, S. (2001) World Bank Development Policy: a SAP in SWAP's clothing, *Current Issues in Comparative Education*, 3(2), 110-121.

Lulat, Y. (1988) Education and National Development: the continuing problem of misdiagnosis and irrelevant prescriptions, *International Journal of Educational Development*, 8(4), 315-328.

Machel, G. (1996) *Impact of Armed Conflict on Children*. Report of the expert of the Secretary-General, Ms Graca Machel, submitted pursuant to General Assembly resolution 48/157. New York: United Nations.

Macrae, J. (2004) Defining the Boundaries: international security and humanitarian engagement in the post-Cold War world, in Office for the Coordination of Humanitarian Affairs (OCHA) (Ed.) *The Humanitarian Decade: challenges for humanitarian assistance in the last decade and into the future*. Vol. 2. New York: United Nations.

Martone, G. & Neighbor, H. (2004) Aid Agencies Must Think about How People are Living, Not Dying, *Humanitarian Affairs Review*.

http://www.reliefweb.int/rw/lib.nsf/db900SID/AMMF-6NHKBM?OpenDocument

Mbembe, A. (2001) *On the Postcolony*. Berkeley, CA: University of California Press.

McMichael, P. (1996) The Rise of the Development Project, in P. McMichael *Development and Social Change: a global perspective*, 15-43. Thousand Oaks, CA: Pine Forge Press.

Nader, L. (2002) Up the Anthropologist – perspectives gained from studying up, in D. Hymes (Ed.) *Reinventing Anthropology*, 284-311. Ann Arbour: University of Michigan Press.

Nickerson, J.A. & Zenger, T.R. (2004) A Knowledge-Based Theory of the Firm: the problem-solving perspective, *Organization Science*, 15(6), 617-632.

Norberg, C. (2000) Development Aid, Humanitarian Assistance and Emergency Relief, in Building Stability in Africa: challenges for the new millennium. Monograph No. 46. http://www.iss.co.za/Pubs/Monographs/No46/Develop.html

Nkurunziza, P. (2008). Address by His Excellency the President of Burundi, Mr Pierre Nkurunziza, in Doha, Qatar.

Office of the United Nations High Commissioner for Refugees (UNHCR) (2000) The Rwandan Genocide and Its Aftermath, in *The State of The World's Refugees 2000: fifty years of humanitarian action*, ch. 10. Geneva: UNHCR.

Organisation for Economic Cooperation and Development-Development Assistance Committee (OECD-DAC) (2007) *Recent and Ongoing Work of the FSG*. Paris: OECD. http://www.oecd.org/document/32/0,3343,en_2649_33693550_35234336_1_1_1_1,00.html

Orwell, G. (1946) Politics and the English Language, in G. Orwell (Ed.) *A Collection of Essays*. Orlando: Harcourt.

Pigozzi, M.J. (1999) *Education in Emergencies and for Reconstruction: a developmental approach*. Working Paper Series, Education Series. New York: UNICEF.

Quasthoff, U.M. (1989) Social Prejudice as a Resource of Power: towards the functional ambivalence of stereotypes, in R. Wodak (Ed.) *Language, Power, and Ideology*. From a series: *Critical Theory: interdisciplinary approaches to language, discourse and ideology*. Vol. 7. Series editors: Iris M. Zavala & Myriam Diaz-Diocaretz. Amsterdam: John Benjamins.

Raisin, J. & Ramsbotham, A. (2001) Relief, Development and Humanitarian Intervention, in The Humanitarian Studies Unit (Ed.) *Reflections on Humanitarian Action: principles, ethics and contradictions*. London: Pluto Press.

Rose, P. & Greeley, M. (2006) Education in Fragile States: capturing lessons and identifying good practice. Prepared for the Development Assistance Committee (DAC) Fragile States Group Service Delivery Workstream Sub-Team for Education Services. Paris: OECD-DAC.

Ryscavage, R. (2003) The Transition from Conflict to Peace, in K.M. Cahill (Ed.) *Emergency Relief Operations*. New York: Fordham University Press & The Centre for International Health and Cooperation.

Saussure, F. (1959) *Course in General Linguistics*. New York: The Philosophical Library.

Save the Children Alliance (2008) Map of Conflict-Affected Fragile States. http://www.unhcr.org/refworld/docid/490591492.html

Schultz, T.W. (1971) *Investment in Human Capital: the role of education and of research.* New York: Free Press.

Slim, H. (1997) International Humanitarianism's Engagement with Civil War in the 1990s: a glance at evolving practice and theory. A Briefing Paper for ActionAid UK. Oxford: ActionAid UK. http://www.jha.ac/articles/a033.htm

Smillie, I. & Minear, L. (2004) *The Charity of Nations: humanitarian action in a calculating world.* Bloomfield, CT: Kumarian Press.

Smith, D.E. (2001) Texts and the Ontology of Organisations and Institutions, *Cultures, Organisations, and Societies*, 7(2), 159-198.

Sollis, P. (1994) The Relief–Development Continuum: some notes on rethinking assistance for civilian victims of conflict, *Journal of International Affairs*, 47(2), 451-471.

Sornig, K. (1989) Some Remarks on Linguistic Strategies of Persuasion, in R. Wodak (Ed.) *Language, Power, and Ideology*. From a series: *Critical Theory: interdisciplinary approaches to language, discourse and ideology*. Vol. 7. Series editors: Iris M. Zavala & Myriam Diaz-Diocaretz. Amsterdam: John Benjamins.

Stepputat, F., Andersen, L. & Moeller, B. (2007) Introduction: Security Arrangements in Fragile States, in L. Andersen, B. Moeller & F. Stepputat (Eds) *Fragile States and Insecure People? Violence, Security, and Statehood in the Twenty-First Century*. New York: Palgrave MacMillan.

UNESCO (2005) *Education for All Global Monitoring Report*. Paris: UNESCO.

UNESCO (2001) *Education in Situations of Emergency and Crisis: challenges for the new century*. World Education Forum. Education for All – 2000 Assessment. Paris: UNESCO.

Uvin, P. (2008) Development and Security: genealogy and typology of an evolving international policy area, in H.G. Brauch, U.O. Spring, C. Mesjasz, et al (Eds) *Globalisation and Environmental Challenges: reconceptualising security in the 21st century*. New York: Springer.

Vavrus, F. & Seghers, M. (2010) Critical Discourse Analysis in Comparative Education: a discursive study of 'partnership' in Tanzania's poverty reduction policies, *Comparative Education Review*, 54(1), 77-103.

Weber, M., Gerth, H.H. & Wright Mills, C. (Eds) (1991) *From Max Weber: essays in sociology*. London: Routledge.

Weiss, H. (1995) Zaire: collapsed society, surviving state, future polity, in I.W. Zartman (Ed.) *Collapsed States: the disintegration and restoration of legitimate authority*. Boulder: Lynne Rienner.

Woodward, S.L. (2004) Fragile States: exploring the concept. Paper presented to the States and Security Learning Group at the Peace and Social Justice meeting of the Ford Foundation, Rio de Janeiro, Brazil, November.

World Bank (2007) *IDA 15 Operational Approaches and Financing in Fragile States*. International Development Association. Operational Policy and Country Services (OPCS) and Resource Mobilization Department (FRM). Washington, DC: World Bank.

Yoffee, N. (1988) Orienting Collapse, in N. Yoffee & G.L. Cowgill (Eds) *The Collapse of Ancient States and Civilisations*. Tucson: University of Arizona Press.

Zartman, I.W. (1995) Introduction: Posing the Problem of State Collapse, in I.W. Zartman (Ed.) *Collapsed States: the disintegration and restoration of legitimate authority*. Boulder: Lynne Rienner.

CHAPTER 3

Different Presumptions about Progress, Divergent Prescriptions for Peace: connections between conflict, 'development' and education in Nepal

JEREMY RAPPLEYE

SUMMARY This chapter argues that the persistent uncertainty about causes and catalysts of both conflict and development creates major fault lines within the research and practitioner community, not merely vis-à-vis Nepal, but the world over. More specifically, it suggests that the immense complexity that inheres in the conflict–development–education nexus has been collapsed into five dominant lines of thought as the opacity of causal relationships comes to be replaced with presumptions about progress. In critically unpacking and explicating each of these five strands it holds that these different presumptions, in turn, lead to divergent prescriptions for fostering peace, educational and otherwise. Built out of a meta-analysis of the flood of recent research on the conflict in Nepal and illustrated with several rich examples of the divergent ways that the rise of the Maoist 'insurgency' has been analysed, the chapter works to provide theoretical and conceptual clarity to the field, but in doing so necessarily challenges some of our most basic assumptions about the relationship between education, conflict and development.

Arguably the relationships between conflict, development and education manifest in infinite ways the world over. Yet, despite the fact that no two conflict contexts are the same, no two development trajectories are congruent, and educational realities vary widely from one country to the next, the immense complexity that inheres in the conflict–development–education equation has been collapsed into, it will be argued here, five primary lines of thought within the research and practitioner community. This chapter seeks to critically unpack, explicate and explore these five strands of thought, showing that the primary reason for these clear fault lines is persistent uncertainty about causes and catalysts of both conflict and development; the replacement of the opacity of causal relationships with presumptions about progress. These presumptions, in turn, lead to divergent prescriptions for fostering peace, educational and otherwise.

The chapter focuses on the decade-long Maoist 'led' civil war in Nepal, deriving these five perspectives from a meta-analysis of the burgeoning literature that conflict has spawned. Although the chapter aspires to provide new perspectives on the specificities of the Nepalese conflict, the overarching goal is far broader: to contemplate how assumptions about progress shape understandings and prefigure 'development' interventions, educational and otherwise, in conflict-affected areas the world over.[1] In this way, the chapter presupposes no prior knowledge of the Nepalese context and aims more to contribute theoretically and conceptually to the academic study of conflict, development and education (increasingly called the *field* of 'education and conflict'). It appeals here at the very outset for some patience from readers interested primarily in education, arguing that understanding the different ways that the conflict/development nexus is conceptualized is a prerequisite to understanding divergent visions of education's catalytic possibilities and mitigating potential vis-à-vis conflict.[2]

Introduction: from 'Shangri-La' to failed state?

> Since the early 1950s Nepal has served as an attractive destination for Westerners for three main reasons, simply characterized as 3 'P's: peaks (towering Himalayan mountains), pot (marijuana and hashish) and poverty (marginal life chances of the Nepali poor). While the peaks attracted mountain climbers and pot brought hordes of hippies, poverty attracted the attention of 'development missionaries'. (Shrestha, 1997, p. 157)

Edmund Hillary's successful ascent of mighty Sagarmatha (English name: Mount Everest) in 1953 certainly put Nepal, that reclusive Himalayan kingdom perched above newly freed India and soon-to-be subjugated Tibet, on the map for a few in the Western world. Yet, arguably, it was the 'hordes of hippies' that began arriving in significant numbers a decade and a half later that made Nepal known to much larger swathes of the Western world, and that gave Nepal its mystique as a land of profound beauty and tranquillity that it enjoyed until quite recently. These affluent young Europeans and Americans left home for the wider world for many reasons: frustration with the materialism of the West, refuge from the apoplectic possibilities of the escalating Cold War, visions of 'finding themselves' as the Christianity (and authority) of their parents no longer held sway, and simple wanderlust and dreams of an adventure to break the monotony of affluent suburban life. Yet Nepal in particular came to be the terminus of a legendary 'hippie trail' of the

1960s that stretched back through Goa, Kabul and eventually Istanbul primarily because of its legendary marijuana and hashish.

Not only were the sub-tropical Himalayan foothills of the Hindu kingdom such an ideal climate for cannabis that it grew wild and abundant, but Hinduism also appeared to celebrate its use as a gateway to transcendental experience. The yogis (itinerant Hindu 'wise men' clad in saffron robes) who came to pay homage at Kathmandu's sacred Pashupatinath temple could be seen, as they still can be today, smoking it freely out of well-worn chillum pipes, one of their few worldly possessions. In doing so, the yogis were following the model of Bhola Nath, one of the myriad manifestations of Shiva who freed himself from material temptation and reached a 'higher' level of spiritual understanding by intoxication with marijuana and hashish, followed by deep contemplation. This suggests that indeed 'Hinduism has a long cultural history of marijuana smoking, transmitting a sense of transcendental beauty, inner peace, and ultimate freedom' (Shresthra, 1997, p. 158), a history that greeted the first Western 'hippies' with marijuana and hashish that was completely legal and traded openly. The quality proved to be such that word quickly spread, attracting more travellers, which, in turn, led to the emergence of a dozen or more hashish shops and restaurants clustered around Jhochen in central Kathmandu. These cultural and religious roots of cannabis use all but negated awareness among most Nepalese that it might be illegal elsewhere in the world (Lindborg & Gersony, 2003). Combined with its majestic peaks and tranquillity, Nepal thus came to take on the mystique of Shangri-La, that mythical Eastern paradise described by the Orientalizing imagination of James Hilton in the 1930s but seemingly forever lost in the vast expanses of the Himalayas.[3]

Yet over the next thirty years the 'hippies' were replaced by more and more development specialists and aid workers who saw Nepal quite differently: a place of poverty, backwardness, suffering and stagnation. Their 'mission' was to *develop* Nepal, to build a physical infrastructure, modernize its economy and society, and rectify the 'backwardness' of Nepalese culture and people. Beginning with modest projects by the United States Government in the early 1950s, by the mid 1970s the Nepal Aid Group was officially established (under the leadership of the World Bank) to try to coordinate a growing number of Western aid projects (Whelpton, 2005). By the late 1980s, the Group included nearly twenty individual donor countries and six international organizations. The People's Movement of 1990 that led to the fall of an authoritarian, inward-looking, Palace-led panchayat system and the 'restoration' of democracy was quickly hailed by these donors as Nepal's 'democratic revolution'. This led to another dramatic influx in aid as Nepal became a donor 'darling': an impoverished 'nation' located in an area of major geopolitical significance that did not take sides during the Cold War, yet now seemed quite committed to the new democracy and free-market ideology of the post-Wall world. Projects abounded and, urged on by donors, Nepal's new leaders enthusiastically committed the country to a range of international covenants (the first, as timing would have it, the Jomtien Education for All declaration), thus unleashing a further rush of donor funds. Aid and 'development' became a booming industry, at least in an increasingly cosmopolitan Kathmandu (Liechty, 2003). For the first half of the 1990s, the image of Shangri-La seemed to return as donors dreamt of a shining development 'success' story perched high up in the majestic Himalayas.

Then civil war broke out. In February 1996, a splinter faction of the Communist Party of Nepal (CPN) announced a Maoist-inspired 'People's War' with attacks on police stations in their stronghold of the Rukum and Rolpa districts in the mid-west hills about 300 kilometres from Kathmandu. From these two districts straddling the Rapti River Valley, the Maoists spread quickly to surrounding areas. Within just four years, the Maoists were believed to control as much as 90% of the Nepalese countryside. In late 2001, after several failed police operations against the 'insurgents' and the breakdown of talks around fulfilment of the '40 Point Demands' (issued by the Maoists as a condition of laying down their arms), the intensity of the conflict rose considerably. The Government declared a 'state of emergency' and mobilized the army against the rebels for the first time but, undaunted, the Maoists launched more brazen attacks on urban areas, killing far larger numbers of security personnel with increasing frequency, punctuated by a high-profile assassination of the head of the Armed Police Force in January 2003.

As the strength of the Maoists increased, so did their power to negotiate the terms of any peace settlement. By the time a fragile ceasefire was signed in late autumn 2006 – one that promised the Maoists protection to run national elections that would elect delegates to rewrite the national Constitution (and thus provided the potential for the Maoists to write 'in' many of their demands if successfully elected) – some 13,000 Nepalese were dead, and an already weak physical infrastructure (including schools) was in shambles. A chronically lethargic economy had heavily contracted. By 2005 the United Nations (UN) appealed for Nepal to undertake the Consolidated Appeals Process (CAP), a move that effectively recognized it as a 'failed state' joining the ranks of Haiti, Sudan, Burundi and Uganda, among others (Ghani and Lockhart, 2008), leading more than a few observers to thus lament 'the end of Shangri-La' (Bloch, 2005; Thapa, 2005).

So what went wrong? What caused Nepal's decline from relative peace and tranquillity to a lack of 'development' and the outbreak of conflict? How should we 'connect the dots' between the various aspects of the last fifty years of Nepal's modern 'development' described above: hippies and hashish, perceptions and poverty, donors and development? The introduction above sets a necessary backdrop for themes utilized and referenced throughout the chapter to address such questions; questions that ultimately point us toward the chapter's overarching puzzle: *what is the relationship between conflict and 'development' and how does education intersect therein?* One good way to approach this immense topic is to first examine key issues and interpretations on a smaller scale, by taking a brief excursion to the heartland of the Maoist insurgency where a little-known (at least outside of Nepal) story of the intersections of marijuana/hashish, 'development' and the outbreak of conflict unfolds.

'District Number One' as Window on the Complexity of Causality: USAID's 'Rapti Development Project' and the rise of the Maoists

As mentioned above, the districts of Rukum and Rolpa straddling the Rapti River Valley in the mid-west hills became the epicentre of the Maoist People's War. Here the Maoist leaders enjoyed such widespread popular support they not only were able to tap a ready pool of recruits to launch the opening moves of the insurgency, but they were relatively impervious to government, army and police infiltration. Although clearly difficult to gauge, it was believed that well over 90% of the population politically supported the Maoists in these areas, as corroborated by the degree of control Maoists enjoyed there and official election results in 2008 that had the Maoists sweeping the election there (Lowati, 2008). Rukum and Rolpa (primarily the north-east parts) were thus very early on dubbed 'District Number One' by the Maoists, announcing their actual base as well as their aspirations to take and remake all of Nepal's districts along such lines.

So what was it about Rukum and Rolpa that made them so amenable to the Maoist message, such fertile ground for the growth of 'revolution'? Rukum and Rolpa is an area that is, like much of Nepal, nestled deep in heavily forested hills climbing up to 6900 metres, with village life centring on the rivers that cut through the rugged terrain as they race towards the Ganges in northern India, in this case the Rapti River. It is a region with few roads; most areas are only accessible by hiking for several days along a traditional network of trails. Many analyses have pointed out that the remoteness of the place provided the Maoists sanctuary, making their base of operations nearly impossible to reach from the outside (de Sales, 2003; Onesto, 2005). Yet, pointing out the fractured, largely impregnable terrain does not explain why the Maoists enjoyed such widespread support in these areas initially. This is why others have turned to look elsewhere for clues to conflict causality.

Rukum and Rolpa are dominated by an ethnic minority group called the Kham Magars, a part of the largest of Nepal's many ethnic groups that trace a Tibeto-Burman, as opposed to Indo-Aryan, lineage. Within the districts the ethnic composition is largely homogeneous and there are few, if any, records of inter-ethnic conflict there. Although Hindu symbols abound, religion is considered to be more animist than Hindu and caste lines are concomitantly less clearly demarcated and enforced (de Sales, 2003). Thus, divisive ethnic, religious and social characteristics would seem to be less than explanatory. Indeed, if ethnicity and religion drove the outbreak of violence, dozens of other districts in Nepal would seem to be more likely candidates for District One status, a conclusion that has led many analysts to instead focus on economic dimensions.

By many accounts only about 10% of Rukum and Rolpa's land is cultivable, translating into small family plots that provide little more than basic subsistence for less than half the year. The food deficit has thus been chronic, as in much of the western hills of Nepal, and exacerbated year-on-year by rapid population growth, forcing families to send male members elsewhere for seasonal work or engage in other money-making activities to generate surplus wealth to buy supplies that could not be made, including clothes, oil and educational supplies (Lindborg & Gersony, 2003). These 'surplus' activities have traditionally included raising sheep and iron mining, but both are said to have declined since the 1970s for several reasons: more and more youth from these areas finding it more lucrative to work abroad (first India, later overseas, especially the Gulf states), competition over markets for these products from cheap imports from India, and the government shuttering of the main iron mine because deforestation made it difficult to find the hardwood needed for smelting the iron ore (Lindborg & Gersony, 2003; see also Burtel & Ali, 2009). A range of additional indicators thus support the view that Rukum and Rolpa was among the poorest economic areas of Nepal by the time the Maoist movement gathered momentum.

Yet, it had not always been such a poor region, primarily because there was another source of 'surplus' income that had once provided more than enough: the cultivation of high-quality marijuana and hash.[4] Although unclear when such surplus production began, the rich hemp textiles from the area reveal that the uses of cannabis had long been an integral part of the culture in the area (Clarke, 2007a). This suggests that when market prices for marijuana/hash eclipsed what farmers could earn from cultivating food on their land, they converted some of their fields to marijuana (Clarke, 2007b) and traded it in market towns along the Indian border for necessary supplies. Such a view is supported by Lindborg & Gersony (2003), who conducted several hundred interviews in Rukum and Rolpa in 2002, where inhabitants 'almost unanimously' reported how:

> Thirty years ago, they said, theirs was the most prosperous area of Nepal's Western Hills. They defined this prosperity as having sufficient cash to bridge the annual food deficit, to buy salt, oil, and several sets of clothes each year for their families, to acquire silver-coin necklaces and bracelets and gold jewelry which Magar women like to wear, and being able to remain at home, rather than migrating to acquire the cash required ... beginning at least in the 1930s and through the 1970s ... they assert [that Rukum and Rolpa] was the principal producer of Nepali hashish, whose quality is renowned throughout the world. (p. 12)

Other sources from the time corroborate the notion that the area was the heartland of Nepal's legendary cannabis production (Fisher, 1975), providing more than enough for the outside market to increasingly become a driver of economic abundance in the otherwise impoverished western hills, especially as the aforementioned 'hippies' boosted demand in the tea houses of Kathmandu.

Yet, this all came to an abrupt halt in 1976 when the Government of Nepal enacted the Drug Trafficking and Abuse Act. The Act came at the behest of Narcotics International, a lesser-known 'control board' of the United Nations charged with coordinating and enforcing UN drug policy. However, the real force and origin of pressure appears to have been the United States (Bewley-Taylor, 1999). Running on a platform of 'law and order' amidst the riots and upheaval of 1968, Richard Nixon was inaugurated in January 1969, promising to 'clean up' a perceived rise in crime, violence, and social disturbances that were seen to be linked, in part, to drug abuse and lower moral standards (as opposed to urban poverty and the civil rights approach of Lyndon B. Johnson's preceding 'Great Society'). The result was the United States' Comprehensive Drug Abuse Prevention and Control Act passed in 1970 and the simultaneous, far more active and assertive role of the United States in pushing for control of 'illegal' substances internationally (Bewley-Taylor, 1999).

This US pressure for an international drug control regime (as opposed to a national policy) quickly crystallized in a major UN conference convened in January 1971 charged with enacting a single international convention on drug control. Yet, the enactment of legislation hit a major roadblock almost immediately as many 'developing' countries that produced cannabis, coca, and opium (organic) opposed lumping such substances together with psychotropic (synthetic) drugs such as LSD that were overwhelmingly produced and consumed in the 'developed' world. These 'developing' states argued that on economic and cultural grounds the production of these organic substances should continue (McAllister, 2000). In the end, however, the developing world could not match the lobbying power and resources of states such as the United States and were further enticed with promises of substantial 'aid' to make up for economic losses (King, 1972). The result was the Convention on Psychotropic Substances passed in February 1971 and scheduled to come into effect in 1976 to give sufficient time for states to prepare. The Nepalese leadership responded with a revocation of all dealers' licences and the shuttering of the tea houses of Kathmandu in July 1973, followed by the official enactment of the aforementioned Drug Trafficking and Abuse Act three years later.

In return for its compliance, the United States offered and awarded Nepal a massive USAID Integrated Rural Development Project (IRDP) in the Rapti River Valley; a region that was comprised of the districts of Rolpa, Rukum, Dang and Salyan – the most renowned cannabis growing region of the country (Fischer, 1975).[5] The USAID Rapti IRDP totalled some 50 million US dollars over 20 years. The project began in 1976, the year the Drug Trafficking and Abuse Act came into effect, and ended in 1995, less than a year before the Maoists launched the People's War from Rukum and Rolpa. Officially, the goal of the project was poverty alleviation through (a) 'increased production and consumption of food by the people of the Rapti Zone', (b) 'construct[ion of] new roads and maintenance of old roads', and (c) 'strengthen[ing] the capacity of Panchayats (now called Village Development Committees) and other local organizations to plan, implement, and sustain local development efforts' (USAID, 1995). The programme also officially included provisions for the enhancement of women's lives, community management of forests, and democratization. Unofficially, the Rapti IRDP was clearly attractive to the United States as a way to facilitate government monitoring and enforcement of the ban on marijuana and hashish, but also to check 'Communist' organization and infiltration (a major geopolitical concern in the context of the height of the Cold War). There were no education or schooling aspects of USAID's Rapti IRDP despite extremely low levels of enrolment and literacy in the region at the time, raising some questions about how significant education itself is in catalysing full-scale conflict.

Completed in two phases, the Rapti Development Project, in the first phase, running from 1976 to 1988, built drinking water and irrigation systems, constructed 180 kilometres of 'farm-to-market' roads and some 15 suspension bridges. In the second phase, running from 1989 to 1994, the building of roads and suspension bridges continued, but more resources were put toward introducing new farming techniques, fertilizers, and seeds to increase apple, onion and radish production that could generate income in market towns bordering India (USAID, 1995). The less obvious by-product of such interventions, however, was the increased visibility and, thus, control of the production, sale and distribution of marijuana and hashish. Police used better roads and bridges to interdict the trafficking of cannabis products, leading to a spate of arrests in the late 1970s. Private property found to have marijuana growing on it was often revoked, officially classified as 'forest land', and thus given back to the State. In other cases, farmers were forced to eradicate their marijuana fields in advance of the arrival of IRDP activities (Lindborg & Gersony, 2003).

Such a 'development' intervention would hardly be remarkable had it not taken place in the region that would become the very epicentre of the Maoist insurgency. Yet, when the Maoists announced the People's War with a brazen attack on the Holeri police station in southern Rolpa on 13 February 1996, the obvious question arose, one that would only grow stronger as the Maoist insurgency spread quickly throughout the region: *what was the relationship between a massive twenty-year external development intervention and the outbreak of violence?* Was it that the USAID project was simply a fine-sounding extension of US foreign policy that thus failed to deliver to local people? Was it that 'development' itself had somehow sparked the unrest? Can and should the cannabis ban and the USAID IRDP intervention be coupled? Was it rather that the USAID project actually helped stave off an inevitable insurgency? Or was there some other intervening factor(s) that might have *caused* the insurgency to erupt from the exact districts where USAID poured enormous sums of aid?

On one level, certain facts appear to be beyond dispute, even though the *causes* of conflict remain unclear. One was the effect of the cannabis ban. In interviews with local residents, Lindborg & Gersony (2003) report, for example, a widespread feeling that for most residents of Rukum and Rolpa:

> the hashish ban was the first substantive action of any kind by the remote Kathmandu government which affected them directly. Between 1976 and 1980, the [relatively high] 'standard of living' of which they had spoken had given way to grinding poverty in which food was shared among neighbors just so they could survive. Women liquidated their silver necklaces and gold jewelry; men migrated in greater numbers to earn the money they needed for their families' survival. In their perception, by banning hashish the government had literally taken the food out of their children's mouths. (p. 14)

That is, according to local residents the cannabis ban created an abrupt slide into poverty, one that came to be linked to the decisions made in Kathmandu and largely unmitigated by USAID's Rapti Development Project. Lindborg & Gersony go on to report that, in Rukum and Rolpa 'allegiance to the Communist Party increased from a nominal 10% to 60% in the four years following the hashish ban. The area's "standard of living" collapsed. People were hungry, without money to buy clothes and, during this adjustment period, without ready alternatives', ultimately leading to the belief 'that only through violent Communist revolt would the neglect and injustices of Nepal's governing system be overcome' (p. 25). These authors are silent as to why democratic solutions were not a possible option, except to say that several delegations from the area appealing to the Government of Nepal were met with little response. The related question is why did it take some twenty years for such discontent to break into open conflict? Here is where the real debate begins and divergent opinions about causality and the concomitant presumptions about 'progress' – the primary point of this chapter – begin to unfold and quickly diverge.

For some authors, 'development' may not have caused the outbreak of violence but it did nothing to stop it, which itself is unacceptable and at odds with 'development's' own rhetoric of 'progress'. Mainali (2003) argues, for example, that:

> I strongly believe that donors, including Americans, should not be allowed to operate in poverty stricken rural areas of Nepal ... and the reason I say so is because of what we saw of the USAID-implemented Rapti Development Rural Area Development

> Project ... The government and donors both say development packages will help eliminate the Maoists. If this were true, why was [the] Rapti Zone so favorable for the development of the Maoist movement? If this is what you get after 15 years of American funded development, we were perhaps better off without it. (pp. 125-126)

Others, such as Gurung (2005), take a similar, albeit a distinctly more critical line, arguing that the 'Rapti Zone presents a telling case of a development intervention with reverse consequence', pointing out that:

> Since [the] mid-1970s, 12 donors have implemented 16 IRDPs covering 41 districts of Nepal ... ironically these efforts made no dent in rural poverty as indicated by the high level of insurgency in districts covered by Rapti, Bheri-Karnali, Seti, and Mahakali IRDPs. On the reverse, districts of Lumbini and Gandaki zone without an IRDP had a low intensity of insurgency. Significantly, Manang and Mustang that had no IRDPs experienced no insurgency deaths.

Gurung is implicitly arguing that IRDPs actually contributed in some ways to the outbreak of violence, but leaves out the fact that perhaps the reason that particular districts originally had no IRDPs was because they were deemed to be relatively less impoverished.

Lieten (2002), however, is explicit in going one step further in arguing that the Rapti Development Project largely *caused* the Maoist insurgency:

> The actual beneficiaries of development and development aid were mainly the high-caste elites from towns and villages ... but local people hardly ever benefited. The polarization between the development-aided rich and the big majority of poor people thus generated resentment in the minds of people. It is interesting to note that ... in the Rapti zone in the Midwestern hills of Nepal, where the 'People's War' movement is at its strongest, the United States had been active in aid projects meant to develop the region ... as soon as the development project, launched with a view to eliminating poverty or backwardness was phased out, the 'People's War' erupted from the very heart of Rapti. The main international donor agencies particularly ... the United States, are perceived as having contributed to the success of the Maoist movement by raising the expectations of rural people for the development of their region and by in fact creating a thin layer of wealthy beneficiaries, leaving the majority with a heightened sense of deprivation and inequality. (p. 444)

Subedi (2009) concurs that the influx of development dollars benefiting the local elites (many with connections to the State), coupled with the ban on marijuana and hashish that cut out the main source of income for peasants, led to an immediate and abrupt spike in inequality. Sharma & Rana (2005; see also Bonino & Donini, 2009) launch a more cutting critique, arguing that it was precisely the combination of rising expectations brought about by the USAID intervention, combined with its failure to produce any substantial replacement for the loss of cannabis, that sparked deep disenchantment in the districts; a loss of faith in 'development' itself amidst crushing poverty that left few options but exit or armed conflict.

Yet, such opinions are by no means dominant. Instead, most accounts of the war avoid engagement with the issue of linkages between USAID development intervention and the rise of the Maoists by eliminating 'development' from the range of possible variables. In effect, there is a de facto opinion that conflict causality derives from factors such as population growth, historical grievances and long-standing poverty (e.g. chronic food shortages) that are unrelated to externally-led 'development' projects. A typical example is the *Final Evaluation of the Rapti Development Project, a* massive 180-page project evaluation prepared for USAID by a Washington-based consultancy, John Mellor Associates. Although it was published in 1995, before the outbreak of violence, not once in the 180-page report is mention made of social unrest, marijuana and/or hashish. Instead the report places the cause of grinding poverty on population growth amid an otherwise sparkling review of the project:

> Since 1970, the rural resources of Nepal have come under immense pressure. The population has nearly doubled ... yet the significant increase in per capita income that reflects sustained growth and keeps fertility rates low has failed to materialize ... [However] The essential shift to a high-growth strategy is now feasible. It requires a sharp departure from past practices ... The RDP [Rapti Development Project] has effectively demonstrated this sharp break. Particularly since the mid-term review the project has emphasized the commercialization of hill agriculture through high-value cash crops such as fruits and vegetables ... Thus, the project is a prototype for sustained development not only in thc Rapti Zone, but throughout Nepal. (USAID, 1995, p. ix)

The irony here is both that conflict would break out within a year (obviously 'high growth' was *not* 'feasible') and that there was arguably no more 'high-value cash crop' than cannabis. Another volume published in 2004 – some eight years after the outbreak of violence – celebrating the achievements of USAID, echoes the *Final Evaluation*, stating that 'during nearly 20 years, from 1976 to 1995, the government of Nepal and USAID worked together to plan and promote rural development in Nepal's remote regions named the Rapti Zone ... the long collaborative effort was largely successful' (Butterfield, 2004, p. 182). Only in a terse final paragraph does it relate that 'in 1998 these Maoists murdered a USAID-funded Nepali specialist working in Rapti ... as a consequence, USAID withdrew its contract staff from the

Rapti Zone ... the insurgents seemed to be using the mountainous Rolpa district of the Rapti Zone as their operational headquarters' (p. 185). In effect, 'development' falls out of the possible causes of conflict; development is taken as a de facto mitigating factor.

Another opinion about what occurred in Rukum and Rolpa that at least engages the possibility of connections between the USAID intervention and the rise of the Maoists, even though still clearly viewing 'development' as positive, is found in the work of Lindborg & Gersony (2003). In a large study in 2003 focusing on the causes of insurgency in the Rapti Zone, they found that:

> The $50 million USAID Rapti Integrated Development Project's successes produced sustainable economic benefits for thousands of families ... where the project was not successful, the impediment was the absence of major roads, a larger central government issue which transcended the scope of USAID's activities. Roads are at the core of this region's political agenda. (Lindborg & Gersony, 2003, p. 97)

They thus go on to conclude that USAID cannot be blamed for the conflict and instead argue that it is the 'Maoists [who] have blocked the development agenda – which is at the heart of local political aspirations – for more than eight years' (p. 97). In effect, they appear to be arguing that a different type of 'development' intervention (namely the construction of roads) could have staved off the conflict, a position that presents development as largely positive, but perhaps in need of tinkering or adjustment. What they leave out is that, although USAID did not discourage road-building (in fact, road-building was an explicit component of the IRDP), other donors such as the World Bank and British Overseas Development Aid (ODA) representatives did. Whelpton (2005, p. 143) describes 'elaborate studies' in the 1970s by both agencies that dissuaded the Government from building roads on the logic that it was 'unlikely to boost agricultural output' and that 'maintenance costs ... were far too high for Nepal to bear'. This raises difficult questions about whether 'development' can be viewed as simply the sum total of the stated goals of individual projects or whether we must talk about 'development' as a coherent phenomenon that transcends the work of any one donor and encompasses both explicit programme goals and implicit drivers of 'development' aid. It is also hard to evaluate how much full funding and 'guidance' by USAID in producing the Lindborg & Gersony (2003) report played a role in its conclusions; conclusions that seem to clearly defy their rich interview data about the impact of the cannabis ban cited above.

The main point here is just as much the specifics of what happened in Rukum and Rolpa as the range of different opinions (and silences, a de facto opinion) that quickly emerges in literature covering events in just two of Nepal's 75 national districts. While the opinions presented above initially appear to be a rather haphazard group of conflicting viewpoints, on closer inspection it is possible to identify fundamental differences over how conflict is implicitly conceptualized and what factors are centred in the analyses (especially 'development'), all founded on divergent hypotheses about causality. For some the Maoists arose because of 'development', for others 'development' failed, for still others aid played a mitigating role. Silences must be listened to here as well: what factors do particular analyses include? Which do they subtly write out of the realm of possibility? What tensions are silenced through such operations? If we ask what creates these different opinions, it seems certain that it is the sheer complexity of the conflict–development puzzle that allows divergent opinions to coexist, as well as unseen ideological and practical imperatives (such as USAID funding of research). The magnitude of possible factors invites onlookers to collapse complexity and thereby hypothesize what made Rukum and Rolpa the epicentre of civil war; self-interest and political motivations largely prefigure the specific ways that this process of collapse and hypothesis take place. From this perspective, it begins to make sense why scholarship on Nepal over the last 15 years has failed to come to any sort of consensus about what caused conflict in Rukum and Rolpa alone.

So, is there any way forward or are we lost in an endless expanse of complexity? This chapter holds that while a definitive answer may prove elusive, we can nevertheless push for awareness, systematization and reordering of divergent opinions. Such an exercise ultimately reveals, it will be argued, a set of five hypothesis-driven perspectives on the relationship between conflict and development (and thus education).[6] Systematization and critical engagement helps to locate silences, assumptions, and the closure of particular possibilities, as well as to suggest reasons for collapse and closure that extend well beyond merely condensing complexity in order to 'act'. This, in turn, helps us make sense of the wider literature on the conflict in Nepal (and probably beyond), and offers much-needed conceptual clarity to the education dimension(s) of the conflict–development–education nexus.

Collapsing Complexity, Conceptualizing Conflict, Hypothesizing Causality: connecting to the wider literature of 'development'

It is rare to find open, frank admission that we are still nowhere close to having sorted out the conflict–development (and education) relationship in the wider literature, notwithstanding increasingly obligatory remarks about 'many factors' that can lead to war. One laudable exception is Mac Ginty & Williams (2009), who have written a 'state-of-the art' of recent conflict and development research that emphatically points out that 'there is no exact science linking conflict to development; the constellation of variables is simply too great given the variations in context and timescales' (p. 42). They hold that as a result 'the conflict analyst is faced with a bewildering array of "evidence" and, ultimately, must make a judgment call on which factors they believe to be the most significant in the escalation of crisis' (p. 27). In effect, observers must reduce – *collapse* – complexity in order to conceptualize conflict. Mac Ginty & Williams continue that the outcome of this is that 'conflict interventions and development programming contain a good deal of guesswork and finger crossing' (p. 42).

While such an observation seems to be a terminus for Mac Ginty & Williams, it can be refashioned as a starting point for this section: we can, in order to advance current research, focus on the broader contours of how conflict observers *collapse* (reduction in variables) complex conflict–development realities, how conflict is *conceptualised* in line with this collapsed reality, and, ultimately, how *causality* is then hypothesized ('judgement calls') to become the basis of 'development' interventions (prescriptions for progress), educational and otherwise. While some risk of overgeneralization attends any such review, moving beyond the muddle of opinions found in the current literature and drawing explicit connections to a wider body of 'development' and social theory would seem one way forward amidst continuing uncertainty.

Let us begin with what we might term a *(neo)classic development* view. This view tends to hold ideological positions such as the pre-eminence of the market and the importance of democracy (mostly to ensure corrections of market excesses) as inviolable development 'truths'. It collapses the complexity of the conflict–development nexus overwhelmingly along economic lines, in effect centring economic growth and decentring non-economic factors. The perspective traces its roots to a combination of human capital (Schultz, 1971) and modernization theories (Rostow, 1960), as well as to a later reworking and further purging of non-economic factors (including the State) by a strain of neoclassical economics mostly closely associated with work at the University of Chicago in the 1970s. Through this (neo)classic lens, the view emerges that development equates with economic growth; a competitive capitalist market is the primary engine of development. Here inequality is viewed as an unfortunate by-product of growth, leading to wealth generation for society as a whole; a necessary intermediary 'step' on a national development trajectory. When linked with conflict, the hypothesis is that (a) generating economic growth can only lessen the risk of violent conflict (and in reverse: economic stagnation heightens the possibility for civil war [see World Bank, 2003a]), and (b) combatants are predominantly motivated by economic deprivation or predation (Mac Ginty & Williams, 2009). *In the classic development view then, more economic development is the solution for conflict; less economic development is the source of it.*

Progress is measured in economic terms; prescriptions become strategies for developing the economy that lessen the drivers of conflict, albeit indirectly. Here, there is no causal link between externally administered 'development' interventions and conflict: development is unequivocally positive; war is fundamentally the result of economic self-interest.

Proponents of this view have traditionally been the major international financial institutions, most prominently the International Monetary Fund (IMF), the World Bank, and regional development banks, although the World Bank has distanced itself, to a degree, from more extreme versions of this view over the past decade or more (see World Bank, 2005). A typical example of the (neo)classical view is the *Final Evaluation* of the USAID Rapti Development Project reviewed above: success is viewed overwhelmingly along economic lines ('cash crops' and commercialization of agriculture) while the potential role of wider geopolitics (the cannabis ban) and the detrimental effects of the USAID intervention itself is removed from the field of possible variables.

A second position is one that we might term a *moderated classic development* view. Maintaining an equally firm conviction in the promise of externally-led 'development', the position diverges from the classic development view because of its tendency to draw non-economic factors to the centre of the analysis, arguing for parity of such issues as human rights, gender mainstreaming, civil liberties, and the inclusion of civil society among others. In its current manifestation, the belief traces much of its recent momentum to a reaction to the dominance of the (neo)classic development view that produced the excesses of 'structural adjustment' in the 1980s, arguing for moderation and heightened sensitivity to non-economic factors in 'development' programming. Theoretical robustness comes from Sen's (1985, 1999) human capabilities approach, while UNICEF's (1997) *Development with a Human Face* and the United Nations Development Programme (UNDP) annual *Human Development Index* (first launched in 1990) can be seen as representative texts. Stewart's (2001) work on horizontal inequalities should be included here as well, as it infuses the (neo)classical economic view with human dimensions of perceptions and *relative* economic deprivation. Many bilateral donors, but especially the Nordic countries, Canada, and the Netherlands and and non-governmental organizations (NGOs) have been at the forefront of operationalizing such an approach (Browne, 2006).

In effect, the moderated (neo)classic development view collapses complexity in a way that, like the former, eliminates 'development' itself as a possible variable even while it does recognize more human variables as significant engines of 'development'. Accordingly, conflict is conceptualized as just as much the result of human factors as it is the result of economics; here factors such as *relative* economic inequality, identity, religion, gender inequity, ethnicity, nationalism and ideology are viewed as causal and thus critical. Still, given the continued belief in the promise of 'development', the hypothesis is that *better development can mitigate conflict and that the relationship between development and conflict flows in only in a single direction: positive and ameliorative*. Progress is still seen to come about through 'development', though more direct interventions focusing on human elements are prescribed. In this way, tinkering, adjusting, viewing more holistically, or creating 'better' development is seen as the imperative; development 'failure' is seen as a result of the wrong kind of intervention. Such a view usually comes to underpin explicit initiatives and 'interventions' for peacebuilding, especially those targeted at the most vulnerable or marginalized populations. One example of the moderated classic development view is found in Lindborg & Gersony's (2003) assertion reviewed above that failing to build roads was the major reason for the less-than-desirable results of the USAID Rapti IRDP, although in a few points that same work begins to approximate the next position by at least considering 'development' as a potential factor.

A third position might be called a *failed development* view, one that begins to more explicitly challenge the view that 'development' programming is altruistic, effective, and unconnected to the origins of conflict, but nonetheless reveals an implicit belief in the ideal of 'development'. Like the moderated classic view, this position tends to centre non-economic factors in the analysis but takes an additional step by considering what role 'development' intervention itself plays in exacerbating pre-existing social divisions that lead to conflict. This inclusion often comes, however, at the cost of pushing other factors preceding or external to 'development' out of the field of possible variables. In another point of departure from the former positions, this view also tends to point out how 'development' is not simply for the benefit of the recipient but is often heavily infused with external agendas, be those foreign policy goals or ideological 'paradigms' of influential actors. *The failed development view thus hypothesizes that 'development' interventions rank among the primary factors in determining if a nation slides to conflict, a view that is achieved by downplaying the history and contemporary context of a particular field of 'development' intervention and thus shifts responsibility for fragile contexts to external donors.* The presumption is that 'development' does not necessarily bring progress, therefore the prescription is to critically consider the ways 'development' catalyses conflict and thus not shy away from the possibility of a complete overhaul of the 'development' status quo.

One representative and popular example is Stiglitz's (2002) scathing critique of those espousing a (neo)classic development view (especially the IMF). Stiglitz argues that 'development' in its (neo)classic manifestation unnecessarily rends a nation-state's pre-existing social fabric. That social fabric, Stiglitz explains, is already brought under severe strain by the processes of 'development'. He points out how many 'developing' states were not only worse off after the 1980s and 1990s primarily because (neo)classic-inspired policies celebrated the 'pain' of breaking down traditional social relations as signs of 'progress', even as one of the biggest assets of 'developing' contexts – a cushioning web of social relations – can now no longer be recouped as slums, crime and social divisions have taken deep root. Commentators included in this failed development group are those who point to the way that donor assistance distorts the local economy, such as Van de Walle (2001), who highlights that 'other than the state itself, the aid business is today the single biggest employer in African states' (p. 58) (see Liechty [2003] for a similar analysis of Nepal). By arguing that the enormous donor presence in fragile states *in its totality* must rank near the top of causal variables, this view in effect tends to answer the earlier question as to whether 'development' should be considered simply the sum of individual projects or 'development' conceptualized as a much larger (distorting) phenomenon in fragile 'developing' countries.

Those subscribing to such a view would thus argue, for example, that one can never separate the cannabis ban from the USAID Rapti IRDP, even if the intervention itself was sound: foreign policy always distorts aid. Others would hold that the cannabis ban and the stratifying effect of delivering the USAID Rapti IRDP are both to blame. Another variation would be that, even if the USAID project itself did not spark conflict, the sum total of forty years of external aid and interventions failing to 'develop' Nepal must be held accountable. The failed development view thus emerges as a much more cutting, self-aware and holistic criticism than the two former positions, within which various strands of critique of external aid co-exist and intermingle. However, all these strands are bound together by the centring of 'development' itself as a key conflict variable (whether causal or corrective), together with a refusal to completely do away with the ameliorative promise of aid and 'development'. Again, this results in prescriptions for fundamental change in the way 'development' itself is administered both globally and locally (see also Uvin, 1998; Browne, 2006).

A fourth position is a *conflict as development success* view, holding that it is the very success of 'development' intervention that catalyses conflict. The logic is that what particular types of 'development' interventions achieve is an elevated awareness among oppressed and marginalized groups of their relative position, followed by support for an oppressed/marginalized population's first tentative steps into a more equitable, empowered space (such as those, say, who adopt a Freirian approach to literacy and community mapping, then tap these new skills to mobilize powerful grass-roots lobbies for greater rights or resources). Such a grass-roots, action-oriented approach obviously confines the primary – although not exclusive – 'development' organizations in this group to international and domestic NGOs. 'Development' creates images, ideas, expectations, networks and so on that soon enable and energize collective action, just as those interventions were designed to do. Yet, if the power structures fail to accommodate this grass-roots ferment or refuse to rectify oppressive conditions, conflict may be inevitable. The position has been largely underdeveloped on both a theoretical and empirical level (although some would point to Freire, 1970; see also Archer, 1990), perhaps because it is frequently assumed (hoped?) that democratic, as opposed to violent, solutions can accommodate the new assertiveness of the oppressed.

In this conflict as development success view, the vast complexity of what creates violent conflict is actually collapsed around the two core propositions: (1) oppression/marginalization fuel conflict, and (2) these tensions rarely translate into open conflict until oppressed/marginalized populations (e.g. the poor, women, ethnic groups) are, through 'development', made conscious of their relative status, latent power, and potential to catalyse change. Through such a lens, 'development' interventions are centred in the analysis and hypothesized as the major cause of conflict, much as in the former failed development hypothesis. *Yet, in contrast to the former position, here conflict is not something to be lamented, but entertained, if not celebrated: despite the tragedy of bloodshed the fundamental structures of oppression are being challenged and the self-perpetuating cycle of passivity and marginalization begins to break down.* That is, 'progress' is fundamentally about challenging oppressive structures and helping give voice to the marginalized, not necessarily eliminating conflict. Prescriptions are thus less concerned with preventing conflict, and more concerned with developing critical consciousness and assertiveness. Like failed development, this conceptualization necessarily sidelines factors such as population growth, scarcity of resources, and other changes that affect entire populations, rather than a particular stratum of oppressor and/or oppressed. This makes it hard to explain, for example, why Rukum and Rolpa became the epicentre of the Maoist insurgency, as opposed to all the other areas in Nepal where 'development' projects were active in grass-roots organizing and consciousness-raising activities. Yet, it does perhaps help in explaining why the Maoists found such an enthusiastic reception and deep pool of recruits among populations that had been involved in 'development', especially women and *dalits* (untouchables).

The final position is surely the most daring, so long as the (neo)classic development and moderated classical development view approximate the mainstream. This fifth perspective might be called *development as cause of conflict*. It centres the impact of 'development' itself in the analysis in much the same way as the previous two positions. Yet, it is distinct from all previous positions because it argues that 'development' itself is such a flawed endeavour from the very outset that it is unsalvageable; that its divisive impacts are built into the very nature of the notion of 'development' and failures that could largely have been forecasted years ago are now bearing fruit in the form of open violence. The origins of the theory can be traced to Escobar's (1995) work entitled *Encountering Development: the making and unmaking of the Third World* in which he challenges the very notion that people were undeveloped, the *raison d'être* of 'development' (and thus all the previous positions). Instead he works with post-structuralism and develops Foucault's notions of power to show how 'development' was largely a construct of the post-World War II world, the need for the West to stay involved in the 'Third World' following the end of colonization and the beginning of a global Cold War that succeeded by fabricating '"abnormalities" (such as the "illiterate," the "underdeveloped," the "malnourished," "small farmers," or "landless peasants"), which it would later treat and reform' (Escobar, 1995, p. 41).

This vision was later powerfully extended and connected to the emergence of conflict by Ferguson (2005), who argued in 'Decomposing Modernity: history and hierarchy after development' that 'development' was a 'powerful narrative that effectively transformed a *spatialized* global hierarchy into a *temporalized* (putative) historical sequence' (p. 167, original italics). This translated into specific propositions for those in the 'developing' world: 'for those at the bottom of the global hierarchy, the message was clear: wait, have your patience, your turn will come' (p. 168). In other words, Ferguson argues that 'development' was a powerful myth that made it possible to avoid issues of global inequality and the legacy of colonization. By suggesting that inequality was to be found in the Third World itself, the solution was patience and a full commitment by those in the 'Third World' to the 'development' endeavour and its underpinning 'modernist' timeline.

Ferguson goes on to argue, however, that with the persistent failure of the litany of development models to deliver 'development's' promised 'catch-up', the current situation is that the myth is breaking down ('decomposing') in the world's most impoverished areas ('nonconvergent holding tanks' that are regressing, not progressing). That is, with 'the economic gulf between the richest and poorest countries ... growing rapidly, and [now that] most African countries are much further from economic parity with the first world than they were twenty or thirty years ago (indeed, many are worse off even in absolute terms)' (p. 172), Ferguson reports a growing trend among people in the 'developing world' to no longer subscribe to the 'development'-truism that if they 'wait patiently, your turn will come'. As a result of its own failures, 'development' is now decreasingly seen as a series of stages (*à la* Rostow and [neo]classical development), and increasingly seen as fixed statuses 'separated from each other by exclusionary walls, rather than development stairways' (p. 176). With the replacement of 'development stairways' those living at the bottom have, according to Ferguson, only two courses of action to move around the 'exclusionary walls': exit or violence. He writes that 'if escape ... is blocked' then 'other avenues may involve violently crashing the gates of the first class, smashing the bricked-up walls and breaking through, if only temporarily, to the other side of privilege and plenty' (p. 179).

In effect, Ferguson is presenting a view that contemporary conflict is driven by increasing desperation and the end of patience with the promises of 'development' as increasing global inequality and the structures of world markets and governance make it all but impossible for some nations, groups and individuals to partake in flows of wealth. As such it is the only position of the five that links conflict to a nation's relative position in a highly unequal global order. *The hypothesis then is that 'development' causes conflict by both its ambition to remake subjects that never really existed ('abnormalities', e.g. the ignorant villager) and by its own (inevitable) failure which has convinced those at the bottom that being 'developed' is a status protected by exclusionary walls, rather than viable development stairways, leading to few options besides violence.* Progress is largely presumed to run in the opposite direction of 'development'; prescriptions are undefined: the more pressing task is to eliminate the blinders that a powerful discourse of 'development' creates. While such a centring of 'development' cannot, as we have seen repeatedly above, avoid sidelining other non-'development' factors that may catalyse conflict, it does raise the haunting spectre of more 'development' being offered as a 'solution' to conflict worldwide even while it actually catalyses it. Although some points of commonality emerge, this critique diverges from the failed development view primarily because it holds that the 'development' enterprise is unsalvageable: prospects for peace are all but non-existent unless we are willing to roll back the 'truth' that 'underdevelopment' is actually found in the 'Third World' itself (instead of being produced in the 'First') and instead tackle global inequality.

Ultimately, this review of the five major positions suggests that the divergent conclusions about the relationship between the cannabis ban and USAID IRDP in Rukum and Rolpa are by no means an anomaly but a rather a typical reflection of the continued uncertainty about cause and effect that infuses the conflict–development (and education) literature. *In other words, uncertainty about causality is at the core of divergent opinions*, rather than, say, a lack of evidence or failure to adequately conceptualize and analyse.[7] This is a critical point. In effect, it seconds the assertion by Mac Ginty & Williams (2009) that 'there is no exact science linking conflict to development; the constellation of variables is simply too great' but extends it by suggesting that, in the face of uncertainty, researchers tend to rely on a finite set of theories, resulting in the centring of particular factors in (and removing others from) the field of possibility. Such a review is crucial, as the chapter now moves to show, through a review of the burgeoning literature on conflict in Nepal, that without greater certainty about causal linkages the result is continued disagreement over the relationship between conflict and 'development'. As such, such notions about 'progress' and prescriptions for peace are little more than presumptions and it is these presumptions that, in turn, determine educational intersections.

The Conflict–Development–Education Nexus in Nepal: a meta-analysis

Let us begin with the (neo)classical development view.[8] As represented clearly in the *Final Evaluation* of the USAID Rapti Development Project highlighted above, this perspective suggests – de facto – that 'development' interventions had no connection to the rise and success of the Maoists. Instead, the outbreak of conflict was due to a combination of overpopulation, endemic corruption, geographic disadvantage, environmental damage, political instability, extreme economic deprivation and so on. A typical example of such a position is a recent IMF report aptly entitled 'Economic Performance over the Conflict Cycle' (Staines, 2004). It articulates well the presumption that poverty and poverty-related despair create conflict, and that 'development' should therefore focus on 'economic stagnation and poverty' rather than 'explanations of civil conflict revolving around the politics of grievance' (Staines, 2004, p. 6). From such a perspective, prescriptions for peace flow naturally: 'more, better, and farther reaching intervention holds the promise of relief', with interventions defined almost wholly in economic and policy terms. The World Bank (2003b) and Asian Development Bank (2005) take very similar positions on events in Nepal, arguing for 'growth-enhancing structural reforms' as the best antidote to the Maoists. Although both tend to give a greater nod than the IMF to a wider range of variables, a more or less similar collapse of the catalysts for war to a lack of economic growth is apparent. Among bilateral donors, USAID in particular takes a similar line (USAID, 1995), arguing that the Maoists 'found fertile ground due to Nepal's ... poverty. The initial pro-people approach, which won the Maoists converts among the disenfranchised of Nepal, [however] has degraded into a campaign of violence, lawlessness, intimidation, and destruction'.[9] Notably, the Government of Nepal seems to support this approach as well, perhaps because of similar convictions or perhaps simply to please international donors (Gordon, 2005). One clear example of this is the National Planning Commission's joint UNDP Millennium Development Goals Needs Assessment published in October 2006 (*before* the November ceasefire) that hardly mentions the conflict in its massive 148-page report: development is, in effect, completely decoupled from conflict (Government of Nepal & UNDP, 2006).[10]

The (neo)classical view thus tends to dominate at the highest echelons of policy and power. Given its centring of economics and removal of 'development' itself from the possible causal factors of conflict, progress is envisaged as more economic growth via more aid-induced 'development'. There is simply no self-reflection on the ways that 'development' may be contributing to Nepal's dysfunction, so the prescription is *peace through economic development* – a presumption that prefigures predominately economic solutions and, importantly, leads to a de facto positioning of education in ways that service the economy. That is, education is not highlighted as a causal factor within these sources except in the sense that a lack of education tends to lead to lower levels of economic growth, for individuals and for society as a whole. This in turn produces a set of educational development policy prescriptions that celebrate enrolments, efficiency, and links to the labour market while simultaneously sidelining considerations of the divisive effects of education on social cohesion. A clear example of this are the decentralization and privatization policies strongly advocated by the IMF and World Bank throughout the conflict in Nepal that were considered necessary because the educational status quo did 'not serve the labor market well' (World Bank, 2001, p. iii; see also Caddell, 2006;

Shields & Rappleye, 2008b). It was a policy package, it must be pointed out, that was explicitly and repeatedly highlighted by the Maoists as something that must be stopped before they would put down arms: '*The commercialization of education should be stopped*' – one of the Maoists' 40-Point Demands that continues to fall on deaf ears even in today's fragile peace.[11]

Despite the immense resources and power that attend the (neo)classical development position, it is the moderated classical development view that perhaps occupies the largest 'share' of the conflict analysis carried out in Nepal. In line with the *moderated* approach of refusing to view 'development' in terms of absolute economic growth, the literature has *relative* economic (Murshed & Gates, 2003; Thapa & Sijapati, 2003; Mancours, 2006; Nepal et al, 2007), political (Brown, 1996; Thapa, 2003; Pfaff-Czarnecka, 2004; Hachhethu, 2006), and social variants (LeComte-Tilouine, 2004; Bennett, 2005; Lowati, 2005). One major work of note in the economic strand is Murshed & Gates's (2003) study that examined horizontal inequalities in Nepalese society, arguing not only that absolute inequality was a major factor contributing to conflict, but that horizontal inequalities were the most critical factor. They then go on to assert that the conflict was catalysed by relative deprivation: inequality 'worsened in the Far-Western and Mid-Western regions between 1996-1999. Thus, these regions, which constitute the starting point of the contemporary Maoist armed struggle in Nepal, have not benefited from recent growth in the rest of the economy, prima facie evidence of worsening horizontal inequality' (Murshed & Gates, 2003, p. 7). Prescriptions for progress flow naturally from such a premise: 'there needs to be an equal focus on tackling horizontal inequalities in addition to the general strategy of poverty reduction' (Murshed & Gates, 2003, p. 11).

In the political strand, Brown (1996) argues that Nepal's shift to democracy in 1990 only led to the further dominance of powerful groups in Nepalese society who were able to legitimate their position through the institutions of democracy. This analysis has been extended by other analysts focusing on the political space as the object to be 'developed' (Hachhethu, 2003), hence prescriptions for cultivating civil society (Dahal, 2006), encouraging democratic participation of marginalized groups (Bhattachan, 2006), and pushing institutional reform (Lowati, 2005). A similar approach is found in the work of authors who point to social factors, specifically the continuing and widening chasm between the dominant Bahun (Brahmin), Chetri and Newar social and ethnic groups, and a strikingly similar line of reasoning emerges for gender (Gautam et al, 2003; Sharma & Prasain, 2004).

Although not always explicit, the premise for these later positions is that solutions to the conflict can come through 'development' of the status and power of marginalized social groups and Nepalese women. That is, prescriptions for peace are more 'development' with a greater focus on the inclusion of marginalized social groups. The approach is probably most clearly associated with the work of the like-minded donors such as the

Danish International Development Agency (DANIDA) (2006), the Norwegian Agency for Development Cooperation (NORAD) (2008), the Finnish ODA, and Canadian International Development Agency (CIDA) (2004), but also with many 'progressive' Nepalese scholars and political commentators. Educationally, such presumptions translate to focus on civic education (Dahal, 2002) – education for the creation of a well-functioning, more inclusive democracy and greater representation of marginalized social groups – and a direct targeting of conflict-affected communities for educational aid (Vaux et al, 2006). Such a position is where we might also locate, rather muted, calls to date for explicit peacebuilding education (Pherali, forthcoming 2011).[12]

The overarching Education Sector Plan (2004-09) can also be located here. Heavily funded by DANIDA and entitled *Education for All*, the plan does not shy away from mentioning its concern with the 'on-going insurgency', thus representing, in many respects, the sorts of educational prescriptions that flow from moderated classic development view (Ministry of Education, 2003). Specifically, it frames, in part, Nepal's next phase of educational 'development' as that which can mitigate the underlying factors leading to conflict: a push for decentralization for democratization (as opposed to efficiency and streamlining of the State *à la* the IMF and World Bank), mainstreaming of disadvantaged communities, 'gender equity and equality', and interventions that 'respond to the diversified clientele groups of the country making it relevant to the learning needs of all ethnic groups, indigenous peoples, Dalit children, and other marginalised populations' (Ministry of Education, 2003, p. 17). It is important to keep in mind, however, that these policy prescriptions only apply to the state education sector, effectively missing nearly 30% of secondary students and upwards of 20% of primary school students enrolled in Nepal's booming private sector.

Attracting far less attention than the previous two positions in absolute terms, the failed development view has nonetheless been championed by an increasing number of observers in Nepal in recent years, as more 'development' dollars flowing in since the outbreak of conflict have clearly failed to stem the violence. This view has two variants. The first concerns the particular policies that were put into place in the 1990s, most clearly articulated in Deraniyagala's (2005) wide-ranging analysis, which concludes that:

> support for the Maoist guerrillas ... [is] traditionally highest in regions and among social groups that are economically disadvantaged. This lends support to the argument that economic deprivation is a key causal factor underlying the Nepal conflict ... however ... given that these patterns of poverty and inequality are the outcome of a historical process of development, violent conflict must be seen, not as an aberration from the country's 'normal' path of development, but as intrinsically linked to that process. (p. 54)

Deraniyagala (2005) goes on to support the case by pointing out that when donors insisted on 'structural adjustment policies' upon entering Nepal with greater force after the 'democratic revolution' of 1990, it produced 'a period in which the incomes of and welfare of the rural population worsened significantly relative to their urban counterparts ... In this sense, the sharp divergence of rural–urban incomes can be seen as an important liberalization-related economic driver of the Nepal conflict' (p. 59). A strikingly similar view is championed by Tiwari (2007), while Sharma (2006) indicts not just the 1990s, but four decades of externally-led 'development' policy (see also Dixit, 1997). All of this suggests some new factors to help explain the timing of the eruption of the Maoist insurgency in Rukum, Rolpa and beyond. The second strain of the failed development critique is represented by researchers like Subedi (2009) and International Alert (2006), the latter writing that 'what positive progress has been made by individual donors in responding to Nepal's conflict context over the past five years is being undermined by the overall aid framework. This is precisely because the current international aid frameworks are counter-productive to enabling sensitivity to the fragile context of Nepal ... aid paradigms cannot just be tinkered with but need a fundamental review' (International Alert, 2006, p. 4). In other words, not isolated policies, but the totality of and contradictions within 'development' must be considered as failing.

Yet undoubtedly the most powerful articulation of this second strand is by Devendra Raj Panday, who served as Nepal's Finance Minister for several years in the 1990s, in his scathing critique aptly entitled *Nepal's Failed Development* (1999). In that volume he rants against the 'absurd' (p. 378) policies of the most powerful development players like the IMF and World Bank, and describes how Nepalese ministers are routinely forced to simply sign off IMF drafts of major policies, but also asserts that even what the 'most sensitive donor representatives ... seek are almost always off the mark' (p. 379).

He elsewhere explains that so long as the 'development' agenda in Nepal is driven by external donor agencies it is out of reach of popular democratic change and therefore 'cannot advance the economic and social development of the country for the benefit of all sections of the society including, in particular, the socially handicapped and the politically powerless' (Panday, 2000). He further argues that 'the growing Maoist movement in Nepal is a case in point' to highlight that failed 'development' policies and democracy compromised by the intransigence of donors ultimately produces conditions ripe for violent alternatives. Thus, while the first strain of the failed development view hypothesizes causality in a way that prefigures much more sensitive, pro-poor educational interventions, the second strain is likely to argue that education-related 'development' interventions are just one part of an entire 'development' enterprise that needs a major overhaul; that a discussion of the content of educational 'development' is largely insignificant as compared to a rethink of the processes and dynamics of delivery. As such, explicit prescriptions for 'progress' through education specifically rarely feature here, but are implicitly included in an entire re-evaluation of dominant aid paradigms and the overall donor–recipient relationship.

The fourth position, conflict as development success, does not feature to near the degree that the previous three positions do, but nevertheless contributes a fresh, if modest, voice in the wider analysis of the Maoist conflict. One example is Gautam et al (2001), who argue that international and domestic NGO involvement in 'Literacy campaigns ... designed to promote the empowerment of women inadvertently encouraged many conscientised young women to choose subsequent empowerment through armed struggle' (p. 222). Leve (2007) concurs and extends this, relating how USAID work in Nepal made 'women's empowerment' a key agency goal in 1996, resulting in a 'huge woman-focused development offensive that enrolled over 100,000 women in six or nine month literacy courses in just one year alone. Nearly 43,000 women "were provided legal awareness and advocacy skills" and the number of microcredit borrowers tripled between 1995 and 1996, reaching a total of 13,450' (p. 132). Leve goes on to convincingly show through sustained ethnographic fieldwork in districts where the USAID programme was active, followed by interviews 10 years later to trace the impact of the interventions, however, that those who received the 'development' interventions, most prominently literacy classes, were decidedly more active and adamant that the Government must 'agree to the Maoists' demands', embracing radical solutions and supporting the Maoists over the Government as compared with those who had not received such training. Hachhethu (2003) makes a somewhat similar case, arguing that the UN's Decade of Indigenous People (1993-2004) unleashed a range of donor funds for ethnic populations in Nepal that translated into more assertive local action that later paved the way for the Maoists to tap increased – and increasingly assertive – ethnic activism.

As opposed to the previous three positions, however, the conflict as development success view does not see conflict in a wholly negative light. Works in this group convey the notion that issues such as gender and ethnic oppression need to be addressed, even violently if the existing power structures fail to recognize those legitimate claims. While none of these authors would seem to favour violent solutions, they are clearly pointing to the fact that on certain points donors' and Maoists' visions of 'progress' aligned and, when met with an unresponsive State, the slide to violence may have been expected and cannot be seen as worse than an indefinite cycle of oppression and passivity. In this conflict as development success view, education actually features quite prominently, as catalysing changes in ways of thinking (making people 'conscious') is held to be fundamental. Yet, educational 'prescriptions' do not serve the end of peace, but instead prioritize the overcoming of oppression/marginalization. Such a position is well articulated in literature on ActionAid-Nepal's Freire-inspired

REFLECT educational intervention that works with some 375,000 Nepalese, focusing on 'challenging the caste system' and 'giving voice to women'; it reveals little explicit interest in the implications of such work vis-à-vis the Maoist conflict: it is simply not taken as the most pressing issue.

The final position, development as cause of conflict, takes a more holistic view, arguing that Nepal was never really the underdeveloped place 'development' framed it as. Therefore, largely as a result, 'development' has failed to deliver, producing such a sorry and sordid history that the Nepalese people's seemingly 'radical' solutions are, in fact, logical. Writing a few years before the outbreak of violence, Pigg (1993) argued in an article entitled 'Unintended Consequences: the ideological impact of development in Nepal':

> Development intensifies social differences in Nepal. Economically, it appears to widen class disparities. At the same time it has altered many of the structures of Nepalese society, it has reworked people's understanding of their society as a nation, their images of change, and their representations of their own place in a national society. Individual development projects may or may not succeed in achieving their goals, but an international development vision does appear to be transforming both the terms in which social identities are cast and the symbols that mark social differences ... [yet now] disillusionment and scepticism towards development may be the single most important source of new social movements with radical potential. (Pigg, 1993, pp. 54-55)

For Pigg, like Escobar (1995) and Ferguson (2005), the whole notion of 'development' and the myriad interventions that flow from it in Nepal, as elsewhere, cut far deeper than mere failed development: 'the asymmetrical development expertise and other knowledges is structural' (p. 53; see also Fujikura, 1996, 2001).

Pigg's conceptualization is later extended by Shrestha (1997), who argues, 'development' became Nepal's 'modern-day intoxicant' (p. 50). He writes, 'the more we drank from the spring of this intoxicant, the less control we had over our own senses, eventually becoming oblivious to the relation that the so-called ladder of modernity, imported and imposed from the West, was actually a trap' (p. 50). Such a conclusion is clearly strikingly similar to Ferguson's (2005), who, as discussed above, traced conflict to a loss of faith in 'development stairways', quickly leading to exit or violence. From this angle it comes as little surprise that Shrestha (1997) argues that true 'progress' in Nepal is not 'possible unless foreign aid is removed first. It has to go, for it is not designed to serve Nepal and its masses irrespective of its claims'. He then adds, contemplatively, 'as much as I believe in ... a non-violent path to societal change, I do not foresee much hope for them to materialize under the Westernized development ideology ... maybe a social revolution is necessary. Maybe violence is inevitable' (p. 213).

From such a standpoint 'development' can never bring about 'progress', so proponents of this view obviously stand in opposition to the usual 'development' prescriptions. Much of this work has emerged in the field of education specifically, starting with Pigg's (1992) early attempts to show how the narrative of 'development' was reproduced in school textbooks, showing, among other things, how UNICEF was explicitly depicted in school textbooks as integral to 'developing' the Nepalese people and how a 'modernity timeline' was overlaid on Nepalese ethnic make-up, ending with urban-Brahmin lifestyles as the epitome of 'developed'. More recent work on educational policy formation has shown how the powerful narrative of 'development' and copious amounts of donor funding-cum-influence has led to the production of certain policy 'truths' that forces closure on alternatives (Carney & Bista, 2009), as well as created a civil society that, despite hopes for an 'authentic' voice of the Nepalese people, only reproduces the same 'development' tropes and donor-led development status quo, pushing the (still) 'discontented into the arms of the Maoists' (Rappleye, forthcoming 2011).

Other works make explicit links to the language of Ferguson (2005), arguing that perhaps schooling functions as one of the primary ways that the broken promises of 'development' are recognized by Nepalese youth:

> Schooling prepares *most* young Nepalis not only to meet the 'exclusionary wall' created by global structures of inequality, but with a level of awareness to know what lies beyond this barrier. Rather than a solution to Nepal's armed conflict, improved schooling – in a World marked by exclusion – may actually intensify it. (Carney & Rappleye, forthcoming 2011)

Such a thesis reveals its centring of (educational) 'development' as well as its implicit opposition to it. It refuses to offer solutions, educational and otherwise, to the host of 'problems' in Nepal articulated by all the former views. While this makes the view unpalatable to most besides critical scholars, such a stance is the only position of the five that is willing to engage with and, indeed, *looks forward to* yet-unknown prescriptions for 'progress' and peace emerging from Nepal itself once the context (and our collective research imaginary) is unburdened of the assumptions, interventions, and distortions of 'development'.

Far from Conclusion: continuing to debate, possibilities for peace

So did the cannabis ban and the subsequent USAID 'development' project cause war to erupt in the Rukum and Rolpa? Did 'development' cause the 10-year civil war in Nepal? Or did 'development' instead mitigate it? Would war have broken out even sooner or been far more violent had 'development' not helped rectify, at least in part, some of the endemic poverty and oppressive structures that persist in Rukum and Rolpa? Instead of offering answers to these fundamental questions, the chapter offered a more modest review of the multiplicity of opinions voiced by wider theories of 'development' and the (now) burgeoning literature on the Maoist insurgency. These five divergent perspectives and presumptions about 'progress' can be summarized, for clarity and review, as presented in Table I. This chapter was premised on the idea that no serious attempt to contemplate the intersection of education in conflict and development contexts could proceed without some notion of causality: identifying causes prefigures prescriptions for peace. The key point for education specifically was that *portrayals of the role of education in catalysing conflict and prescriptions for its role in contributing to peace derive from, instead of stand independent of, the wider conceptualization of conflict and hypotheses about causality.* It was tentatively suggested that as such these fault lines that cut through the literature on Nepal might well characterize fault lines inherent in debates around the world. Future research will be necessary to determine to what degree this is true, as well as to find new hypotheses and tease out nuances.

Amid this continued uncertainty what does seems clear is that we are far from conclusion: given the immense complexity of the conflict–development–education equation, the catalysing and mitigating potential will continue to be debated. Pessimistically, the thesis presented here that the educational piece of this paramount equation derives from mere hypotheses about causality, many of which are underpinned by 'development' ideology, suggests that the field of 'education and conflict', the area of academic inquiry most heavily invested in the equation, is likely to remain confined to a field built on ideological, as opposed to empirical, foundations for the foreseeable future. This position is exacerbated by the overwhelming stakes of the 'development' apparatus itself (aid agencies, multinational organizations, 'development' research think tanks, departments and networks) in the conflict–development–education nexus; involvement that has and will continue to skew analysis of conflict–development–education toward positions that remove development's own presence from the list of possible catalysts of conflict: (neo)classical development and moderated classic development. Supported by copious amounts of research funding and backed by powerful 'development' players, these positions are likely to crowd out the other three more critical positions in the literature purely in terms of material-cum-quantitative output. Complexity will be increasingly collapsed according to the logic of power, political imperatives, *ideals* of 'development' and sources of funding.

More optimistically, researchers might continue to push for a multiplicity of opinions about the drivers of conflict. Practitioners can refuse to allow those they work for to reduce the immense complexity of the conflict–development–education equation to a limited range of factors. Scholars can continue to develop theoretical directions and increasingly complex conceptual models, refusing to succumb to the dictates of 'third-income' funding (consultancies and the like) and their own academic disciplines (say, the need to use statistics and/or rational choice theory to get published in top journals) and thereby keep open the possibilities for what might initially appear to be counter-intuitive linkages and seemingly radical alternatives. The Maoists sweeping election victory in nationwide elections in April 2008 that sent such shock waves through the 'development' set in Kathmandu is good proof that it is only the theory-dependency of our judgements that define 'radical' and 'alternative', not actual events on the ground. Here the promise for future studies of conflict and education is not simply the inclusion of a wider range of variables (most of all 'development' itself!) and refined understandings of linkages. It is instead to work against those who would collapse such complexity in their naïve confidence and rush to intervene and/or their unwillingness to raise politically uncomfortable linkages. Only then can research make a real contribution by challenging us to consider all possibilities, rather than reproduce the same blinkered view of conflict proffered by 'development' agencies and their academic collaborators.

Yet, make no mistake that such a stance necessitates a far deeper problematization of the 'usual' ways of seeing the 'developing' world and conflict-affected areas of the globe, one that moves beyond old stereotypes and well-worn images of poverty versus wealth, oppression versus oppressor, greed versus grievance.

That is, such a shift requires – if we take the case of Nepal specifically – moving from a view of the place as simply the land of majestic mountains and potent 'pot' whose own ignorance and poverty caused it to collapse into civil war towards one that reflects critically on the history of how those images have been constructed, brings in a much wider range of factors and alternative perspectives, and attempts to investigate initially counter-intuitive connections between them. This was the purpose of leading the chapter with the little-known story of the links between the cannabis ban, the USAID IRDP and the rise of the Maoists. Put another way, when we seek to understand conflict in Nepal we must replace the outward-looking, essentialist '3Ps' we began with – *peaks, pot and poverty* – with a more self-aware, dynamic '3Ps'*: perspectives, presumptions and prescriptions*. Only then are we likely to move closer in Nepal, and probably the rest of the world, toward a fourth: *peace*.

View of 'development' and conflict	Theorists and representative texts	Dominant assumptions and hypothesis about causality	Prescribed intervention	Education implications
(Neo) Classic Development	Schultz (1971) Rostow (1960) Chicago School (1970s)	• Centering of economic factors, democracy to correct market • Conflict as result of poverty, economic growth reduces likelihood of conflict (Collier et al, 2003) • 'Development' as unequivocally positive; more 'development' reduces the likelihood of conflict; conflict as 'development in reverse' (WB, 2003)	• More 'development' for greater *economic* growth, market-based solutions • 'structural adjustment', despite short-term 'pain', inequalities • Conflict resolution indirectly through economic growth; few direct interventions	• Education for economic growth, linking education to the needs of the economy: labor markets, etc. • Greater internal and external efficiency for educational system, usually through market solutions: private schools, school choice (increased enrolments viewed as gains in human capital)
Moderated Classic Development	Sen (1985,1997) UNICEF (1997) UNDP HDI	• Parity of non-economic factors • Conflict equally the result of human factors such as relative economic inequality; non-parity of religion, gender, ethnicity; ideology, etc. • 'Development' as unequivocally positive; *right kind* of 'development' reduces likelihood of conflict	• More 'development', but one adjusted to focus on human factors: horizontal inequality, human rights, democracy, inclusion • Direct conflict resolution, targeting of pockets/ populations of inequality or oppression	• Education for wider political and social 'development'; education that combats economic inequality • Decentralization for democratization, focus on marginalized communities, curricula and delivery that responds to diverse groups • Aid to *Peacebuilding* Education

Failed Development	Stiglitz (2002) Browne (2006)	• Centering of 'development' itself in the analysis, focus on its distortion of local economy, society, and culture; aid exacerbates divisions/inequality • External donors bear responsibility for failure to develop; aid never sheer altruism but linked to ideological and geopolitical agendas	• Not tinkering, but a major overhaul of modus operandi of aid • Much more context sensitivity in delivery • Consideration of the way that interventions exacerbate conflict	• 'Educational 'development' considered holistically as part of a major rethink of dominant aid paradigms, total impact of 'development' and overall donor–recipient relationship • Few prescriptions, education cannot be uncoupled from 'dev'
Conflict as Development Success	Freire (1970) Archer (1990)	• Oppression/marginalization fuels a latent pool of angst and indignation • 'Development' helps spark collective action by oppressed groups • If power structures do not accommodate demands for equity then conflict may emerge *but* conflict a lesser evil than the perpetuation of a cycle of oppression and passivity	• 'Development' for conscientization, local empowerment, and catalysing collective action • Focus on adults and oppressed/marginalized populations	• More educational intervention focusing on 'conscientization' and ownership of 'development' and 'education • More of the same for NGOs and other organizations working at grass-roots levels making local populations aware of oppression
'Development' as Cause of Conflict	Escobar (1995) Ferguson (2005) Pigg (1993)	• The narrative 'development' a powerful myth that structures reality failing to approximate conditions on the ground; perpetuates 'underdevelopment', fabricates 'abnormalities', 'Third World' • The 50+ year failure of 'development' caused the idea of 'development stairways' to break down, replaced by belief in 'exclusionary walls' where the only way around is *exit or violence*	• End of 'development'; critical re-evaluation of most fundamental truths of development • Wider global inequalities • Refusal to specify solutions, preferring to see what emerges once contexts are unburdened of 'development'	?

Table I. Five different perspectives on conflict, development, and education.

Notes

[1] The term 'development' is rendered in quotations throughout the chapter to gain some critical distance from this central term. Alone, the term development signifies evolution, movement forward, betterment and progress. Such an idea has been co-opted by international aid organizations to describe their own work and has been accepted as such to such a degree that a positive relationship now goes largely unquestioned, something this chapter seeks to problematize. Hence the need for critical distance. At points 'progress' is rendered similarly, signifying the same.

[2] Readers interested in work focused more tightly on the impact of the insurgency on education (and vice versa) will find such descriptions in Caddell (2006), Shields & Rappleye (2008a, b) and Pherali (forthcoming 2011).

[3] This is not to say that Nepal was either the spiritual or tranquil 'Shangri-La' that outside observers (be they 'hippies' or development workers) have imagined it to be, only to point out that this was a dominant image associated with Nepal by the outside world. At the same time, the scale and intensity of the Maoist conflict clearly dwarfs any prior social upheaval since Nepal's unification-through-conquest in 1743, making it not 'just another' episode in the continued search for a stable and durable 'modern' political system (see Whelpton [2005] for further historical details).

[4] Hash derives from the cannabis plant, but it is a collection (usually by hand in Nepal) of the resin produced by the plant as opposed to harvesting the leaves or buds. Hash thus appears as a hard, dark, pasty substance, often with a more powerful effect (higher THC levels) than smoking other parts of the plant.

[5] In fact, the United States Agency for International Development (USAID; then USOM) initiated a malaria eradication project in the Rapti Zone as early as April 1954, but it was largely deemed a failure. Mihaly (1965, pp. 42-47) argues that 'all areas sprayed by this [US] group had to be redone' (p. 43) and the 'failure was a disaster' (p. 45) leading to a situation where, in addition to a reduction in US prestige, the fledgling Nepalese 'government was blamed, and corruption and ineptitude were cited as the main causes of failure' (p. 45). These early US efforts also included a 'Community Development' component that several decades later was evaluated by USAID itself as largely a failure due to 'implementation problems' and some 'fundamentally flawed assumptions' about villagers and their lives (Skerry et al, 1992, cited in Fujikura, 1996). Although a fuller account would include a look at how these earlier 'failures' became the base upon which the USAID Rapti IRDP built, such an account would arguably only further strengthen the hypothesis of the *detrimental* effects of 'development'.

[6] Given more space this review would encompass two more prominent positions found in the current literature. The first would be one we might call a *Greed, Extremism and Terrorism* position. It would hold that insurgencies are fundamentally about insatiable or extremist political, religious, and/or social

views. More crudely: insurgents are simply 'terrorists'. Progress means physically eliminating such groups who prey on and terrorize an unsympathetic wider population; prescriptions usually thus mean military or policy operations. A second *Identity Conflict* position will not be covered here either, despite gaining considerable salience in the academic literature over the past few decades. Huntington's *Clash of Civilizations* (1996) represents a well-known, if crude, version of a position better articulated by Young (2003) and gaining much popular support after the horrors of Rwanda and Kosovo (see also Ignatieff, 2001; Sen, 2006). The former is excluded in this chapter because the Maoists' well-articulated political agenda and sweeping election victory in 2008 suggest that an extremist or terrorism position does not apply in the case of Nepal (if it does anywhere else!) Similarly, the latter position is not dealt with because the combined lack of a history of extreme ethnic tensions/conflict in Nepal, and the widespread support the (multi-ethnic) Maoist movement enjoyed makes it extremely hard to view the conflict in Nepal in terms of identity/ethnicity. Please see note 8 for a brief review of how these positions have attempted, rather unconvincingly, to be articulated in the Nepalese context. Please also note that both of these views write 'development' out of the realm of possibility, not the least because greed, extremism and identity politics are, in these views, essentialized: viewed as fixed in the minds of combatants and not derivatives of socio-economic configurations (marginalization, horizontal inequality, etc.)

[7] However, political imperatives and personal motivations clearly dictate which major strand of thought is articulated by which institutions and actors; more on this in note 10 and the Conclusion.

[8] As mentioned in note 6, provided more space this review would have engaged the *Greed, Extremism and Terrorism* and the *Identity Conflict* positions to total seven major strands of thought. Briefly, the *Greed, Extremism and Terrorism* view is well articulated by the US Government. Speaking just four months after September 11, 2001, the US Ambassador to Nepal, Michael Malinowski, discussed the Maoists, arguing that they were no different from Al Qaeda:

Nepal is currently plagued with a terrorism that is shaking its very foundation as a nation. These terrorists, under the guise of Maoism ... are fundamentally the same as terrorists elsewhere – be they members of the Shining Path, Abu Sayaf, the Khmer Rouge, or Al Qaeda ... Having failed to receive the popular support of the Nepali people at the ballot box, the Maoists now seek to achieve their aims through the use of force, violence, extortion, intimidation, and murder. (Cited in Lindborg & Gersony, 2003, p. 81)

Following the speech, the US Department of State added the Maoists to its list of global 'Terrorist' organizations, a classification – it is interesting to note – the Maoists still hold even today years *after* winning free and fair national elections (that obviously made a farce of Malinowski's comments about lack of support at the 'ballot box'). Current trends in conflict research would demand a review of the *identity conflict*, but that literature is all but non-existent in Nepal, good proof that its applicability to the Maoist insurgency is highly tenuous (of the few who mention ethnicity, see Bohara et al, 2006). This is not to say that the Maoist insurgency lacks an ethnic dimension, but simply to point out that the literature suggests that the major momentum for the Maoist insurgency does not come from long-standing ethnic/identity tensions.

[9] Note, however, how this shades into the *Greed, Extremism and Terrorism* position, a straddling of two different positions that approximates rather well USAID's tenuous position as a 'development' agency operating within a broader, post-9/11 US foreign policy framework.

[10] A critical question to consider vis-à-vis this position is why such perspectives emerge. Although there is little space to delve into these issues here and the Conclusion points out some salient points for further research, an argument that action demands simplification seems highly inadequate. Certainly simplification is necessary and inevitable to a degree, but there are strong political and material reasons why simplification (collapse) happens along particular lines. Obviously, those heavily invested in 'development' cannot risk their own legitimacy by including 'development' among factors that might cause conflict, but the reasons and beliefs that lead to patterns of simplification are indeed complex. Those who work at, say, the World Bank tend to be economists, work quantitatively, and think in terms of bounded States, an approach that largely prefigures economic solutions, writes out that which is hard to quantify, and disregards transnational factors (including the 'development' apparatus) in conflict analyses. Likewise, those working in the government have a difficult time criticizing 'development' for political reasons, including relations with donors, superiors and powerful national politicians who campaign on delivering 'development'. Critiques of 'development' also close off possibilities to one day work in lucrative 'development' jobs. The point is that it is far more than a mere seeking of simplicity for the sake of action (the common response of practitioners to the critique of academics) that determines the ways that complexity is collapsed and 'development' is written out of the conflict equation. Again, the Conclusion will touch upon this, but more research in this area is urgent, though fraught with methodological challenges as it must trace the circulation of information and ideas and somehow manage to get candid, reflective interviews/insights from those with the most at stake in presenting particular ideas as 'truth'.

[11] A full English translation of the Maoists' 40-Point Demands that was issued in February 1996 can be found in Hutt (2006, pp. 285-287).

[12] It is somewhat unclear why explicit peacebuilding initiatives, educational and otherwise, have not featured heavily in Nepal to date. Possibilities are: (a) that the conflict continues to be highly unstable and there was never the 'collapse' of total war that provides a window for reconciliation, but instead low-intensity conflict spread over a decade, (b) with the election of the Maoists to power in 2008, it is unclear what peacebuilding would look like – the Maoists seem less interested in 'peace' and more in overturning oppressive structures, and (c) few donors or international and domestic NGOs have shown much interest.

References

Archer, D. (1990) *Literacy and Power: the Latin America battleground*. London: Earthscan.

Asian Development Bank (2005) *Measuring the Economic Costs of Conflict: the effect of declining development expenditure*. Kathmandu: Asian Development Bank.

Bennett, L. (2005) Gender, Caste, and Ethnic Exclusion: following the policy process from analysis to action. Paper presented at the conference, New Frontiers of Social Action, December, Arusha. http://siteresources.worldbank.org/INTRANETSOCIALDEVELOPMENT/Resources/Bennett.rev.pdf (accessed 10 March 2010).

Bewley-Taylor, D. (1999) *The United States and International Drug Control, 1909-1997*. New York: Pinter.

Bhattachan, (2006) Expected Model and Process of Inclusive Democracy in Nepal. Paper presented at the conference, 'The Agenda of Transformation: inclusion in Nepali democracy', Birendra International Convention Centre, Kathmandu. http://www.nepalresearch.de/publications/bhattachan_inclusive_democracy.pdf (accessed 15 April 2010).

Bloch, J. (2005) Nepal: the end of Shangri-La, *Liberal Democracy Nepal Bulletin*, 1, 1-13.

Bohara, A., Mitchell, M. & Nepal, M. (2006) Opportunity, Democracy, and the Exchange of Political Violence: a subnational analysis of conflict in Nepal, *Journal of Conflict Resolution*, 50(1), 108-128.

Bonino, F. & Donini, A. (2009) Aid and Violence: development policies and conflict in Nepal. Boston: Tufts/Feinstein International Center. https://wikis.uit.tufts.edu/confluence/display/FIC/Aid+and+Violence (accessed 15 April 2010).

Brown, T.L. (1996) *The Challenge to Democracy in Nepal: a political history*. New York: Routledge.

Browne, S. (2006) *Aid and Influence: do donors help or hinder?* London: Earthscan.

Burtel, J. & Ali., S.H. (2009) Green Roots of Red Rebellion: environmental degradation as the ultimate cause of social vulnerability and militancy in Nepal. Paper presented at the Georgetown School of Foreign Service in Qatar. http://www.uvm.edu/~shali/Maoist.pdf

Butterfield, S. (2004) *US Development Aid – an historic first: achievements and failures in the twentieth century*. Westport: Praeger.

Caddell, M. (2006) Private Schools as Battlefields: contested visions of learning and livelihood in Nepal, *Compare*, 36(4), 463-479.

Canadian International Development Agency (CIDA) (2004) Peace and Conflict Impact Assessment: summary. Kathmandu: CIDA. http://www.cconepal.org.np/pdf/CIDA-PCIASR.pdf

Carney, S. & Bista, M. (2009) Community Schooling in Nepal: a genealogy of education reform since 1990, *Comparative Education Review*, 53(2), 189-211.

Carney, S. & Rappleye, J. (forthcoming 2011) Editorial Introduction: From Modernity to Conflict, *Globalisation, Societies, and Education*.

Clarke, R (2007a) Traditional Nepali Hemp Textiles, *Journal of Industrial Hemp*, 12(2), 97-113.

Clarke, R. (2007b) Traditional Cannabis Cultivation in Darchula District, Nepal: seed, resin and textiles, *Journal of Industrial Hemp*, 12(2), 19-42.

Dahal, D.R. (2006) Civil Society Groups in Nepal: their roles in conflict and peace building. Paper presented at the United Nations Development Programme sponsored Support for Peace and Development Initiative, May, Kathmandu. http://www.nepaldemocracy.org/conflict_resolution/Peacebuilding.pdf (accessed 10 January 2010).

Dahal, D.R. (2002) Civic Education: the problems and possibilities of a democratic public life in Nepal. Paper presented at the Society for the Promotion of Civic Education in Nepal, Kathmandu. http://www.nepaldemocracy.org/civic_education/civic_education.PDF (accessed 15 February 2010).

Danish International Development Agency (DANIDA) (2006) How Political and Institutional Factors have Impacted on the Implementation of the Human Rights and Good Governance Programme in Nepal. Kathmandu: DANIDA. http://www.danidadevforum.um.dk/NR/rdonlyres/820D2D66-2214-4F5A-A326-7B01476266DB/0/Nepal.pdf (accessed 10 March 2010).

Deraniyagala, S. (2005) The Political Economy of Civil Conflict in Nepal, *Oxford Development Studies*, 33(1): 47-62.

De Sales, A. (2003) The Kham Magar Country, Nepal: between ethnic claims and Maoism, in D. Thapa (Ed.) *Understanding the Maoist Movement of Nepal*, 59-89. Kathmandu: Martin Chautari.

Dixit, K. (1997) Foreign Aid in Nepal: no bang for the buck, *Studies in Nepali History and Society*, 2(1), 173-186.

Escobar, A. (1995) *Encountering Development: the making and unmaking of the Third World*. Princeton: Princeton University Press.

Ferguson, J. (2005) Decomposing Modernity: history and hierarchy after development, in A. Loomba, S. Kaul, M. Bunzi, A.M. Burton & J. Esty (Eds) *Postcolonial Studies and Beyond*, 166-181. Durham, NC: Duke University Press.

Fisher, J. (1975) Cannabis in Nepal: an overview, in V. Rubin (Ed.) *Cannabis and Culture*, 247-258. The Hague: Mouton.

Freire, P. (1970) *Pedagogy of the Oppressed*. New York: Continuum.

Fujikura, T. (1996) Technologies of Improvement, Locations of Culture: American discourses of democracy and 'community development' in Nepal, *Studies in Nepali History and Society (SINHAS)*, 1(2), 271-311.

Fujikura, T. (2001) Discourses of Awareness: notes for a criticism of development in Nepal, *Studies in Nepali History and Society (SINHAS)*, 6(2), 15-32.

Gautam, S., Banskota, A. & Manchanda, R. (2001) Where There Are No Men: women in the Maoist insurgency in Nepal, in R. Manchanda (Ed.) *Women, War and Peace in South Asia: beyond victimhood to agency*, 214-251. New Delhi: Sage.

Gautam, S., Banskota, A. & Manchanda, R. (2003) Women in the Maoist Insurgency in Nepal, in D. Thapa (Ed.) *Understanding the Maoist Movement of Nepal*, 93-124. Kathmandu: Martin Chautari.

Ghani, A. & Lockhart, C. (2008) *Fixing Failed States: a framework for rebuilding a fractured world.* Oxford: Oxford University Press.

Gordon, S. (2005) Evaluating Nepal's Integrated 'Security' and 'Development' Policy: development, democracy, and couterinsurgency, *Asian Survey*, 45(4), 581-602.

Government of Nepal and United Nations Development Programme (2006) Millennium Development Goals: needs assessment for Nepal. Kathmandu: National Planning Commission and UNDP. http://www.undp.org.np/publication/html/mdg_NAN/MDG_NeedsAssessmentNepal.pdf (accessed 1 May 2010).

Gurung, H. (2005) Social Exclusion and Maoist Insurgency. Paper presented at the National Dialogue Conference on the ILO Convention 169 regarding Indigenous and Tribal Peoples, January, Kathmandu. http://ilo-mirror.library.cornell.edu/public/english/standards/norm/egalite/itpp/activity/nepal/maoist.pdf

Hachhethu, K. (2003, April) The Question of Inclusion and Exclusion in Nepal: interface between state and ethnicity. Paper presented at the conference, 'The Agenda of Transformation: inclusion in Nepali democracy', April, Kathmandu. http://www.uni-bielefeld.de/midea/pdf/harticle1.pdf (accessed 15 February 2010).

Hachhethu, K. (2006) The Nepali State and the Maoist Insurgency, in M. Hutt (Ed.) *Himalayan People's War: Nepal's Maoist rebellion*, 58-78. Bloomington: Indiana University Press.

Huntington, S. (1996) *The Clash of Civilisations and the Remaking of the World Order.* New York: Simon & Schuster.

Hutt, M. (Ed.) (2006) *Himalayan People's War: Nepal's Maoist rebellion*, 58-78. Bloomington: Indiana University Press.

Ignatieff, M. (2001) *Virtual War: Kosovo and beyond.* New York: Picador.

International Alert (2006) Donor Aid Strategies in Post-Peace Settlement Environments. London/Kathmandu: International Alert. http://www.international-alert.org/pdf/Donor_Aid_Strategies_in_Post_Peace_settlement_environments.pdf (accessed 1 March 2010).

King, R. (1972) *The Drug Hang-Up: America's fifty year folly*. Springfield, IL: Charles Thomas.

LeComte-Tilouine, M. (2004) Ethnic Demands within Maoism: questions of Magar territorial autonomy, nationality and class, in M. Hutt (Ed.) *Himalayan People's War: Nepal's Maoist rebellion*, 112-135. Bloomington: Indiana University Press.

Leve, L. (2007) 'Failed Development' and Rural Revolution in Nepal: rethinking subaltern consciousness and women's empowerment, *Anthropological Quarterly*, 80(1), 127-172.

Liechty, M. (2003) *Suitably Modern: making a middle-class culture in a new consumer society*. Princeton: Princeton University Press.

Lieten, K. (2002) Nepal: Maoist insurgency against lopsided development, in M. Mekencamp, P. van Tongeren & H. van de Veen (Eds) *Searching for Peace in*

Central and South Asia: an overview of conflict prevention and peacebuilding activities, 443-446. London: Lynne Reinner.

Lindborg, N. & Gersony, R. (2003) *Sowing the Wind ... History and Dynamics of the Maoist revolt in Nepal's Rapti Hills*. Kathmandu: Mercy Corps.

Lowati, M. (2005) *Towards a Democratic Nepal: inclusive political institutions for a multicultural society*. New Delhi: Sage.

Lowati, M. (2008, October) Bullets, Ballots, and Bounty: Maoist victory in the twenty-first century, Nepal. Paper presented at the Third Annual Himalayan Policy Research Conference, October, Madison, Wisconsin. https://repository.unm.edu/dspace/bitstream/1928/6935/1/Lawoti_Bullets,%20Ballots,%20Bounty.pdf (accessed 5 April 2010).

Mac Ginty, R. & Williams, A. (2009) *Conflict and Development*. London: Routledge.

Mainali, M. (2003) 'Development' vs the Maobaadis, in D. Thapa (Ed.) *Understanding the Maoist Movement of Nepal*, 125-128. Kathmandu: Martin Chautari.

Mancours, K. (2006, March) Relative Deprivation and Civil Conflict in Nepal. Paper presented at School of Advanced International Studies, Johns Hopkins University. http://www.csae.ox.ac.uk/conferences/2006-eoi-rpi/papers/gprg/macours.pdf

McAllister, W. (2000) *Drug Diplomacy in the Twentieth Century: an international history*. New York: Routledge.

Mihaly, E.B. (1965) *Foreign Aid and Politics in Nepal: a case study*. Oxford: Oxford University Press.

Ministry of Education (2003) Education for All, 2004-2009 – Core Document. Kathmandu: Ministry of Education. http://www.esat.org.np/documents/Programmes_Plans/EFA/EFA_Core.pdf (accessed 1 April 2010).

Murshed, S.M. & Gates, S. (2003) Spatial-Horizontal Inequality and the Maoist Insurgency in Nepal. Tokyo: United Nations University/World Institute for Development Economics Research. http://siteresources.worldbank.org/INTDECINEQ/Resources/NepalConflict.pdf

Nepal, M., Bohara, A.K. & Gwande, K. (2007) Inequality, Polarization, and Violent Conflict: the Maoist insurgency in Nepal. https://repository.unm.edu/dspace/bitstream/1928/3295/1/ManiNepal_Inequality&Conflict2.pdf

Norwegian Agency for Development Cooperation (NORAD) (2008) Final Evaluation of the Program for Strengthening Central Child Welfare Board (CCWB) and District Child Welfare Boards (DCWBS). Kathmandu: NORAD/Plan Norway. http://www.norad.no/en/Tools+and+publications/Publications/Publication+Page?key=117510 (accessed 20 March 2010)

Onesto, L. (2005) *Dispatches from the People's War in Nepal*. London: Pluto Press.

Panday, D.R. (1999) *Nepal's Failed Development: reflections on the missions and the maladies*. Kathmandu: Nepal South Asia Centre.

Panday, D.R. (2000) Matching Democracy and Developmental Policymaking in an Aid-Dependent Country, *Harvard Asia Quarterly*, 4(1), 1-24.

Pfaff-Czarnecka, J. (2004) High Expectations, Deep Disappointment: politics, state, and society in Nepal after 1990, in M. Hutt (Ed.) *Himalayan People's War: Nepal's Maoist rebellion*, 166-191. Bloomington: Indiana University Press.

Pherali, T. (forthcoming 2011) Education and Conflict in Nepal: possibilities for reconstruction, *Globalisation, Societies, and Education.*

Pigg, S. (1993) Unintended Consequences: the ideological impact of development in Nepal, *South Asia Bulletin*, 13(1/2), 45-58.

Pigg, S. (1992) Inventing Social Categories through Place: social representations and development in Nepal, *Comparative Studies in Society and History*, 34(3), 491-513.

Rappleye, J. (forthcoming 2011) Catalyzing Educational Development or Institutionalizing External Influence? Donors, Civil Society, and Educational Policy Formation in Nepal, *Globalisation, Societies, and Education.*

Rostow, W. (1960) *The Stages of Economic Growth: a non-Communist manifesto.* Cambridge: Cambridge University Press.

Sen, A. (1985) *Commodities and Capabilities.* New York: Elsevier.

Sen, A. (1999) *Development as Freedom.* New York: Anchor Books.

Sen, A. (2006) *Identity and Violence.* New York: Norton.

Sharma, K. (2006) Development Policy, Inequity, and Civil War in Nepal, *Journal of International Development*, 18, 553-569.

Sharma, M. & Prasain, D. (2004) Gender Dimensions of the People's War: some reflections on the experiences of rural women, in M. Hutt (Ed.) *Himalayan People's War: Nepal's Maoist rebellion*, 152-165. Bloomington: Indiana University Press.

Sharma, S. & Rana, S. (2005) The Maoist Insurgency in Nepal: a monograph. Program for the Study of International Organizations Occasional Papers, no. 5. Geneva: Institute of Graduate Studies.

Shrestha, N. (1997) *In the Name of Development: a reflection on Nepal.* New York: University Press of America.

Shields, R. & Rappleye, J. (2008a) Differentiation, Development, (Dis)Integration: education in Nepal's 'People's War', *Research in Comparative and International Education*, 3(1), 91-102.

Shields, R. & Rappleye, J. (2008b) Uneven Terrain: educational policy and equity in Nepal, *Asia Pacific Journal of Education*, Special Issue on Education in South Asia – Equity, Policy, and Pedagogy, 28(3), 265-276.

Shultz, T. (1971) *Investment in Human Capital.* New York: The Free Press.

Staines, N (2004) Economic Performance over the Conflict Cycle. IMF Working Paper no. 95. Washington: International Monetary Fund. http://imf.org/external/pubs/ft/wp/2004/wp0495.pdf (accessed 10 April 2010).

Stewart, F. (2001) Horizontal Inequalities: a neglected dimension of development. Centre for Research on Inequality, Human Security, and Ethnicity, Queen Elizabeth House, Oxford University. Working Paper 1. http://www.crise.ox.ac.uk/pubs/workingpaper1.pdf

Stiglitz, J. (2002) *Globalization and its Discontents.* New York: Norton.

Subedi, M. (2009) Foreign Aid, Sustainable Development, and the Rapti IRDP. Occasional Papers in Sociology and Anthropology, 9, 231-257. http://www.digitalhimalaya.com/collections/journals/opsa/index.php?selection=9 (accessed 10 May 2010).

Thapa, D. (2003) Introduction, in D. Thapa (Ed.) *Understanding the Maoist Movement in Nepal*, ix-xx. Kathmandu: Martin Chautari.

Thapa, D. & Sijapati, S. (2003) *Kingdom under Siege: Nepal's Maoist insurgency, 1996-2003*. London: Zed Books.

Thapa, M. (2005) *Forget Kathmandu: an elegy for democracy*. New Delhi: Penguin.

Tiwari, B.N. (2007) An Assessment of the Causes of Conflict in Nepal. Paper presented at the Second Annual Himalayan Policy Research Conference, October, Madison, Wisconsin. https://repository.unm.edu/dspace/bitstream/1928/3294/1/BishwaNathTiwari_Nepal_CausesofConflict_pdf.pdf (accessed 10 April 2010).

UNICEF (1997) *Development with a Human Face: experiences in social achievement and economic growth*. Oxford: Oxford University Press.

United States Agency for International Development (USAID) (1995) *The Rapti Development Project: final evaluation*. Washington, DC: USAID. http://www.rmportal.net/library/content/tools/community-based-natural-forest-management/cbnfm/USAID-BDB-cd-2-data/the-rapti-development-project-final-evaluation/view?searchterm=livestock

Uvin, P. (1998) *Aiding Violence: the development enterprise in Rwanda*. West Hartford, CT: Kumarian Press.

Van de Walle, N. (2001) *African Economies and the Politics of Permanent Crisis, 1979-1999*. Cambridge: Cambridge University Press.

Vaux, T., Smith, A. & Subba, S. (2006) *Education for All – Nepal review from a conflict perspective*. Kathmandu: International Alert. http://www.international-alert.org/pdf/Education_4all_Nepal.pdf

Whelpton, J. (2005) *A History of Nepal*. Cambridge: Cambridge University Press.

World Bank (2001) *Nepal: priorities and strategies for education reform*. Report no. 22065-NEP. Washington, DC: World Bank.

World Bank (2003a) *Breaking the Conflict Trap: civil war and development policy*. Washington: World Bank.

World Bank (2003b) *Country Assistance Strategy for Nepal*. Washington/Kathmandu: World Bank.

World Bank (2005) *Reshaping the Future: education and post-conflict reconstruction*. Washington: World Bank.

Young, C. (2003) Explaining the Conflict Potential of Ethnicity, in J. Darby & R. Mac Ginty (Eds) *Contemporary Peacemaking: conflict, violence, and peace processes*, 9-18. Basingstoke: Palgrave Macmillan.

PART 2

Understanding Relationships: country case studies

CHAPTER 4

Sources of Learning about Human Rights and Democracy in Southern Sudan

CHRISTINE PAGEN

SUMMARY After conflict, social structures are often completely or partially destroyed; post-conflict reconstruction is the process of rebuilding those systems. This path may be influenced by a combination of factors that are contextually internal or external, including armed parties to conflict, neighbouring countries and international organizations. In this process, international norms may also shape the interaction and interests of actors. Conceptual examples of such ideational influences may include democracy or human rights. If reconstruction is affected by these international norms, then it is important to understand the different ways that individuals may learn about democracy and human rights in and after conflict. This chapter explores sources of learning about these ideas in the post-conflict context of Sudan. Using a combination of qualitative and quantitative research conducted in southern Sudan, this chapter explores how the ideas of democracy and human rights may be passed on through formal, non-formal and informal education. The findings suggest that a better understanding of these sources of learning could shape democracy-building efforts in southern Sudan, with the dynamic role of international non-governmental organizations in this process emerging as a critical topic for future research.

Introduction

After conflict, previously existing social structures are often completely or partially destroyed; post-conflict reconstruction is the process of rebuilding those systems. The path of reconstruction may be influenced by a combination of factors that are contextually internal or external, including armed parties to the conflict, neighbouring countries and international organizations. In this process, international norms, ideas and values that are collectively and intersubjectively held, may also shape the interaction and interests of actors (Finnemore & Sikkink, 2001). Conceptual examples of such norms would include democracy or human rights as possible ideational influences during reconstruction. If reconstruction is affected by these international norms, then it is important to understand the different ways that individuals may learn about democracy and human rights in and after conflict. Because of the dependence of social structures on such ideas (Wendt, 1992), this chapter explores sources of learning about them in the post-conflict context of southern Sudan.

The protracted civil war in Sudan exacerbated widespread poverty in the south, creating a complex emergency situation that demanded immediate attention from the international community (United Nations Office for the Coordination of Humanitarian Affairs [UNOCHA], 2005). The situation was intensified by the violence of the civil war and drought-induced famine conditions over several decades. More than 90% of the population currently lives below the international poverty line of less than one dollar a day; during the civil war, this number is estimated to have reached almost 100% (Deng, 2003). In response to this post-conflict situation, multilateral and governmental agencies have directed large financial resources into humanitarian and development projects in southern Sudan; the US Government is the leading international donor to Sudan, in part through the US Agency for International Development (USAID) (USAID, 2005b; US Government, 2007a).[1] More than $6 billion in support for humanitarian relief, reconstruction and assistance has been invested by the US Government in Sudan since 2005.[2]

The US policy strategy in Sudan has assumed that high levels of investment in democratic reform during conflict and reconstruction will contribute to sustainable peace (USAID, 2002, 2004, 2005b). According to the US Foreign Assistance Framework (US Government, 2007b), Sudan is a *rebuilding country*, meaning that it is 'in or emerging from and rebuilding after internal or external conflict' (p. 1). Rebuilding countries need a 'stable environment for good governance, increased availability of essential social services, and initial progress to create policies and institutions upon which future progress will rest' (p. 1). In the USAID Strategic Framework for Africa, Sudan is considered a *fragile state*, meaning it is 'vulnerable to crisis, in crisis or emerging from crisis and either cannot assume, will not assure, or demonstrate a growing ability to assure the provision of basic services and security' (USAID, 2006, p. 3; USAID 2005a). In these contexts, the goals are to 'avert and resolve conflict' and 'promote stability, recovery, and democratic reform' (p. 2).

Given this focus in US policy on democratic reform as the path towards a stable, sustainable and secure peace in southern Sudan, it is critical to illuminate the process by which southern Sudanese learn about the international norms that ground such reform. Using a combination of qualitative and quantitative research conducted in southern Sudan, this chapter explores how the ideas of democracy and human rights may be passed on through formal, non-formal and informal education. The findings suggest that a better understanding of these sources of learning could shape democracy-building efforts in southern Sudan, with the dynamic role of international non-governmental organizations (INGOs) in this process emerging as a critical topic for future research.

Conflict and Peace in Southern Sudan

The conflict in Sudan has raged nearly continuously since the country's 1956 independence from Anglo-Egyptian rule. Seeking to end the latest surge of violence, the northern government in Khartoum and the leading rebel group from southern Sudan, the Sudan People's Liberation Movement/Army (SPLM/A), signed the Comprehensive Peace Agreement (CPA) in 2005 with the intention to end 21 years of civil war that led to some two million deaths (Armed Conflict Database, 2008). The CPA delineated an interim period of six years in which Khartoum and the SPLM/A would share power and oil revenues in a unified government. The resulting Government of National Unity (GNU) is now jointly operated by the National Congress Party (NCP) and the SPLM/A as the leading party of the nascent Government of Southern Sudan (GOSS), along with the representation of several other parties (Central Intelligence Agency [CIA], 2008). In 2011, voters from the south have the opportunity to participate in a referendum to decide whether southern Sudan is to remain part of Sudan or to secede into a separate nation-state.

Well before these recent developments, between the fifteenth and nineteenth centuries, Arab influence spread from Egypt into the Nubian civilization located in what is currently northern Sudan through widened trading patterns (Petterson, 2003). Islam followed, driving Christian missionaries down into the south. In time, Egyptian administration also stretched south through Sudan and into Uganda via the slave trade (Johnson, 2003). In 1882, the Mahdist rebellion movement under the leadership of Muhammad Ahmad bin Abdallah overthrew Egyptian rule, and the Mahdists assassinated a British General in Khartoum (Petterson, 2003). As a result, the British conducted a number of military campaigns in Sudan, culminating in an official declaration in 1889 that the British and Egyptians would jointly rule the country after defeating the Mahdist state.

Britain's focus and interest in northern Sudan continued to effectively bifurcate the country into a predominantly (though not entirely) Arab north and non-Arab south, home to a diverse composition of African ethnic groups. Colonial policy fostered the growth and education of northern Sudan and protected its Islamic culture. At the same time, development was obstructed in the south, and investment in social services was minimal, thus reinforcing existing tensions from the slave trade (Johnson, 2003). Christian missionaries from Europe made the primary social and economic investment in southern Sudan at this time (Ali & Matthews, 1999; Petterson, 2003).

In June 1947, southern Sudanese leaders held a conference to discuss the prospect of independence and how the south might participate in a new form of governance (Petterson, 2003). In reaction to the threat of continued colonial rule, the conference attendees decided to support unification as one nation with northern Sudan. In the next decade, however, southerners increasingly believed that Arabs from the north would merely take over colonial rule in the south, leaving little to no opportunity for southern participation in Sudan's government.

Starting with a mutiny in Torit, in the south of Sudan, in 1955 that sparked much violence in both north and south, violence in Sudan has continued with very little respite (Ali & Matthews, 1999). Since Sudan gained its independence in 1956, there have been three formal attempts at settling the conflict between the northern government and southern opposition groups: 1965, 1972 and 1986. None of them, however, provided enough incentive for the hostile parties to maintain long-term peace. The Khartoum Round Table Conference of 1965 brought actors together during a period when labour unions and trade organizations were competing with sectarian groups for power. The conference failed because of a lack of cohesiveness within both the political parties and geographical regions, complicated by contentious struggles over leadership (Ali & Matthews, 1999).

In 1969, Colonel Gaafar Muhammed Nimairi took control of the country via a military coup. He initially embraced radical socialism but became increasingly unpopular as he failed to enact promised economic reforms. In a desperate play for allies, Nimairi signed the 1972 Addis Ababa agreement, which granted some regional autonomy to the south. Because the south's regional autonomy made it more difficult for the north to access minerals and other natural resources in the south, Nimairi redrew the border in 1980. When this change was met with resistance from the southern regional authority, Nimairi formed and occupied a new province that held all of the oil fields. At the same time, Nimairi forced Islamic law on the south, which led to renewed civil war in 1983 with the recently-founded SPLM/A, commanded by Dr John Garang de Mabior.

The early 1980s was a period of extreme violence during which the people of both north and south Sudan suffered. Nimieri was deposed in a 1985 coup, after which parties from across the country came together to sign the Kokadam Declaration of 1986. It was believed by the leaders of the SPLM/A and others that this agreement was a major step towards securing peace in Sudan. However, the northern government that followed Nimairi mirrored many of his actions. Peace promises were broken by the then Prime Minister Sadiq el Mahdi, and popular protests in the south were quickly organized, leading to another extremely volatile and violent environment. El Mahdi was overthrown without resolving the conflict with the south.

Using harsh military tactics, General Omar al-Bashir came to power in 1989 with the support of Hassan al-Turabi of the hard-line National Islamic Front (NIF) (Petterson, 2003); al-Bashir is the current president of Sudan and leader of the NCP (CIA, 2008). Under al-Bashir and the NCP, the northern government continued to systematically under-develop the south (Cobham, 2005). It enacted social and economic policies of Arabization, Islamization and slavery (Deng, 2006). These processes over time, in addition to the British and Egyptian colonial legacies and existing tribal lines, created a mix of religious, racial, economic and ethnic identities that have complicated the country's civil war and its post-conflict reconstruction (Deng, 2006; Branch & Mampilly, 2005).

After a failed coup within the liberation movement of the SPLM/A in 1991, the group splintered into numerous factions, including SPLA-United and the Southern Sudan Independence Movement/Army (Nyaba, 1997). In 1994, the SPLM/A held a national convention in the south and elected Garang and Commander Salva Kiir Mayardit to the positions of SPLM/A chairman and deputy chairman, respectively. The disparate political movements in the south reunified under this leadership team within several years, despite some lingering dissent among certain political leaders at the time (Nyaba, 1997).

In the mid 1990s, the Intergovernmental Authority on Development (IGAD), a regional development organization comprised of Djibouti, Eritrea, Ethiopia, Kenya, Somalia, Sudan and Uganda, attempted to mediate the conflict between the north and south with the support of Australia, Canada, Britain, Norway, Italy and the USA (Johnson, 2003). The northern NCP and the southern SPLM/A finally signed a Declaration of Principles (DOP) in 1997 that prioritized the unity of Sudan under a secular democratic system, although Khartoum did so with reservations (Petterson, 2003). Under the terms of the DOP, if this governmental transformation did not occur concurrently with an equitable distribution of resources, then southern Sudan would be permitted to hold a referendum of self-determination at some point in the future (IGAD, 1997).

Despite the signing of the DOP, violence continued until 2002, when Khartoum and the SPLM/A finally declared a ceasefire and signed the Machakos Protocol (2002), which laid the groundwork yet again for a peace agreement between north and south. In 2003, however, aggressive attacks were launched by both the Khartoum government in northern Sudan and the SPLM/A, which was then a consolidation of southern rebel factions. This re-emergence of fighting after the 2002 peace agreement aggravated the already dire humanitarian circumstances in southern Sudan.

Since the CPA was signed in 2005, the peace in Sudan has been fragile at best, as evidenced by the removal of GOSS ministers from the GNU after allegations that Khartoum was not honouring the CPA. SPLM/A leader Garang's death in a helicopter crash in July 2005, three weeks after he was sworn in as First Vice President of Sudan, caused an eruption of violence in the Sudanese urban centres of Juba and Khartoum, despite evidence suggesting that the crash was an accident. The transition of southern leadership to Commander Kiir has been precarious but hopeful, as he has continued to try to integrate different ethnicities within the government (Young, 2005). Continuing rebel activity in eastern Sudan and in the disputed areas in the centre of the country, the conflict in northern Uganda, and the genocide in Darfur to the west have also been threatening the peace in southern Sudan. Throughout its history, southern Sudan has been underdeveloped and affected by conflict and poverty. In its environment of limited schooling, opportunities to learn formally about democracy and human rights were unavailable. However, clearly the persistent political struggle for greater participation in its own governance indicates some knowledge and understanding of these underlying principles coming from sources other than formal education.

Situating USAID Policy in Southern Sudan

Democratization in southern Sudan is the overarching goal of American foreign policy in the region. From the US National Security Strategy (US Government, 2002) to the USAID Strategy Statement for Sudan (2005b), democratic reform is the top priority. The primary road to this objective is democratic institution-building. However, the importance of individuals and the role they must play in a sustainable democracy is also recognized in country-specific policies.

Peace in Sudan is also of critical interest to the USA from a national security standpoint. The Sudan Strategy Statement indicates that Sudan 'is the U.S. government's highest priority country in Africa due to its importance for counterterrorism and regional stability, as well as the magnitude of human rights and humanitarian abuses' (USAID, 2005b, p. 1). This policy sits within a larger policy framework that is grounded in the national security concerns of the US Government.

The Bush administration released its version of the US National Security Strategy in September 2002. Section VII of this document situates development within the country's overarching security framework. It asserts that aid has been ineffective in terms of assisting vulnerable populations and promoting global security. The Strategy argues that American foreign assistance should, instead, demonstrably value democratic reforms and transparency by focusing on long-term outcomes and emphasizing support to governments that have embraced institutional change. In other words, programmes should be funded that foster the 'subcomponents of democracy, including civic participation, good governance, rule of law, and human rights' (Windsor, 2006, p. 25).

As mentioned above, while some policy documents highlight institutional governance, the role of southern Sudanese individuals is also recognized. Indeed, this is explicitly discussed in the framework for the south. According to the Sudan Strategy Statement, '[a]verting and resolving conflict by consolidating peace, managing crises, and promoting stability, recovery, and democratic reform are monumental tasks for the GNU, the GOSS, [the] Three Areas state governments, and *Sudanese citizens* and civil society organizations' (USAID, 2005b, p. 3, emphasis added). This assertion reflects the wording and spirit of other US government documents, including, most directly, the Strategic Framework for Africa (USAID, 2006). It is significant in its recognition that responsibility for peace in Sudan extends beyond the institutional reach of the GOSS and other governmental structures; civil society and the citizens of southern Sudan themselves are also active players in this process.

Because of the primacy of democracy in US foreign assistance, and because of the critical role that individuals in southern Sudan play in its reconstruction, it is important to better understand sources of learning about democracy and human rights. Certainly, formal education is a location in which this transmission of ideas may take place. However, the war in Sudan prevented many Sudanese from accessing formal education, and therefore it is also critical to look beyond the school setting towards where learning occurs in non-formal and informal contexts.

Categories of Education

Often, the term *education* is associated with learning that takes place in schools or other formal settings; however, there are processes of learning that occur outside of a classroom setting that also merit attention (Bentley, 1998). Education is, then, more broadly defined in this chapter as the transmission and communication of ideas and knowledge (Dewey, 1916). It is the process through which learning takes place, and it can take place in different contexts.

In 1974, Coombs & Ahmed delineated three categories of education: formal, non-formal and informal; today, this rubric is almost always reflected in discussions of education as it occurs inside and outside of schools (Jeffs & Smith, 1990). Formal education is the 'hierarchically structured, chronologically graded "educational system" running from primary school through the university' (Coombs, 1973, p. 11). It possesses a 'rigidity of rules and regulations' (Chandra & Shah, 1987, p. 1). My research is concerned with formal education because I am interested in learning that occurs inside of the classroom, as well as other potential sources of learning about democracy and human rights outside of a formal school setting.

The conceptualization of non-formal education grew from the work of Philip Coombs and others in the late 1960s and early 1970s (Coombs, 1968). The term refers to 'any organized educational activity outside the established formal system – whether operating separately or as an important feature of some broader activity – that is intended to serve identifiable learning clienteles and learning objectives' (Coombs & Ahmed, 1974, p. 11).

For example, such learning may take place in spaces in a community that are not necessarily dedicated to or designed for education (McGivney, 1999), and associations and social groups can serve as educators, as can institutions (Galbraith, 1990). Rather than focusing on official state-driven curricula, non-formal education commonly emphasizes the learning of skills and knowledge that have practical application for the learner and that vary from one region to another (Chandra & Shah, 1987).

Development theorists and academics alike embraced the term 'non-formal education' as part of larger debates over education reform in developing countries (Rogers, 2005). Substantive funding followed for decades, as did programming and research initiatives. Rogers found that the exact meaning of the term 'non-formal education' has been increasingly blurred. Many development initiatives have employed the term as that which encompasses primary schooling but takes place outside of the formal school setting. Essentially, non-formal education is comprised of '[f]lexible modes of providing schooling for young people ... especially in the light of growing populations, the escalating costs of education combined with more limited funding, the search for partnerships with civil society, and new educational targets set internationally' (p. 3). It has also been applied to supplemental programming outside of the typical school day that is targeted at adult learners who are or who could be in the workforce (Chandra & Shah, 1987).

Dejene (1980) draws on multiple earlier definitions of non-formal education to conclude that it involves a strategy in which a particular subject is being taught that, dependent upon programme design, may also be taught in formal settings but is not because of varying circumstances. He argues that non-formal education is more autonomous and flexible than formal education tends to be, and it often seeks to provide training in particular life skills. Non-formal education is, according to Dejene, 'not as formless as its name might imply' (p. 19). Non-formal education programmes generally ceased to be grouped under that term in the 1990s, 'non-formal' having been eschewed for terms such as 'basic, continuing, recurrent or lifelong education or learning', mirroring trends in development theory and programming (Rogers, 2005, p. 4).

Informal education, by contrast, is understood as that which takes places outside of the curricula, institutions and programmes of formal and non-formal education (Schugurensky, 2000). It is 'the truly lifelong process whereby every individual acquires attitudes, values, skills and knowledge from daily experience and the educative influences and resources in his or her environment' (Coombs & Ahmed, 1974, p. 10), and these attitudes, values and skills are not likely to be taught in formal settings. As such, informal education differs from non-formal education, which also occurs outside of a formal setting, but which specifically includes skills and knowledge that are purposefully taught in school curricula. The informal education process is considered to be 'relatively unorganized and unsystematic (hence the rubric "informal")' (Coombs & Ahmed, 1974, p. 11). Similarly, Dejene (1980) summarizes Paulston's definition of informal education as one 'where people learn in a non-systematic manner from generally unstructured exposure to cultural facilities, social institutions, political process, personal media, and the mass media' (as paraphrased in Dejene, 1980, p. 17).

There is, of course, overlap between these three formulations of education, and there have been criticisms of the distinctions because they often suggest differences based primarily on institutional context. For instance, Smith argues that the variation among these categories of education relies too heavily on setting and administration. In other words, '[f]ormal education is linked with schools and training institutions; non-formal with community groups and other organizations; and informal covers what is left, e.g. interactions with friends, family and work colleagues' (2006, para. 10). In these cases, 'there is an over-concern with institutional setting or sponsorship as against process and content' (2006, para. 5). However, when exploring *sources* of learning about particular ideas – meaning *from where* the ideas come from – it is the setting that is particularly of interest.

Methods of Data Collection

This research is grounded in a mixed methods approach that combines both qualitative and quantitative strategies. It follows educational researchers Johnson & Onwuegbuzie, who argue that 'methodological pluralism ... frequently results in superior research (compared to monomethod research)' (2004, p. 14). These approaches can be complementary, rigorous, and held to high standards of research without losing the context of qualitative data (Brady & Collier, 2004). Thus, this research was designed to approach the research question into sources of learning from multiple perspectives and to incorporate qualitative and quantitative approaches.

The data emerges from surveys, interviews and informal conversations. A field-based survey of 271 randomly selected Sudanese men and women was conducted in Yei, a town in the southern Sudanese state of Central Equatoria whose surrounding lands were peppered with landmines during the war. Throughout the past several decades, violence in Yei has been aggravated by its proximity both to Juba, the last-held northern government garrison town, and to Uganda, whose rebels committed atrocities against Yei's people at the behest of the northern government in Khartoum. Of those interviewed, 70% had completed primary school, but only 25% had completed secondary school. Qualitative data comes from interviews with a total of five national (Sudanese) and 16 expatriate INGO staff in Yei and Juba, in Nairobi, Kenya, and in Washington, DC, using convenience and opportunistic sampling (Marshall & Rossman, 1999). In addition to these interviews, this chapter draws upon informal conversations held with six USAID and 14 INGO and staff members that were recorded in field notes. A total of nine INGOs were included in this study.

Findings on Sources of Learning

This section presents findings from research conducted in southern Sudan on where people learn about democracy and human rights. It first explores the sources of learning indicated by the survey responses of participants from Yei, and then presents the sources of learning that emerged primarily through interviews with USAID and INGO staff. The purpose of the analysis is to identify the organizations and people from which someone in southern Sudan may have learned about democracy and human rights in order to illuminate the process of democracy-building after conflict.

The survey asked respondents to provide up to four sources from which or from whom they learned about democracy and human rights. The question was open-ended to gather all answers, rather than limiting the possibilities with fixed multiple choices. Upon analysis, these answers fell into six groupings: schooling, relatives and friends, government and political leaders, INGOs (including seminars and workshops), tribal and community leaders, and churches. The percentages of respondents who made references to the respective sources of learning are given in Table I.

Origin of learning	%
Government and political leaders	72.79
Relatives and friends	43.38
Churches and religious leaders	37.87
Schooling	36.40
INGOs	31.99
Tribal and community leaders	5.15

Table I. Sources of learning about democracy.

Government and political leaders were listed as a source of learning about democracy and human rights by the highest percentage: 72.79% of the respondents. However, it was unclear whether this percentage was high only because people assume they learn about government *from* government or whether they learned about government from other sources. For instance, this result may indicate that the USAID focus on strengthening political infrastructure in southern Sudan is a good investment because nearly three-quarters of the respondents indicated that they learned about democracy and human rights from their government and political leaders. Such an elevated percentage may also suggest that, throughout the civil war, the rhetoric of democracy and human rights was used by military forces (including but not exclusively the SPLA) to garner support even though these principles were not necessarily enacted by either party to the conflict. Further research on this point could be undertaken by interviews with those who stayed at home during the war as well as with ex-combatants.

The informal education that occurs in the home is also clearly very important in terms of learning about international norms. In the survey question that asked where respondents learned about democracy and human rights, 43.38% identified relatives and friends as sources of information. When in a separate question they were asked how frequently the respondent discussed political issues with friends and family, 39.5% indicated that such conversations occurred more often than monthly. Table II provides information on frequency of these discussions. The similarity in these two percentages (those who mentioned friends and relatives as sources of information and those who discuss political issues with friends and relatives) may indicate that more frequent discussions must take place in informal settings for a person to consider them educational. Encouraging these personal interactions may be a critical component of successful democracy-building efforts, and additional research should explore the degree to which gender impacts this factor.

Frequency	%
Never	41.1
Monthly	19.4
Weekly	21.3
Daily	18.2

Table II. Frequency of political discussions with friends and family.

Learning certainly may also take place in religious settings. Of the survey respondents, 37.87% answered that their religious leaders were a source of learning about democracy and human rights. In this survey, data was not captured on the amount of time spent in religious settings or the degree of religiosity of a respondent. In addition, as 97% of the participants indicated their religion as Christianity, there is not sufficient variance to differentiate between sites of worship in southern Sudan and how they may be used to promote democracy and human rights. Organizations seeking to promote democracy may consider how to integrate democracy-building into the existing social settings that are grounded in religious belief. The number of respondents who reported that their tribal and community leaders are a primary source of information about democracy and human rights, on the other hand, was quite small, being only 5.15%.

It is intuitive that formal schooling may serve as a learning source that shapes the respondents' attitudes towards democracy and human rights, as indicated by the answers of 36.4% of the survey respondents. However, this is a fairly low percentage, given how much emphasis is put on formal schooling as a mechanism through which to educate about democracy and human rights. It is a good reminder that, in and after conflict, formal education is often disrupted, and thus schools may not be the most effective setting through which to transmit messages – whether about security issues like landmine awareness, health concerns regarding water quality or malaria, or international norms such as democracy and human rights. If schools are to be used as centres of social services delivery and a mechanism through which to educate on any issue, including those of interest in this chapter, however, focusing on access – getting children into classrooms – will be a critical component of any programme. In addition, education programming should consider the quality of learning in post-conflict environments, including the degree to which democracy and human rights are incorporated into the curriculum being used and whether teachers are opting to include these lessons.

Almost 32% of respondents indicated that INGOs were sources of learning about democracy and human rights. This could mean that respondents participated in civic education programmes or other training of which democracy-building was a desired result, but it may also include education about these international norms that was unintended by the organization but occurs through the interaction between aid provider and recipient. Further analysis should consider whether meanings and messages about the concepts of democracy and human rights may be passed on through the experience of participating in a seed distribution, for example, or another aid scenario without explicit political goals. INGOs may provide a setting for the transmission of ideas, such as democracy and human rights, but this may or may not be aligned with the actual programming and/or political intentions of these organizations.

Interviews with USAID and INGO staff members, in addition to experiences of the researcher, suggested two additional sources of learning about international norms. These are media and personal exposure to places beyond Sudan. In the USAID and INGO interviews, media exposure was a clear matter of importance. However, not one Sudanese survey respondent listed media or radio as a significant source of learning about democracy and human rights. This is particularly surprising given that USAID funding was being directed into radio programming in Sudan, and several INGOs were working on media projects related to civic education. These initiatives are generally thought to be an effective means of communicating with populations who are remotely located or otherwise isolated from more direct efforts, but survey findings may suggest otherwise. Further research on media programmes with political messaging might further explore how such efforts are being perceived by their intended or unintended audiences. Despite it not being mentioned as a source of information in the survey, 50% of the respondents accessed at least two different types of media (radio, television, newspaper and web-based sources) once per week or more often. This indicates that exposure to media does exist and could indeed be a source of learning about democracy and human rights, even if the audience does not consider it as such.

In addition, some staff suggested that influences from outside of Sudan might have an impact on this learning process, specifically from family members abroad and personal time spent outside of the country. The data that captured personal influences from outside of Sudan was a combination of the degree to which someone has family living abroad, receives remittances from family abroad, or has themself lived outside of the country. Of the respondents, 80.4% had at least one of these characteristics. As with media, these answers did not arise in the surveys of southern Sudanese, but such a high percentage of respondents having influences outside of Sudan – and thus in the international arena – may be significant when discussing how international norms are learned.

Discussion

In this research, multiple potential sources were identified from which southern Sudanese adults may have learned about democracy and human rights. These include relatives and friends, government and political leaders, media, churches and religious leaders, tribal or community leaders, schooling, personal outside influences and INGOs. In order to gain a better understanding about how such international norms are learned, it is useful to consider whether these sources would be considered formal, non-formal or informal education. Doing so can feed into the design of programmes focusing on democracy-building in and after conflict by encouraging a framework that draws upon different sites of learning available in a given context.

School is the mechanism by which a person would be taught directly and purposefully about democracy and human rights. This structured environment with a set curriculum is formal education, and it has a clear role to play in the transmission of knowledge. For the people surveyed in Yei, over a third suggested that their formal experience was a key factor in their understanding of these issues. Such civic education may not take place in schools frequently, as about two-thirds of the population did not indicate that formal education was a source of learning about democracy and human rights. Those organizations that strive to promote an understanding of these concepts may wish to support the development and implementation of a formal curriculum on the federal level that focuses on them.

Non-formal educational contexts are those that operate outside of the formal sphere but still possess tangible learning goals. In other words, there is an intention to teach inherent in the interaction. It is not possible in each case to determine universally whether the remaining sources of learning possess the objective of teaching about democracy and human rights. However, it is likely that leaders from government, political parties, ethnic groups, particular geographic areas, or religious organizations may have a particular agenda in terms of educating their communities about these concepts.

It follows that, in order to promote democratic attitudes and behaviour and a respect for human rights, a stronger focus on incorporating the community into aid efforts should be considered. Identifying individuals who can both lead socio-political change efforts and encourage engagement of other community members may help to engender democratic norms. Aid organizations interested in democracy-building – and a donor agency like USAID with clear political goals in this area – would probably be well served to identify these leaders and support their efforts to teach democracy and human rights, through non-formal means, to the populations over whom they hold influence. Finnemore & Sikkink's model explains the spread of internationally accepted ideas through the actions of effective norm entrepreneurs, meaning those minority advocates 'who use international norms to strengthen their position in domestic debates' (1998, p. 893). These actors catalyse a norm cascade, the embrace of an idea by a critical mass, after which the norm is legitimized through international socialization and institutionalized, making it part of the political development process. It may be that, in international response in and after conflict, such persons should be supported in order to best encourage democratic behaviour and respect for the globally agreed-upon rights of all humans. Mobilization of and support for such individuals could represent an enormous opportunity in relief and development as a key component to be added to future aid efforts, regardless of sector.

The relatively high percentage of participating southern Sudanese adults who responded that their churches and religious leaders were sources of learning about democracy and human rights indicates that this may be another effective avenue for teaching these issues. As community leaders were mentioned by a much smaller percentage of participants, accessing populations through their religious organizations may be more effective than using ethnic avenues. Additional research could explore the different messages transmitted through these different types of leadership. INGO programmes should consider that each community will probably have its own leadership structure where, in some places, churches will be more influential, and in others, leaders of ethnic groupings will fill that role. Understanding these underlying socio-cultural and political complexities in a community will be critical to effectively providing social services, as well as to effectively creating democratic change.

The remaining sources of learning that were identified in this research can be categorized as informal educators. These include relatives and friends of survey respondents, the media, personal influences outside of Sudan, and INGOs. The learning that takes place in these instances is informal; in other words, it is 'non-systematic' and from 'generally unstructured exposure' (Dejene, 1980).

That almost 60% of respondents included friends and family as sources of information regarding democracy and human rights highlights the importance of facilitating these informal dialogues. Heretofore there has not been a focus in the aid community on the construction and maintenance of safe spaces in which communities can share their own ideas. However, should these environments be created – or if existing spaces were supported – they could become part of successful efforts to promote democracy-building.

The resulting environment would look different from current civic training programmes because there would not be a necessary end goal in which participants might gain an understanding of specific democratic institutions or concepts. Rather, these spaces might model democracy on the individual level in the way in which INGOs already speak; they could be open, participatory and transparent. In this way, the growth of democracy in southern Sudan may be more organic and community-appropriate.

Media is a resource that is heavily relied upon in programmes in southern Sudan to serve civic education purposes; radio programming, in particular, is the medium of choice. However, the survey found that participating southern Sudanese adults did not identify media as a place from which they learned about democracy and human rights. Further research into the effectiveness of radio programmes as a civic education tool should be conducted as the reach of radio programming may not be as wide as previously assumed, or the content may not be presented in an effective or easily absorbable manner. Alternatively, these programmes may be quite effective at attracting listeners, but evaluations may focus more on attitudinal and behavioural change on the individual level, rather than relying on the number of listeners as an indicator of success.

Scholarship on the intersection of informal learning and politics has focused on the direct educative effect of participation in democratic processes; for example, how the process of voting in an election can educate the voter on democracy (Smith & Tolbert, 2004). This may be confirmed by the high percentage of survey respondents who identified government actors as sources of learning. However, INGOs were also cited as a source of learning about democracy and human rights. Further research should explore this important point, particularly given the political goals USAID seeks to achieve through its development efforts.

While it may be that respondents were referring to civic education, training, or other actual INGO programmes that have the goal of transmitting knowledge on these international norms, there may also be informal learning occurring in the space of the interaction between aid organization and recipient. Some INGO staff suggested that they may indirectly train communities in an 'unstructured' way in which 'interaction' with the organization helps with empowerment, as these concepts are 'absorbed, whether we acknowledge it or not' (personal communication, 2007). In other words, 'being involved in relief/development programmes exposes southern Sudanese to new ideas and concepts which changes how they feel politically' (personal communication, 2007). An interesting parallel may be found within public health in those studies which find that a programme has a particular educative effect on individuals beyond their medical treatment. McFadden & Sunkara (2004) offer an example of this behaviour change after participation in malarial prevention programmes in Guinea. In other words, participation in the aid relationship may also educate the recipient in international norms such as democracy and human rights, which would be particularly of interest to USAID – given its focus on democracy-building – and the organizations it funds. Aid may be conceptualized as *an educative force*, rather than purely an operational or programmatic one. This may be particularly relevant for democracy-building in the case of Sudan and other countries affected by conflict in which INGOs are the primary providers of social services. Additional research should illuminate the nature of the relationship between international aid organizations and aid recipients and how interactions between them may be sites of learning.

Conclusion

During this research, a Sudanese staff member of an INGO remarked that 'we Sudanese want to have democracy, and it is good that you Americans are here to show us how to do it' (personal communication, 2007). This quote begins to highlight the relationship between INGOs and recipient populations, which has implications for education and development efforts in and after conflict. To promote democracy and respect for human rights, multiple sources of learning could be supported, including community leaders and media, among others discussed in this chapter. Perhaps most interesting, however, will be future research exploring how interactions with INGOs are shaping attitudes and behaviour in southern Sudan and similar contexts.

Notes

[1] These funds include money earmarked for Darfur as well as for southern Sudan. See http://www.reliefweb.int/rw/rwb.nsf/db900SID/KHII-6VS92C?OpenDocument

[2] http://www.usaid.gov/locations/sub-saharan_africa/countries/sudan/index.html

References

Ali, T. & Matthews, R. (1999) Civil War and Peace Efforts in Sudan, in T. Ali & R. Matthews (Eds) *Civil Wars in Africa: roots and resolution*, 193-222. Montreal: McGill-Queen's University Press.

Armed Conflict Database (2008) *Sudan (SPLM and NDA)*. London: International Institute for Strategic Studies.

Bentley, T. (1998) *Learning beyond the Classroom: education for a changing world.* London: Routledge.

Brady, H. & Collier, D. (Eds) (2004) *Rethinking Social Inquiry: diverse tools, shared standards.* London: Rowman & Littlefield.

Branch, A. & Mampilly, Z. (2005) Winning the War, but Losing the Peace? The Dilemma of SPLM/A Civil Administration and the Tasks Ahead, *Journal of Modern African Studies*, 43(1), 1-20.

Central Intelligence Agency (2008) *World Factbook: Sudan.* https://www.cia.gov/cia/publications/factbook/geos/su.html

Chandra, A. & Shah, A. (1987) *Non-formal Education for All.* New Delhi: Sterling.

Cobham, A. (2005) Causes of Conflict in Sudan: testing the black book, *European Journal of Development Research*, 17(3), 462-480.

Coombs, P. (1968) *World Educational Crisis: a systems approach.* New York: Oxford University Press.

Coombs, P. (1973) *New Paths to Learning for Rural Children and Youth.* New York: International Council for Educational Development.

Coombs, P. & Ahmed, M. (1974) *Attacking Rural Poverty: how non-formal education can help.* Baltimore: Johns Hopkins University Press.

Dejene, A. (1980) *Non-formal Education as a Strategy in Development: comparative analysis of rural development projects.* Lanham: University Press of America.

Deng, F. (2006) Sudan: a nation in turbulent search of itself, *Annals of the American Academy of Political and Social Science*, 603, 155-162.

Deng, L. (2003) *Education in Southern Sudan: war, status and challenges of achieving Education for All goals.* Brighton: Institute of Development Studies, University of Sussex.

Dewey, J. (1916) *Democracy and Education: an introduction to the philosophy of education.* New York: Macmillan.

Finnemore, M. & Sikkink, K. (1998) International Norm Dynamics and Political Change, *International Organization*, 52(4), 887-917.

Finnemore, M. & Sikkink, K. (2001) Taking Stock: the constructivist research program in IR and comparative politics, *Annual Review of Political Science*, 4, 391-416.

Galbraith, M.W. (1990) *Education through Community Organizations.* San Francisco: Jossey-Bass.

Intergovernmental Authority on Development (1997) *Declaration of Principles.* Dated July 20, 1994, signed by the Government of Sudan in July 1997. http://www.c-r.org/our-work/accord/sudan/key-texts-igad-dop.php

Jeffs, T. & Smith, M. (Eds) (1990) *Using Informal Education.* Milton Keynes: Open University Press.

Johnson, D. (2003) *The Root Causes of Sudan's Civil Wars.* Bloomington: Indiana University Press.

Johnson, R. & Onwuegbuzie, A. (2004) Mixed Methods Research: a research paradigm whose time has come, *Educational Researcher*, 33(7), 14-26.

Marshall, C. & Rossman, G. (1999) *Designing Qualitative Research*, 3rd ed. Thousand Oaks: Sage.

McFadden, D. & Sunkara, V. (2004) The Educative Impact of Health Care Treatment on Malarial Prevention Behavior for the Poor in Guinea, West Africa, in *Proceedings of the National Academy of Sciences of the United States of America*, 101(31), 11523-11525.

McGivney, V. (1999) *Informal Learning in the Community: a trigger for change and development.* Leicester: National Institute of Adult Continuing Education.

Nyaba, P. (1997) *The Politics of Liberation in South Sudan*. Kampala: Fountain Publishers.

Petterson, D. (2003) *Inside Sudan: political Islam, conflict, and* catastrophe, 2nd ed. Oxford and Colorado: Westview Press.

Rogers, A. (2005) *Non-formal Education*. CERC Studies in Comparative Education 15. Hong Kong: Comparative Education Research Centre of the University of Hong Kong and Kluwer.

Schugurensky, D. (2000) The Forms of Informal Learning: towards a conceptualization of the field. NALL Working Paper no. 19. Centre for the Study of Education and Work. Toronto: Ontario Institute for Studies in Education.

Smith, D. & Tolbert, C. (2004) *Educated by Initiative: the effects of direct democracy on citizens and political organizations in the American states*. Ann Arbor: University of Michigan Press.

Smith, M. (2006) Informal Learning, in *Encyclopaedia of Informal Education*. London: Infed. http://www.infed.org/biblio/inf-lrn.htm

United Nations Office for the Coordination of Humanitarian Affairs (2005) *Sudan Humanitarian Overview*, 1, 1. http://www.unsudanig.org/docs/Sudan%20Humanitarian%20Overview%20Vol1%20Iss1%20Sept05.pdf

US Agency for International Development (USAID) (2002) *Foreign Aid in the National Interest: promoting freedom, security, and opportunity*. Washington, DC: USAID.

US Agency for International Development (USAID) (2004) *US Foreign Aid: meeting the challenges of the twenty-first century*. White Paper. Washington, DC: USAID.

US Agency for International Development (USAID) (2005a) *Fragile States Strategy*. Washington, DC: USAID.

US Agency for International Development (USAID) (2005b) *Sudan Strategy Statement 2006-08*. Washington, DC: USAID.

US Agency for International Development (USAID) (2006) *Strategic Framework for Africa*. Washington, DC: USAID.

US Government (2002) *The National Security Strategy of the United States of America*. Washington, DC: USG Printing Office.

US Government (2007a) *Fiscal Year 2008 Budget Request. Summary and Highlights. International Affairs, Function 150*. Washington, DC: USG Printing Office.

US Government (2007b) *Foreign Assistance Framework*. Washington, DC: USG Printing Office.

Wendt, A. (1992) Anarchy is What States Make of it: the social construction of power politics, *International Organization*, 46(2), 391-425.

Windsor, J. (2006) Advancing the Freedom Agenda: time for a recalibration? *Washington Quarterly*, 29(3), 21-34.

Young, J. (2005) John Garang's Legacy to the Peace Process, the SPLM/A, and the South, *Review of African Political Economy*, 106, 535-548.

CHAPTER 5

Expectations and Realities of Education in Post-conflict Sierra Leone: a reflection of society or a driver for peacebuilding?

MITSUKO MATSUMOTO

SUMMARY Education is increasingly seen as a key tool for peacebuilding efforts in the post-conflict context. However, to what extent are such expectations for education being met in reality? A more fundamental question is whether education *can* bear such expectations. This chapter looks into the role of education in Sierra Leone in the pursuit of these questions. The approach focuses on examining adolescents' experiences and perceptions of education – including adolescents who are presently in formal schooling, who are in vocational training centres, and who are out of school– utilising interviews and participatory task-based methods. These young people are central to understanding the relationship of education to society and the state, a relationship that is suggested to have played into underlying fragility and, as a result, into the decade-long civil war. This chapter suggests that the role of education in Sierra Leone has not been reformed fundamentally in society since the conflict. The chapter problematizes approaches that understand education as an independent institution; it instead calls for a more contextualised approach that situates education in the socioeconomic reality of society.

Introduction

The international community has been paying increasing attention to the provision of education in conflict-affected areas (see UNESCO, 2000; Education for All Global Monitoring Report Team, 2010). This trend is demonstrated by growing support from bilateral donors to education in fragile states; for example, the United Kingdom Department for International

Development (DFID) has recently committed to increase the volume and proportion of aid to the educational sector in fragile and conflict-affected states by around 50% (DFID, 2010). This focus on education in conflict-affected countries is partly driven by the recognition that the right of children in such areas to access education, in particular primary schooling, has not been ensured. With these children out of school, Education for All (EFA) goals cannot be achieved. On the other hand, there is also interest in this area because education is seen as a key tool for promoting long-term stability, peace and development in conflict-affected areas (UNESCO, 2000; DFID, 2010). For example, DFID's recent education strategy (2010) states that:

> Education can play an important part in the emergency response to conflict or fragility, in the long term process of reconstruction and building stability and in promoting civil engagement and democracy. Empirical evidence links levels and distribution of education achievement to indicators of democracy, stability and security. (DFID, 2010)

Various arguments, often normative, have been put forth in support of the role of education in peacebuilding [1], ensuring long-term stability and promoting development. One approach is to look at education as an institution that has both the potential of contributing to the stability of society as well as of exacerbating tensions in society; Bush & Saltarelli (2000) refer to these as the 'positive face' and 'negative face' of education. This approach to the 'positive face' of education includes arguments such as: education can help restore normalcy (Nicolai & Triplehorn, 2003); education can provide psychosocial support (Wessells & Monteiro, 2006); education can act as 'peace dividend' to buttress support for peace (Buckland, 2005); education can promote social cohesion (Tawil & Harley, 2004); education can contribute to reconciliation (Smith & Vaux, 2003); classrooms can be a place to promote tolerance (Bush & Saltarelli, 2000) or 'conflict resolution' skills (Davies, 2004); or more broadly, educational institutions can be a 'driver of change' and prevent the future reoccurrence of conflict (Rose & Greeley, 2006).

A second approach towards the peacebuilding potential of education for development asserts that education will drive economic and social development, thereby alleviating poverty and bringing about stability in society (e.g. Psacharopoulos & Woodhall, 1985; Sen, 1999; Annan, 2005). Here theories of human capital and human capabilities are mobilised, with education as key in building these and supporting growing economies.

A final approach derives from a security agenda. Failure to provide youth, who are often the largest population cohort in conflict-affected states, with education or training, if not employment (leaving them 'idle'), is feared to present the risk of widespread disillusionment, social tensions and, potentially, conflict. Education or training is seen a way to meaningfully engage youth and to reduce conflict risk by promoting tolerance of other members in society or by increasing the opportunity cost for young people's involvement in conflict (e.g. Collier & Hoeffler, 2004; Thyne, 2006; World Bank, 2006, 2009). This is often also the rationale behind the focus on education and training in the reintegration of young former combatants (Krech & Maclure, 2003).

What is common among the three approaches is the lofty expectation on 'education', which is portrayed as capable of making a positive change in societies affected by conflict, or at the very least, of bringing that society into equilibrium and maintaining it. Behind such expectation seems to be an assumption of or a normative approach to the educational institution as independent of or detached from the rest of society which is devastated by conflict. The presumed detached independence of education is what imbues it with the capacity to meet such expectations. These high aspirations for education to create or contribute to social change raise the question of whether education is meeting expectations in reality. The more fundamental question of whether education can realistically bear such expectations is also raised.

In order to begin to unravel the education = peacebuilding equation, I believe it is essential to undertake deeply-contextualised analyses in situations affected by conflict where education has been heralded with peacebuilding potential. Deeply contextualised analyses enable us to illuminate in the actual lives of people and in communities how and whether education might be meeting or failing to meet the expectations for peace, stability and development. In such cases, a first question from which to begin analysis is *what role does education play in the lives of young people who are and who are not involved in it?* A picture of how education may (or may not) be contributing towards the expected societal responsibilities – the responsibilities that have been attached to education in post-conflict societies– can emerge from understanding the meanings that individuals give to education and the experiences in which it is enabling (or not) individual aspirations. In this chapter, therefore, I shall look into a single case, Sierra Leone, a country in transition and recovery from the experience of a decade-long civil war (1991-2002) where educational reconstruction has been a key part of post-conflict peacebuilding initiatives. I will first establish the background by looking into the civil war and the role of education in pre-conflict Sierra Leone.

From 'Athens of West Africa' to the Civil War in Sierra Leone

Sierra Leone's civil war broke out when a small group of rebels, the Revolutionary United Front (RUF), entered into Kailahun district near the Liberian border in March 1991. By the time the war ended in 2002, perhaps two-thirds of Sierra Leone's population had been displaced and more than 50,000 were killed (Keen, 2005). The civil war is notorious not only for its horrific violence but also for the enormous involvement of young people in the war; of a total of the 137,865 members of Sierra Leone's armed forces who fought in the conflict, 48,216 were estimated to be children (McKay & Mazurana, 2004). The RUF was considered to be the 'army of children and youth', as the majority of command and control structures were made up of individuals under 30, and great atrocities were committed by children themselves (Rosen, 2005). Furthermore, the forceful recruitment, or abduction, of many children, both girls and boys, into the RUF has made this civil war even more notorious.

In stark contrast to the image of this brutal civil war is the image of Sierra Leone as the 'Athens of West Africa' where students and scholars from all over sub-Saharan Africa used to gather to study at the first university in West Africa, Fourah Bay College (FBC) established in 1827 (Paracka, 2003). Not only in higher education, but in general the level of educational enrolment was high in Freetown, a colony of Britain at that time (1808-1961). By 1900, 7000 students were enrolled in primary school out of an estimated 14,000 children of primary school age (Sumner, 1963). If we follow the discourse of 'education for development', the question that may emerge is why has this country that should have benefited from the early intervention of education deteriorated into a brutal civil war involving many children and young people? Was there something wrong in the educational system? When we look into this, educational issues can be seen to hold an evident but ambiguous role in the emergence of conflict in Sierra Leone (Krech & Maclure, 2003).

One evident role is the place that education held in the mobilisation of young people into the fighting forces. The origins of the RUF can be traced to a radical student group at FBC, who since the 1970s were mingling with 'lumpen youth' in the capital city (Abdullah, 1998; Rashid, 2004; Yusuf, 2004; Keen, 2005).[2] 'Lumpen youth' is a term used to describe young people, mostly male, who are unemployed but who often work in the underground economy in the city. They are seen in association with deviance in society, such as petty theft and drugs (Abdullah, 1998; Rashid, 2004). Since the 1970s the lumpen population has changed significantly. Young people benefited from the expansion of schooling at primary and secondary levels after the independence of the country in 1961, but were faced with bleak employment opportunities (Rashid, 2004). In relation to this, one of the major groups of young people who were mobilised into the fighting forces on both sides of the conflict were 'drop-outs' from the school system: those who dropped out from schooling, especially at the secondary level, or those who completed schooling but failed to achieve qualifications (Richards, 1996; Wright, 1997; Keen, 2005).

In a more indirect but fundamental sense, it was through its exclusive and elitist nature that the educational system is considered to have contributed towards conflict in Sierra Leone (Sierra Leone Truth and Reconciliation Commission [SLTRC], 2004). While by 1900 50% of children in Freetown were enrolled in primary school, in the 'hinterland' there were less than 900 children enrolled out of an estimated population of 1,500,000 (Corby, 1990). Even in the rural hinterland there was a great discrepancy between regions. According to the 1931 Census, there were 26 schools in the Northern Province compared to 143 in the Southern Province. The percentage of children attending school was 0.97 in the North while it was 4.75 in the South (Sumner, 1963, p. 228). Furthermore, the curriculum was a British-style 'bookish' one, (for instance, Greek was taught) (Banya, 1993), and was neither relevant nor useful to the lives of many students.

The unequal distribution and provision of education was exacerbated in the 1980s. As Sierra Leone declined into a long era of repressive rule after its independence, the economy worsened and political corruption increased. The educational system was not an exception; the exclusive and elitist nature of education was magnified. Census data from 1992 show a 35% enrolment rate in primary and an 11% rate in secondary education (cited in Government of Sierra Leone, 1995). Great regional discrepancies still existed; the primary enrolment for the Southern Province was more than double that of the Northern Province in 1989, and as for the secondary level, the enrolment in the South was more than triple that of the North (Government of Sierra Leone, 1989, cited in Banya, 1993).[3] Former president Momoh, in power from 1985 to 1992, stated that education was a 'privilege' and not a right (quoted in Richards, 1996, p. 19). This demonstrates the degree of exclusivity inherent in Sierra Leone's state education system prior to the civil war.

Moreover, by the time the conflict began in 1991, the whole educational system was dysfunctional. Teachers' salaries were delayed for many months. As a result, teachers were busy trying to make ends meet, for instance by engaging in farming (Banya, 1991), and there were many 'ghost' teachers who were on the payroll, but not actually teaching (Keen, 2005). In addition, dilapidation of buildings, lack of essential school supplies, and closure of boarding schools were commonly observed (Banya, 1991). From parents' perspectives, they could not even afford to send their children to school, where fees were still charged, due to the dramatic and sustained inflation of Sierra Leonean currency since 1978 (Keen, 2005).

While there is little disagreement about the dramatic collapse of education in the country, there are different views among scholars with regard to the degree to which and the way in which education came to play into the conflict itself and in the conditions that enabled it. Some scholars state rather strongly that the RUF was led by 'highly educated' excluded dissidents (Richards, 1996). Some more moderately claim that the promise of free education was consistently high on the RUF agenda because of the rebels' perceptions of how state education had failed them. These scholars also argue that attacks on educational institutions were premeditated (Wright, 1997; Keen, 2005). Some suggest that lack of access to schooling offers a reliable proxy for the participation of combatants in the war (Humphreys & Weinstein, 2008), and that the hierarchy among combatants was affected by their levels of schooling (Peters & Richards, 1998; Humphreys & Weinstein, 2004). This may not be extraneous to the fact that many of the RUF fighters may have been excluded by the elitist and increasingly failing educational system. Yet others take less account of education in their explanations of civil war, stating that the rebel group or the original radical student group was formed not out of frustration with education per se, but because of their more general grievances towards the political system (Abdullah, 1998; Rashid, 2004; Yusuf, 2004). In the interviews that I conducted with academics, educationalists and journalists in Sierra Leone, most respondents took the latter view.

This ambiguity in the relationship between the educational system and the combatants in the civil war can be better explained when we focus our attention on what 'education' had come to represent and imply for young people and their lives through the course of Sierra Leonean history (Krech & Maclure, 2003). In the course of Sierra Leone's rich history of education, it became apparent that educational advantage was essential in achieving higher social, political and economic status. The Creoles, or Krios, the descendants of repatriated Africans from the Caribbean, North America and England, received education to the highest level in Sierra Leonean society. It was these Creoles and the secondary-schooled hinterland Africans who gained success in the form of government employment during the colonial period and who took over the roles held by expatriate Europeans after independence (Corby, 1990; Banya, 1993). Furthermore, alumni networks of schooling began to play a pivotal role when seeking jobs. For example, Bo Government Boys' School has a strong association, the Old Bo Boys' Association (OBBA), and graduates ask for favours from older graduates with successful careers (Corby, 1990). In the political arena as well, Bo graduates have played prominent roles at national level by producing politicians in the Sierra Leonean People's Party (SLPP), a party based in the southern and Mende regions of the country (Corby, 1990). In this way, 'success' came to be strongly defined by academic qualification (Wright, 1997). Consequently, the importance of education was not much to do with what was learned in the classroom, but the available opportunities in the economy and social structure that were only accessible with particular qualifications and connections (Shepler, 1998). Education created a powerful identity in society and became a source of 'symbolic capital' (Bourdieu, 1986) – a resource that has symbolic value on the basis of honour, prestige, or recognition– in the economy of Sierra Leone (Shepler, 1998).

Examining education as symbolic capital suggests two links of education to the underlying fragility of the state that ultimately enabled the outbreak of the war. Firstly, the established credentialism was of a 'high' or exclusive standard. Only when one was successful in graduating from college was one considered to be fully 'educated' (Interview, Sierra Leone Teachers' Union [SLTU] President, 25 October, 2010). Additionally, in the prevailing paradigm where education was seen as the symbolic capital, the education of girls was not seen to be important, especially in the Northern Province; girls were not seen to have much to do with economic and social advancement and instead were to be married early and take care of the house (e.g. Keen, 2005). The second factor is the gradual collapse of education as a symbolic capital in reality, in contrast to the expectation. By the 1980s, as political corruption increased and economic deterioration worsened, even many of the university graduates could not get the jobs they desired (i.e. public sector jobs); only those who had a politically influential patron were able to secure a prestigious job. Therefore, prior to the conflict, the promise of education – as symbolic capital – was no longer being realised for many young people (Krech & Maclure, 2003). The collaboration between radical student group members at FBC and 'lumpen youth' can perhaps be attributed to their realisation, and attendant frustration, that regardless of education levels, employment was no longer available to them without strong political connection.

In summary, 'education' can be seen to have played into the political and economic marginalisation and grievances of young people in three ways. First is the elitist and exclusive nature of the educational system, in particular the unequal and scarce distribution of access to schooling and the less than relevant curriculum. Second is the elitism and exclusion that arises from the representation of education as symbolic capital. And third is the fact that the realities of education were not meeting the expectations of it as symbolic capital; many who received educational qualifications were unable to translate these into jobs and social mobility. Therefore, it is not accurate to state that the educational system per se was a direct cause of conflict. However, we could assert that the relationship that was built around what 'education' had come to represent in Sierra Leonean society facilitated state fragility. In other words, it created a situation where young people could be easily mobilised when there was a trigger in the form of rebellion against the state.

Planned Educational Reform after the Civil War

With this background in mind, I now turn to post-conflict Sierra Leone. After the war ended, the educational system became one of the focal areas for reform. The share of total expenditure on education was increased considerably to 20% in 2003, compared to 14% in 1996, and the share of spending on education and general public services is the largest in the Sierra Leonean budget (excluding debt payments) (World Bank, 2007). In part this derives from the recognition that the educational system played a role in the war. The SLTRC identified the historically elitist and divisive nature of the educational system as one of the key 'historical antecedents to conflict' (SLTRC, 2004). However, an equally powerful impetus for the focus on educational reform is the idea that education is one of the key instruments for peacebuilding in Sierra Leone, which aligns with the drive towards EFA and

Millennium Development Goals (MDG). President Koroma, in his 2010 speech at the African Union Summit, stated, 'by making all children attend school, we will be ensuring that our people have the knowledge, skills and confidence to make informed choices to sustain our achievement and secure the future of this continent. Getting all our children to school is a moral and developmental imperative' (Koroma, 2010). The education for peacebuilding impetus, as discussed before, links with different rationales behind it. As a short-term response various educational programmes were employed for the reintegration of child combatants into society. For example, the Disarmament, Demobilisation, and Reintegration (DDR) programme included the Reintegration Opportunity Programme (ROP) where former combatants could learn skills through vocational training and formal education (Disarmament, Demobilisation and Reintegration Resource Centre, 2010).[4] As a longer-term strategy, education comprises an essential part of Sierra Leone's Poverty Reduction Strategy Programme, which aligns the country's development goals with meeting the MDGs (International Monetary Fund, 2001, 2005, 2008).

With such a rationale, various initiatives were undertaken to reconstruct and reform the educational system in collaboration with international agencies, such as the World Bank and UNICEF. As an immediate and temporary measure, the major priority was to provide education to ex-combatants and other young people who missed educational opportunities during the war. Initiatives included (partly in conjunction with the DDR programming): the Complementary Rapid Education for Primary Schools (CREPS), which compressed six years of primary into three years and served youth aged 16 and over; the Rapid Response Education Programme (RREP), which provided children with six months of intensive schooling to prepare them for their reinsertion into the regular system; and the Community Education Investment Programme (CEIP), which waived school fees for former child combatants by providing teaching, learning, or recreation materials to schools that admitted them(see Women's Commission for Refugee Women and Children, 2002).

Medium-term priorities were addressed through the Rehabilitation of Basic Education Project/SABABU Education Project in 2003, funded by the Government of Sierra Leone, the World Bank and the African Development Bank, which focused on reconstruction and construction of schools, provision of teaching and learning materials, and teacher education over a seven-year period (Ministry of Education, Science and Technology [MEST], 2007a). The Girls Education Support Program was launched in 2003, committed to providing all girl pupils with free junior secondary education in the Northern and Eastern regions (where traditionally gender inequality was severest), and a modified version is planned for all the regions in 2010 (Interview, a Deputy Minister of MEST, 14 December 2009). Finally, the Education Act 2004 is an essential long-term legal framework for reforming the educational system after the war. It legalised a 6-3-3-4 system that now forms the basic structure of Sierra Leonean education. It also commits the Government to free and compulsory basic education (six years of primary and three years of junior secondary schooling) and to have at least one junior secondary school per chiefdom to enable access to basic education over the whole country (Government of Sierra Leone, 2004). And, as the essential practice in the attempt to expand access to schooling, 'free' primary education was introduced from class 1 to 3 in 1999 and extended to class 4 to 6 in 2001 (MEST, 2007a).

The key post-conflict educational change was the launch of the 6-3-3-4 system (six years in primary, three years in junior secondary, three years in senior secondary, and four years in tertiary education) which replaced the previous 7-5-2-4 system (seven years in primary, five years up to GCE [General Certificate of Education] O level followed by two years for the A level and four years in tertiary).[5] This change was put forward in order to move away from the grammar school model and to give prominence to the technical and vocational track that caters for middle-level skilled employment. The new system also aimed to increase the relevance of education and to reduce the number of 'drop-outs' – including those who completed secondary schooling but did not pass the Basic Education Certificate Examination (BECE) that marks the completion of basic education in Sierra Leone. Those who do not succeed in the academic track by the end of basic education (junior secondary school, JSS) could proceed to the vocational track at senior secondary school (SSS) level.

As a result of the introduction of free primary education, by the 2003/04 academic year, the gross enrolment rate for primary schools had risen to 104% and JSS enrolment also increased to 41% (Dupigny et al, 2006). The total number of schools also doubled from 2240 in 1989 to 4578 in 2004 (World Bank, 2007). Referencing this massive expansion in primary enrolment, which occurred without lowering the National Primary School Exam (NPSE) results, the World Bank (2007) described a 'remarkable recovery' in Sierra Leonean education.

It is important to note here the large involvement of donors and international agencies behind the 'remarkable recovery' of the educational system in Sierra Leone. Almost 40% of the total governmental budget comes from external support (World Bank, 2007). This fact is important to mention because such support rarely comes without conditionalities. The focus on primary education is influenced by the international drive towards EFA and the MDGs. As such, the majority of donor funding is aimed at basic education: more than 90% of the 2002-03 commitments, and 75% of those for 2004 (World Bank, 2007). Additionally, for example, the International Monetary Fund (IMF) introduced wage bill ceilings that set limits on teachers' wages as part of the poverty reduction strategy. This entails limiting the total number of teachers on the Government's payroll, which is causing concerns about the possibility of lowering the quality of the educational system significantly (Fedelino et al, 2006; ActionAid, 2007; McDonald, 2007).

Having summarised these sector-wide changes, the question we return to is whether and how education actually plays a role in peacebuilding, especially in the lives of beneficiaries of education in the post-conflict environment. In considering this, the first question to be approached is whether the role of education in indirectly contributing to the deterioration of society, and thus ultimately to the civil war, has been essentially transformed. If the answer to this is not positive then it is doubtful that education can fundamentally contribute to peacebuilding in Sierra Leone.

Reflecting on the role that education played in the conflict, it appears that the approach that the educational reformers took was inadequate. The elitist and exclusive nature of the educational system has certainly been approached through efforts to expand access and increase relevance, although whether the implementation of these measures has transformed the experience of educational beneficiaries has yet to be examined. The elitism and exclusivity arising from the representation of education and the gap between expectations and the realities of education as symbolic capital do not seem to be approached or even identified as educational issues within the current post-conflict reform initiatives. More fundamentally, the approach that treats education as a self-contained institution remains behind post-conflict educational prescriptions. In a simple sense, reformers appear to assume that fixing the educational system will be sufficient to alter the role of education in Sierra Leone from a contributor to the civil war to a key contributor to peacebuilding.

Methodology

The data incorporated in this chapter is drawn from seven months of fieldwork in Sierra Leone in 2009. My main participants were adolescents. Their cohort a generation earlier were the ones who dropped out of the school system, in particular at the secondary school level, and became involved in the civil war. Therefore, I presumed that today's young people would be a key group within the broader population for ensuring the long-term stability of society after the war; if they are not satisfied with the education they are (or they are not) receiving, they might be easily mobilised like the adolescents before them. My approach was to focus on the perceptions and experiences of these young people since it was not only the educational system per se, but also its representation and meaning for young people that were essential to understanding the role of education in Sierra Leone historically and in Sierra Leone's recent conflict. By understanding the current representations and meanings that young people attribute to education, we can assess whether these have been transformed from those pre-conflict representations that enabled exclusion and resentment. Should such a transformation be identified, it would be reasonable to think it might contribute towards stability and peacebuilding.

The majority of data were collected in Makeni town in the Northern Province. Makeni is the capital of Bombali district and has a population of about 82,840 (Sessay et al, 2006). Historically, as discussed above, the Northern Province has been a deprived area, and this includes the provision of educational services. Furthermore, after the conflict many children who were deeply affected by the conflict, especially ex-combatants, remained and still reside in Makeni and in surrounding towns in Northern Province. These were important criteria for the selection of a case study site, as I anticipated that the experiences of young people who are in relatively deprived positions would illuminate the role that education plays in the lives of those likely be denied its symbolic capital. In addition, as it is the largest city in the Northern Province and the fifth largest city in Sierra Leone, young people from rural areas came to Makeni seeking educational and other opportunities before the conflict and continue to do so in the present. I anticipated, therefore, that I could encounter in Makeni young people who have or have had educational opportunities as well as those who have not had such opportunities.

Qualitative case-study methodology was employed. Three groups of the adolescents with different educational experiences became the units of study: (1) a group of adolescents who are in senior secondary school (15 respondents); (2) a group of adolescents who are in a vocational training programme (15 respondents); and (3) adolescents who are out of school (10 respondents). I selected three different groups based on educational categories because, if education, or strictly speaking formal schooling, is the symbolic capital, I anticipated differences in these young people's socio-economic profiles and future prospects (perceived and actual), and their views of other groups who have different educational profiles.

With a total of 40 respondents, I met with each group once a week (sometimes dividing one group into two) for three months to conduct focus group discussions, individual interviews, or task-based activities such as writing or drawing on a particular topic. In addition, I conducted 49 interviews with key adult informants under three categories: (1) key informants in understanding the relationship between education and society before and after the war at the national level; (2) informants who work closely with adolescents on a daily basis; and (3) informants who experienced secondary schooling immediately before the war. Together with documents collected, the adult interviews serve as the 'context' to the adolescents' perceptions and experiences in this study.

The Actual Role of Education after the War

For the pre-conflict role of education in Sierra Leone – a role that facilitated education to contribute indirectly towards the war – to be transformed (i.e.

for education to intersect heartily with peacebuilding), at least three elements would have to be reformed. The first is the elitist and divisive nature of the educational system itself, by expanding access and making it relevant. The second is the elitism and exclusiveness that arises from the conception and representation of education among young people themselves. The third is the gap between the expectations and the realities of the representation of education as symbolic capital for those who have gained access to schooling. Therefore, I shall present my findings according to these three themes.

The Stark Reality of the Educational System

With regard to reforming the nature of the educational system itself, responses from both adults and adolescents give mixed reports on the status of the educational system. On the positive side, all respondents agreed that access to schooling has been expanded massively since the war, and that the discrepancies in access in different regions have been reduced. However, many adolescents responded that schooling was available for only those who can afford it. Though 'free' education was introduced at the primary level, it is known that there are 'hidden' fees and indirect costs, which are estimated to be as high as US$39.15 per year (UNICEF, 2009).[6] At the secondary level, there are school fees (60,000 Leone, equivalent to US$15 for JSS, and 75,000 Leone, equivalent to US$19 for SSS) plus higher hidden fees than at primary school.

Grim retention figures attest to the struggles of children to climb the academic ladder. Only half of class 1 pupils are expected to reach class 6, and only 22% of those who enter JSS1 are expected to reach SSS3 (World Bank, 2007). The low retention of girls is particularly evident in rural areas. When we look at the parity index by locality and gender together, the enrolment of rural girls at SSS is 15% that of urban boys (World Bank, 2007). Such a low rate of retention of girls was repeatedly explained by respondents as being due to pregnancy or early marriage.

The implementation of a more relevant curriculum appears to be poor as well. The majority of adult interviewees stated that the implementation of 6-3-3-4 has not been successful, though by intention it should be relevant to the lives of ordinary Sierra Leoneans. The President of Sierra Leone Teachers' Union (SLTU) commented that:

> It is [relevant], if only it is fully allowed to operate according to the merits it deserves. But ... much of the properties are lacking. Textbooks are not available. Teachers are not there ... About JSS 3, they are allowed to go into different careers. We have a good a number of carpenters, masons, but they don't have tools again. (Interview, 25 September 2009)

The lack of equipment and support for the vocational track in particular was seen to be detrimental to the effective implementation of a relevant curriculum. The failure to implement the technical and vocational elements of the new educational system is apparent in the ratio of existing vocational centres to secondary schools; there are only 70 vocational centres in total compared to 466 secondary schools in the country, and no vocational schools that are equivalent to academic track SSS exist in Makeni, the provincial headquarters of the Northern region (MEST, 2007b).[7]

Despite the perception among adults of irrelevant education, most of the adolescents responded that the schooling was relevant and useful. For example, Abdul [8], an SSS student in the commercial stream, said:

> All of [the subjects] are useful ... [People in my village] just take stone to counting [rice in order to sell], perhaps more than four hours they will be there, but when I'm around when they tell me the amount of rice and the money I will just multiply it ... when I started to do that in the first place they won't believe me, and so they just checked it. But till now ...they follow.

This comment seems to suggest that Abdul feels he is receiving a reasonable quality of education, having learned to multiply correctly. He also thinks he is learning subjects that are important for his future. Indeed, when asked, most SSS pupils said that all the subjects they were studying were useful.

At the same time, adolescents were concerned about quality. Their concern for the quality of education mainly revolved around whether their schooling was good enough to enable them to pass the public examinations and to proceed to higher education. Another pupil in the commercial stream, Ibrahim, said: 'Some who were at class 3 could write letter in the old time, but now for SSS3 students to write a simple letter is difficult'. Additionally, the examination results confirm the low quality of Sierra Leone's education system. Less than 4% of SSS3 pupils who took the West Africa Senior School Certificate Examination (WASSCE) passed, and therefore only this very small proportion of students was qualified to enter a university in 2009 (data provided by West Africa Examination Council).[9] Two young male motorbike taxi drivers, Mohamed and Amadu, who participated in my research, both failed the WASSCE twice. Mohamed has been working as a motorbike taxi driver ever since he entered JSS1 in order to fund himself to continue schooling. Out of his 14 brothers and sisters, only three brothers and one sister are in school currently. Mohamed wants to go to a college to read for a Higher Teaching Certificate to be qualified to teach at secondary level, but explains that this would only be possible by bribing a lecturer with 300,000 Leones (US$75), which he does not have. The massive failure at public examinations is a critical issue in the current educational system in Sierra Leone. As such, President Koroma established a review commission in 2009 that investigated the causes of poor performance, and it made recommendations for reform (Government of Sierra Leone, 2009).

The stark condition of the educational system, with poor implementation capacity and poor quality, can be seen as a reflection of the conditions that the country faces after the war. The wages of teachers are very low (on average 180,000 Leones in primary schools and 270,000 Leones at JSS and SSS levels, the equivalent of US$73-110 per month in 2004) (World Bank, 2007). Yet they are the highest for civil servants in Sierra Leone (Interview, SLTU President, 25 October 2009). Other civil servants, such as police officers, make ends meet by receiving bribes. That practice has also become widespread in the educational sector, with teachers asking for and receiving extra money from pupils for their own survival. Some partly attribute this to the effects of conflict; moral sensibilities were degenerated by the conflict, and thus the teachers' moral standards have been lowered as well (e.g. Interview, the Director of a college in Makeni, 5 September 2009). Regardless of the cause, this small-scale corruption, as well as more major corruption in the educational system, is so rampant that the Anti-Corruption Commission held a recent enquiry into the education sector (see Anti-Corruption Commission, 2009). The 'ceiling' system of teacher recruitment due to the conditionality set by the IMF is also profoundly affecting the poor quality and corruption in the educational system. These realities in the educational sector go back to the fact that Sierra Leone is a country that is coming out of conflict and that the reform and reconstruction efforts there are driven by donors. Additionally, the economic recession and destruction of economic infrastructure affects many families; the basic foundation for economic stability has not been recovered after the war, and it is difficult for families to meet the basic educational needs of their children, including essential textbooks.

Thus, the portrayal we get from the experiences and perceptions of adolescents, as well as adult interviewees, on the actual condition of education differs greatly from the optimism that characterises international and government reports about the policies for reform and reconstruction of the system. Though access has been expanded greatly, the issues of quality and poor implementation of a more relevant curriculum are profoundly affected by the condition of Sierra Leone as a post-conflict society.

Continuity in the Representation of Education

In terms of conception of 'education' among young people, not much change has been seen. Education may not be seen as an exclusive privilege any more, but basic education has not become a right that everyone is entitled to. As we discussed in the previous section, respondents considered that access to higher levels of education is granted only to those who can afford it. Adolescent respondents – both those who are in schooling or training and those who are out of school – expressed that only those who have 'an opportunity' or 'a chance' can go up the ladder of the academic stream. Ibrahim, when asked about friends who are out of school, answered, 'I don't feel good, because I am coming to school every day but they don't have that opportunity. They want to educate [themselves] but because of financial reason or [not having] somebody to help them [they can't come to school]'.

The perception of education as symbolic capital has not been changed either. Education is certainly perceived as the key to success for adolescents. For example, Musa, who completed SSS but has no prospect to go to college stated, 'Education is the light and key to success ... you need to learn before, then you will be lucky to have a job'. Many senior school students believe they can achieve their lofty dreams, becoming a lawyer, a doctor, or a bank manager, with a university degree. In contrast, adult respondents see education more as the key to the development of the country. In particular it was commented that the 6-3-3-4 system is intended to play a pivotal role in the development of the country, building a middle-level skilled labour force (e.g. Interview, President of Principals' Conference, 25 October 2009).

Indeed, since the conflict the perception of education as symbolic capital has perhaps even been enhanced. One aspect of it is that the awareness of the importance of education seems to have increased after the war, as some adult respondents commented. A reason raised was the exposition of difference between the educated and uneducated during the war. Musa's father used to be a rich businessman, going to trade in Guinea, but most of his property, including his machinery and cars, were destroyed or raided by the rebels. Now the family lives in poverty without any prospect to restart the business. Musa said:

> If he had been educated, after the process, let me say, he can go to any institution to apply himself, and maybe he can have job and then able to cater for us, but now just look at him. He doesn't have enough money to further my education. That is why people who are educated are better than those who are not educated.

In refugee camps those educated as teachers were observed to have been working while those without education remained unemployed and without resources. Those who had family abroad, often with high educational achievement, received money or materials or were even themselves called to go abroad. In addition, sensitisation after the war by various non-governmental organisations (NGOs) undeniably contributed to the increased awareness of the importance of education. The fact that many job advertisements since the war require qualifications contributed also to the growing perception of education as very important for one's future. For example, one respondent explained that while you could become a security guard without any educational background before the war, now they ask for at least the BECE result.

Another aspect of the enhancement of the perception of education as symbolic capital lies in the maintained and even growing credentialism in Sierra Leonean society. As exemplified by the requirement of BECE for the security job, more employment requires credentials. Furthermore, for most of the adolescents who participated in this study, being educated in Sierra

Leone means you have to get a 'paper' from tertiary institutions, because, like Mohamed, the motorbike taxi driver, without at least being qualified to enter tertiary education, opportunities for employment and engagement in society, beyond jobs like driving a motorcycle taxi, remain limited for young people. A number of adult respondents shared concern for young people like Mohamed who have not achieved sufficient qualifications and thus have limited employment prospects. The President of the Sierra Leone Association of Journalists (SLAJ) commented:

> One thing it does is that it makes people not too qualified or not too skilled to be employed at offices where they would love to work, but then they are left to labour or manual jobs, which they don't earn much or not even much available. It leaves them disgruntled. It turns them to thieves. And if there is a slightest opportunity of civil unrest they capitalise on it and vandalise. (Interview, 15 December 2009)

In relation to the maintained and growing credentialism, academic and vocational qualifications continue to be perceived differently in status. Many of the students in vocational training told me that if they had the chance they want to go back to formal schooling. Isatu, in masonry, plans to go back to school to sit the BECE and WASCCE exams if possible after getting her certificate in masonry. She expressed the necessity to 'defend' her certificate; if somebody else has the same qualification along with a WASCCE result, then they will be employed over Isatu.

Along with the value clearly attached to being educated, the devaluation of those who are not educated was observed. When asked to draw the image of an uneducated person, many adolescents illustrated a person, often a farmer, without decent clothes or shoes. On an occasion when a group of children, many of whom are currently out of school, held a radio discussion on the importance of education, a community worker at the radio station joined the discussion and made the comment that, if a person is not educated he or she is 'nothing to the community.'

The perception of educational qualifications as indicators of social status continues to affect social networks as well. The OBBA's strong ties still exist, though the degree of influence might have lessened due to the development of other prestigious schools.[10] John, a student in masonry, who had stopped schooling at class 4 and worked as a mason for some years in Kabala, a remote area in the North, said: 'I can get money but educated people interact with people who are well educated ... when you get money, people don't care about you'.[11] John's reasoning for coming to learn at the vocational centre in Makeni is to receive a certificate in masonry with which he believes he can get better employment. He has been recently allocated to job training in Freetown as part of the programme, and he hopes to acquire a job in Freetown subsequently. A number of adolescents noted that it is more through schooling than through the ethnic group or family relations that one can establish contacts – called 'Sababu' by Sierra Leoneans – with people who have influence in society.

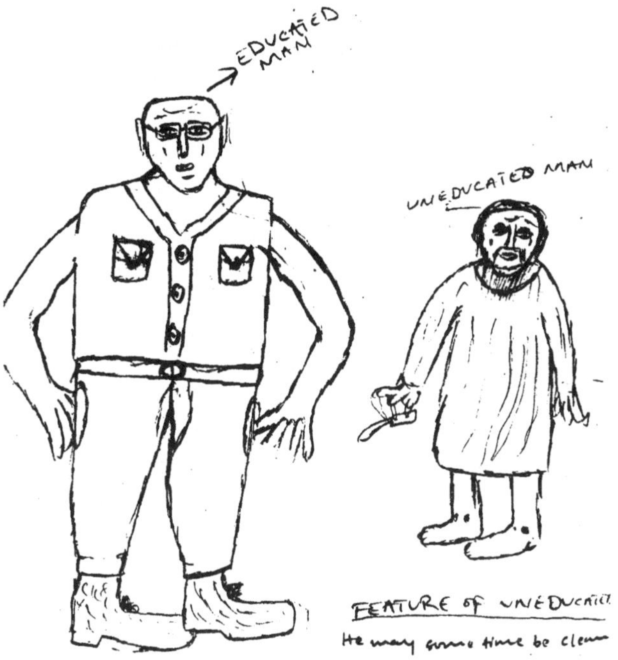

Figure 1. A drawing by Abdul, an SSS2 pupil on the image of an 'educated person' and an 'uneducated person'.

Continuity in the Gap between Expectations and Reality

Considerable divergence continues to exist between what education is expected to do for the lives of educational beneficiaries and what education actually enables in reality. As we have seen in the previous section, adolescents believe that education is the key to individual success. For them the opportunity to attend higher education is critical. However, such an opportunity is only brought about through connections and/or money. For example, Alexis' father was killed in front of him during the war and Alexis was abducted to fight with the RUF. He had completed SSS, with good results from WASSCE, but did not have a prospect to go to college. He stated that unless people have money or have a connection with an influential person in society, they cannot continue their education. The gross enrolment rate for tertiary institutions was merely 4% in 2005 (World Bank, 2007), and this attests to the difficulty of acquiring tertiary education.

When asked about alternatives to entering higher education, adolescents' most frequent responses were to work as a teacher or to find another job and save the money to be able to go to a college later on. Most of the students did not give 'creative' answers that did not depend on educational credentials, such as starting a business. Out-of-school adolescents as well, except one female, expressed desire to go back to formal schooling or proceed to college.[12] The only 'realistic' answers, given the realities of access to tertiary institutions in the country, came from students in a vocational institute; a number of them mentioned that they want to open a business or find a job with the skills they have learned. Yet some others want to go back to schooling or proceed to a college if opportunities are available.

In contrast to the optimistic expectations of young people is the persistence of bleak employment possibilities both for the educated as well the semi-educated and uneducated in Sierra Leone. The youth unemployment rate is estimated to be as high as 65% (Humanitarian News and Analysis [IRIN], 2007), and the census report in 2004 states that educated youth, particularly those who enter the labour force for the first time after their education, are 'at risk' of unemployment (Braima et al, 2006).[13] A number of adult interviewees stated that the gap between education and employment – meaning the unemployment or underemployment of the educated – has not changed since the war, and might be widening. The contributing factors raised are: decrease in the presence of NGOs (and the jobs associated with them) as Sierra Leone has moved away from a period of intense humanitarian intervention towards a development stage (Interview, SLAJ President, 15 December 2009); the 'ceiling system' that places large restrictions on the number of teachers recruited by the Government in arrangement with the IMF (e.g. Interview, SLTU President, 25 October 2009)[14]; and the rapid increase in the number of college graduates (Interview, a principal of an SSS, 2 December 2009).[15]

Nonetheless, some were more optimistic that the gap between education and employment is being reduced due to intervention by the Government or by other agencies such as United Nations Development Programme (UNDP) (Interview, a lecturer at FBC, 15 December 2009) or due to the development of the financial sector (Interview, President of Principals' Union, 26 October 2009). Some believe students are responsible for unemployment by being 'picky' in selecting a job and by the types of fields they choose to study (Interview, President of Principals' Union, 26 October 2009).

In comparison, the perceptions of adolescents about the employment prospects of the educated were found to be overly hopeful. When asked if they are worried about unemployment or were confident to find a job, many of the adolescents stated that they are not worried and believe they will get a job. The types of jobs that SSS pupils are confident that they can get are the typical well-respected jobs with high salaries. They are convinced they can get these types of jobs, so long as they attend college. Nonetheless, young people did seem to have a grasp of the reality that they face. When asked why many university graduates are not getting jobs, more 'realistic' points were made as well as lofty answers. The lofty answers appear to be based on the assumption that the good graduates from college should find a job. Good students imply those with a 'blessing' as well as with good results. 'Blessing' is a religious concept gained by obeying teachers and the principal, as well as by serving parents and elderly in the community. Gladys, a student in home management, who stopped schooling at JSS2 when the war started, commented:

> People say when you are learning you should have blessing ... You should obey your teacher, instructor, principal ... so that the end of the day your results will be blessed ... Anywhere you present your certificate or result they will take you for the job.

Therefore, those who cannot get a job are understood by respondents to be people without blessing, those who did not perform well, or those who did not get the certificate legally but by bribing or having Sababu with an influential person.

Despite the desirability of an educational 'blessing', the majority of young people acknowledged that the job availability for college graduates is limited. In that scarcity it is Sababu that came up a number of times as a determining factor for employment. Only those who have good Sababu – i.e. having somebody who knows you well in the office where you are applying to– will get hired, even if they have a lower qualification than someone without Sababu. Josephine, a student at the vocational training institute, who had worked as a commercial sex worker in the past and has a son, said, 'sometimes you may be well educated but if you don't have strong relationship they won't consider you. In fact somebody in the office will tear up and throw your application away'. Many respondents consider that the economic decline experienced during the fieldwork period was heightening the role that Sababu played in job opportunities. The more limited the job places, the more office workers want to bring in their family members or those they are strongly connected to. For many respondents, a realistic strategy when one does not have job prospects after graduation was to go to classroom teaching 'as a waiting room'.

Interestingly, I did not encounter many responses that blame the Government excessively for not providing jobs. Many adolescents attributed the small number of employment prospects for college graduates to economic decline more than to the Government or to faults in educational institutions. Some held the Government accountable, but for not having managed to provide electricity nationally so that foreign investors could come and open job opportunities for young people.

A Reflection of Societal Problems or a Driver for Peacebuilding?

The findings presented above show that the relational effect of education that contributed to the collapse of Sierra Leonean society and thus to the civil war has not been reformed comprehensively. This is partly due to the poor implementation of the reform plan. However, even if the reform plan were implemented well, it would not have reformed the negative role played by education, because it did not aim to or provide the means for the transformation of education's representation in Sierra Leone or the ways in which this representation configures opportunities (or lack thereof). As a result, the conception of education in Sierra Leone has not changed, and the gap between the expectations of what education can do and what it actually enables in reality in the lives of young people continues to be substantial. Therefore, I suggest that education presently does not contribute heartily to peacebuilding in Sierra Leone and would not do so even if the reform plan were well implemented.

Furthermore, what surfaces from these findings is that 'education' is deeply embedded within the post-conflict context. As we have seen, the stark condition of the educational system is linked to and largely constrained by the realities of post-conflict society and state (i.e. the high reliance on external support, destruction of infrastructure, heightened corruption, and poverty, to name but a few). On the other hand, there are some effects of conflict on the representation of education that are not entirely negative. The conflict raised the value of education for those who previously did not value it so highly (e.g. families in rural areas), especially with regard to sending a girl to school. If we take the view that pre-war youth had only overtly optimistic views on education leading to government jobs and then blaming the Government for not realising these goals, the adolescents in this study may have developed more nuanced understandings of the realities of the power of education. This is visible in the adolescents' seemingly contradictory views – overly optimistic but insightful into the realities they face – on the gap between education and employment.

In the case of Sierra Leone, where the post-conflict condition of society and state affect education and its representations, the three normative approaches that advocate the role of education in peacebuilding are met with pessimistic outcomes. Some of 'positive faces' of education may be surfacing in post-conflict Sierra Leone, such as helping children restore normalcy and by doing so providing them with some psychosocial support. However, these positive effects seem to be minimal and are counterbalanced by 'positive faces' that have not been realised, particularly the fact that education is not fulfilling its expectation as a driver of change. From a development lens, the extent to which education is promoting economic development in Sierra Leone is limited. The gap between education and employment appears to have not been significantly reduced even with the policies on increasing the relevance of the curriculum and increasing the employment opportunities for the young. It may even have widened as more graduates have been produced while the economic infrastructure remains devastated. As for the security agenda, education may be playing a role, but more as a stop-gap measure than as a source of long-term stability; giving young people hope that once they complete college they can get well-paid jobs, and meanwhile they have something meaningful (i.e. schooling or training) in which to engage themselves. Some young people have 'opportunities' to find jobs, but those who do not get a job blame themselves for not having enough or a good enough education.

However, I am not suggesting in this chapter that education cannot play a role for peacebuilding, and indeed it is wrong to suggest that education is not making a difference to the lives of adolescents in Sierra Leone. Despite the limitations there are positive stories that came from the interviewees. For example, Josephine told me that she quit 'the dirty game' (the sex work she previously engaged in) when she got a scholarship to continue her training at the vocational centre. Later on, she received another scholarship from an international agency to attend a workshop abroad, and was the only girl selected. Josephine's story draws attention to the agency of adolescents; despite this chapter's focus on the relationship between post-conflict society and the educational system, the young people who do and do not participate in education are not mere recipients of the stark conditions presented to them, but are attempting to find ways through the system for their own survival and success. It is also erroneous to state that the Sierra Leonean Government is not aware of the importance of equilibrium between the education sector and other sectors of society; it is illustrated as one of the visions in the Education Sector Plan for 2007-2015 (MEST, 2007a). However, the question remains to what extent this vision weighs in the actual planning and implementation of educational system.

To reiterate, assuming education is able to operate independently outside the constraints of society and effect transformative change while doing so may lead to disillusionment and discord with other sectors of society. Ultimately such approach to educational intervention might result in further fragility. It is essential therefore to begin with understanding the role and effects of 'education' situated in society, more precisely in the lives of young people, i.e. what education does and does not do for young people and what young people expect of education in conflict-affected societies. Should such an approach be taken, education would then begin to play a constructive and perhaps transformative role in their lives, which should consequently contribute to stability and the development of society.

Notes

[1] Peacebuilding, for the purpose of this chapter, refers to the process of preventing the reoccurrence of violence after the cessation of violent conflict

and reconstructing the society where long-term peace and stability can be achieved.

[2] However, it is not agreed whether this group became part of the RUF since there seems to have been a split within the group before the formation of the RUF (Abdullah, 1998; Rashid, 2004; Yusuf, 2004).

[3] The primary enrolment for Southern Province was 141, 280 compared to 65,040 in the Northern Province in 1989. For the secondary level, it was 25,352 in the South and 7856 in the North (Government of Sierra Leone, 1989, cited in Banya, 1993).

[4] By 31 January 2004, a total of 51,122 young people had been supported in the following categories: Vocational/Apprenticeship (28,901); Formal Education (12,182); Agriculture (9,231); Job Placement (444); Others (364) (Disarmament, Demobilisation and Reintegration Resource Centre, 2010).

[5] This was originally launched in 1993, but the full implementation did not begin until after the conflict.

[6] A group of respondents in the Home Management class said that for 'catering practical' they are responsible for getting all the ingredients. Sometimes it will cost 30,000 or 60,000 Leones (US$8-15) for one practical. The way they manage to get the money is by doing some work, such as selling in the market. A few of them said that they worked at a nightclub to earn enough money.

[7] There are three vocational centres in Makeni, but they are not for those who went through the basic education to JSS and recommended for the vocational track at the senior secondary level for three years' training. These three existing centres are for young adults with 1-2 year' training.

[8] For adolescent participants I am using pseudonyms so that their anonymity is protected.

[9] In 2009, out of 28,224 who sat on WASSCE, 990 candidates passed in four subjects or more, which is the minimum requirement to enter tertiary institutions.

[10] I have observed this from my encounters with various graduates from Bo School throughout my fieldwork.

[11] This quote was translated by his course mate from Krio to English.

[12] Isata, who does not want to go to formal schooling, still wants to receive skills training if an opportunity arises.

[13] The percentage of youth in 'paid labour' – referring to 'the economically active population that is in regular wage or salary employment' – is 3.5% out of the total youth labour force according to the census in 2004 (Braima et al, 2006).

[14] The Government hired only 2000 new teachers in 2009.

[15] The number of those enrolled in tertiary institutions has more than doubled in 2004 compared to 1998 (World Bank, 2007).

References

Abdullah, I. (1998) Bush Path to Destruction: the origin and character of the Revolutionary United Front Sierra Leone, *Journal of Modern African Studies*, 36(2), 203-235.

ActionAid (2007) *Confronting the Contradictions: the IMF, wage bill caps and the case for teachers*. London: ActionAid.

Annan, K. (2005) *In Larger Freedom: towards development, security and human rights for all*. Report of the Secretary-General. New York: United Nations.

Anti-Corruption Commission (2009) From the Abyss back to the Athens of West Africa. A Report on Systems Review of Ministry of Education. http://www.anticorruption.sl/drwebsite/uploads/from_the_abyss_back_to_the_athens_of_west_africa_1_.pdf (accessed 15 December 2009).

Banya, K. (1991) Economic Decline and the Education System: the case of Sierra Leone, *Compare*, 21(2), 127-143.

Banya, K. (1993) Illiteracy, Colonial Legacy and Education: the case of modern Sierra Leone, *Comparative Education*, 29(2), 159-170.

Bourdieu, P. (1986) The Forms of Capital, in J.E. Richardson (Ed.) *Handbook of Theory for Research in the Sociology of Education*, 46-58. Westport: Greenwood Press.

Braima, S.J., Amara, P.S., Kargo, B.B. & Moseray, B. (2006) 2004 Population and Housing Census: analytical report on employment and labour force. Statistics Sierra Leone. http://www.statistics.sl/2004%20Pop.%20&%20Hou.%20Census%20Analytical%20Reports/2004%20Population%20and%20Housing%20Census%20Report%20on%20Employment%20and%20Labour.pdf (accessed 30 November 2009).

Buckland, P. (2005) *Reshaping the future and postconflict reconstruction*. Washington, DC: World Bank.

Bush, K.D. & Saltarelli, D. (2000) *The Two Faces of Education in Ethnic Conflict: towards a peacebuilding education for children*. Florence: UNICEF Innocenti Research Centre.

Collier, P. & Hoeffler, A. (2004) Greed and Grievance in Civil War, *Oxford Economic Papers*, 56(4), 563-595.

Corby, R.A. (1990) Educating Africans for Inferiority under British Rule: Bo School in Sierra Leone, *Comparative Education Review*, 34(3), 314-349.

Davies, L. (2004) *Conflict and Education: complexity and chaos*. London: RoutledgeFalmer.

Department for International Development (DFID) (2010) *Learning for All: DFID's education strategy 2010-2015*. London: DFID.

Disarmament, Demobilisation and Reintegration Resource Centre (2010) Country Program Sierra Leone. United Nations Inter-Agency Working Group on Disarmament, Demobilisation and Reintegration. http://www.unddr.org/countryprogrammes.php?c=60#approach (accessed 1 May 2010).

Dupigny, A.C., Kargbo, I.G. & Yallancy, A. (2006) 2004 Population and Housing Census: analytical report on education and literacy. Statistics Sierra Leone.

http://www.statistics.sl/2004%20Pop.%20&%20Hou.%20Census%20Analytical%20Reports/2004%20Population%20and%20Housing%20Census%20Report%20on%20Education%20and%20Literacy.pdf (accessed 30 November 2009).

Education for All Global Monitoring Report Team (2010) Education for All Global Monitoring Report 2011: Education and Violent Conflict. Concept Note. http://www.unesco.org/fileadmin/MULTIMEDIA/HQ/ED/GMR/pdf/gmr2011/gmr2011-concept-note.pdf

Fedelino, A., Schwartz, G. & Verhoeven, M. (2006) Aid Scaling Up: do wages bill ceilings stand in the way? International Monetary Fund. http://www.imf.org/external/pubs/ft/wp/2006/wp06106.pdf (accessed 20 April 2010, 2010).

Government of Sierra Leone (1995) *New Education Policy for Sierra Leone.* Freetown: Government of Sierra Leone.

Government of Sierra Leone (2004) *The Education Act 2004.* Freetown: Government of Sierra Leone.

Government of Sierra Leone (2009) *Commission of Inquiry on Poor Educational Standard Set up in Sierra Leone.* Freetown: Government of Sierra Leone.

Humanitarian News and Analysis (IRIN) (2007) Sierra Leone: 'An idle mind is a devil's workshop'. UN Office for the Coordination of Humanitarian Affairs. http://www.irinnews.org/report.aspx?ReportId=71831 (accessed 6 October 2008).

Humphreys, M. & Weinstein, J.M. (2004) *What the Fighters Say: a survey of ex-combatants in Sierra Leone June-August 2003.* http://www.columbia.edu/~mh2245/Report1_BW.pdf (accessed 10 October 2010).

Humphreys, M. & Weinstein, J.M. (2008) Who Fights? The Determinants of Participation in Civil War, *American Journal of Political Science*, 52(2), 436-455.

International Monetary Fund (2001) Interim Poverty Reduction Strategy Paper. http://www.imf.org/external/np/prsp/2001/sle/01/063101.pdf (accessed 1 May 2010).

International Monetary Fund (2005) Sierra Leone: Poverty Reduction Strategy Paper. http://www.imf.org/external/pubs/ft/scr/2005/cr05191.pdf (accessed 1 May 2010).

International Monetary Fund (2008) *The Republic of Sierra Leone: an agenda for change; Second Poverty Reduction Strategy (PRSP II) 2008-2012.* Washington, DC: International Monetary Fund.

Keen, D. (2005) *Conflict and Collusion in Sierra Leone.* Oxford: James Currey.

Koroma, E.B. (2010) *Statement by His Excellency, Dr. Ernest Bai Koroma, President of the Republic of Sierra Leone, on the topic 1: Education for All at the 14th African Union Summit in Addis Ababa, Ethiopia.* Freetown: The Patriotic Vanguard.

Krech, R. & Maclure, R. (2003) Education and Human Security in Sierra Leone: discourses of failure and reconstruction, in W. Nelles (Ed.) *Comparative Education, Terrorism and Human Security*, 141-158. New York: Palgrave Macmillan.

McDonald, C. (2007) *A Response to ActionAid International.* International Monetary Fund. http://www.imf.org/external/np/vc/2007/051707.htm (accessed 30 April 2010).

McKay, S. & Mazurana, D. (2004) *Where Are the Girls? Girls in Fighting Forces in Northern Uganda, Sierra Leone, and Mozambique: their lives during and after war.* Montreal: Rights & Democracy.

Ministry of Education, Science and Technology (MEST) (2007a) *Sierra Leone Education Sector Plan: a road map to a better future 2007-2015.* Freetown: MEST.

Ministry of Education, Science and Technology (MEST) (2007b) *School Level Data 2006/07.* Freetown: MEST.

Nicolai, S. & Triplehorn, C. (2003) *The Role of Education in Protecting Children in Conflict.* London: Humanitarian Practice Network.

Paracka, D.J., Jr (2003) *The Athens of West Africa: a history of international education at Fourah Bay College, Freetown, Sierra Leone.* New York: Routledge.

Peters, K. & Richards, P. (1998) 'Why We Fight': voices of youth combatants in Sierra Leone, *Africa: Journal of the International African Institute,* 68(2), 183-210.

Psacharopoulos, G. & Woodhall, M. (1985) *Education for Development: an analysis of investment choices.* Oxford and New York: Oxford University Place.

Rashid, I. (2004) Student Radicals, Lumpen Youth, and the Origins of Revolutionary Groups in Sierra Leone, 1977-1996, in I. Abdullah (Ed.) *Between Democracy and Terror: the Sierra Leonean civil war.*, 66-89. Dakar: Council for the Development of Social Science Research in Africa (CODESRIA).

Richards, P. (1996) *Fighting for the Rain Forest: war, youth and resources in Sierra Leone.* Oxford: James Currey.

Rose, P. & Greeley, M. (2006) *Education in Fragile States: capturing lessons and identifying good practices.* Prepared for the DAC Fragile States Group Service Delivery Workstream Sub-Team for Education Services. http://ineesite.org/uploads/documents/store/doc_1_82_doc_1_48_Education_in_Fragile_States_DAC_final_draft.doc (accessed 15 October 2010).

Rosen, D. (2005) *Armies of the Young: child soldiers in war and terrorism.* Piscataway NJ: Rutgers University Press.

Sen, A. (1999) *Development as Freedom.* New York: Random House.

Sessay, I.M., Kamara, A.A. & Ngobeh, J.J. (2006) 2004 Population and Housing Census: analytical report on population distribution, migration and urbanisation in Sierra Leone. Statistics Sierra Leone. http://www.statistics.sl/2004%20Pop.%20&%20Hou.%20Census%20Analytical%20Reports/2004%20Population%20and%20Housing%20Census%20Report%20on%20Migration%20and%20Ubarnisation%20in%20Sierra%20Leone.PDF (accessed 31 January 2010).

Shepler, S. (1998) Education as a Site for Political Struggle in Sierra Leone, *Antropológicas,* 2, 3-14.

Sierra Leone Truth and Reconciliation Commission (SLTRC) (2004) *Witness to Truth.* Report of the Sierra Leone Truth and Reconciliation Commission, vol. 3A. Accra: SLTRC.

Smith, A. & Vaux, T. (2003) *Education, Conflict and International Development.* London: Department for International Development.

Sumner, D.L. (1963) *Education in Sierra Leone.* Freetown: Government Printer.

Tawil, S. & Harley, A. (Eds) (2004) *Education, Conflict and Social Cohesion.* Geneva: UNESCO International Bureau of Education.

Thyne, C.L. (2006) ABC's, 123's, and the Golden Rule: the pacifying effect of education on civil war, 1980-1999, *International Studies Quarterly*, 50, 733-754.

UNESCO (2000) *Dakar Framework for Action: Education for All: meeting our collective commitments.* Paris: UNESCO.

UNICEF (2009) Out-of-School Children of Sierra Leone. http://www.educationfasttrack.org/media/library/Final_Out_of_School_Study_Sierra_Leone_012009.pdf (accessed 1 May 2010).

Wessells, M. & Monteiro, C. (2006) Psychosocial Assistance to Youth: towards reconstruction for peace in Angola, *Journal of Social Justice*, 62(1), 121-139.

Women's Commission for Refugee Women and Children (2002) *Precious Resources: adolescents in the reconstruction of Sierra Leone.* New York: Women's Commission for Refugee Women and Children.

World Bank (2006) *World Development Report 2007: Development and the Next Generation.* Washington DC: World Bank.

World Bank (2007) *Education in Sierra Leone: present challenges, future opportunities.* Washington DC: World Bank.

World Bank (2009) *Africa Development Indicators 2008/2009: Youth and Employment in Africa: the potential, the problem, and the promise.* Washington DC: World Bank.

Wright, C. (1997) Reflections on Sierra Leone: a case study, in S. Tawil (Ed.) *Final Report and Case Studies on Educational Disruption and Reconstruction in Disrupted Societies*, 17-30. Geneva: International Bureau of Education.

Yusuf, B. (2004) The Political and Cultural Dynamics of the Sierra Leone War: a critique of Paul Richards, in I. Abdullah (Ed.) *Between Democracy and Terror: the Sierra Leone civil war*, 13-40. Dakar: Council for the Development of Social Science Research in Africa (CODESRIA).

CHAPTER 6

A Point of Connection through Transnational History Textbooks? An Examination of *History that Opens to the Future*, the Joint History Textbook Initiative of China, Japan and South Korea

TOMOE OTSUKI

SUMMARY In the last several decades, a number of studies have discussed the role of common history textbooks between the former adversaries in Europe as a symbolic tool to facilitate the process of historical reconciliation and to develop a common European identity. However, it is not well known that China, South Korea and Japan, too, have begun to work towards historical reconciliation through the establishment of joint history commissions or working groups at both official and non-official levels over the last decade. This chapter examines the history textbook jointly developed by Chinese, South Korean and Japanese scholars, educators and civil society members, called *History [that] Opens to the Future: the contemporary and modern history of the three nations in East Asia* (2005, 2006). This study critically engages with the presence of persistent nationalism in this trilateral history textbook, and yet argues that East Asia's joint history textbook indicates that the practice of remembrance through historical dialogue can act as a communicative force through which responsibility for the past becomes a democratic and ethical relationship with Others in the present time. The chapter also discusses the concept of 'intergenerational responsibility' for the past and raises the question of what kind of historical consciousness is required to assume responsibility for the past.

Introduction

For many years the question of how Japanese aggression during World War II ought to be remembered has elicited contentious, politicized and emotionally charged responses in China, Japan and South Korea. This question also raises unresolved issues regarding Japan's war legacy, such as the numerous lawsuits launched by Japan's former colonial subjects against the Government of Japan and Japanese corporations for their use of slave labour during the war period, and Japan's continuing failure to respond to the cries of former 'comfort women' for a sincere official apology and reparations. Arguably, however, the most intractable issue in East Asia's historical dispute is the controversy surrounding Japanese history textbooks that allegedly downplay the brutality of Japanese war crimes or even omit references to Japanese aggression altogether; an issue that has stirred diplomatic tensions between Japan and its neighbours since the early 1980s while simultaneously inspiring ethnic nationalism based on an anti-Japanese sentiment in both China and South Korea.

In an effort to map out shared ground and areas of dispute in their historical understandings, the Japanese and the South Korean governments initiated an officially sanctioned bilateral history commission in 2001 with the goal of producing a report from their collaborative study. This collaborative history project was followed by another official bilateral history commission in 2006, this time involving China and Japan. This suggests that the official bilateral efforts have been perceived as a testing ground for the possible creation of a future common history textbook between the three countries.[1] In March 2010, the two bilateral commissions respectively announced the status of their projects. Neither commission was able to indicate any common historical recognition with respect to the war period in the twentieth century. Both bilateral commissions agreed that the gaps between their members' respective historical interpretations and historiography are so deep that the development of a common historical recognition appears elusive.

Despite these challenges, however, a group of concerned scholars and educators from China, South Korea and Japan completed the first trilateral joint history textbook between these three countries, entitled *History that Opens to the Future: the contemporary and modern history of the three nations in East Asia* (hereafter *Future*). This textbook was simultaneously published in all the three countries in 2005 and revised in 2006. *Future* is not a government-sanctioned textbook. It was written by a group of scholars, schoolteachers and civil society members from the three countries. According to the authors/editors, *Future* was an attempt to overcome conventional historiography – the narrative of which centres on a single nation's perspective – by co-authoring a common transnational history textbook. By so doing, *Future* expected the students/readers from the three countries to develop a shared 'Asian historical recognition' that transcends nation-state borders and develops a common vision of a peaceful and prosperous 'East Asian community'.

This chapter intends to open up a pedagogical question around the possibility for the writing of a transnational history textbook to become a vehicle towards a 'point of connection' between oneself and the Other's historical memory (Simon, 2000, p. 12). This potential connection between the Other's past and one's present might become a driving force to pursue a common project and communal futurity with the Other in the present. I show here that the authors/editors of *Future* from the three countries encountered and engaged with the myriad differences of the Other in order to establish a common ground to pursue 'historical justice'. Through their constant confrontation, dialogue and negotiation with the Other, I argue, the members of *Future* formed a 'responsible community', which Sharon Todd (2004) defines as a *come-together*, in spite of the radical difference of the Other, 'in order to promote a shared understanding that has moral and political implications' (p. 338). It is my contention that *Future*'s consistent attempt to respond to the Other's call indicates that the practice of remembrance through historical dialogue can act as a communicative force through which our responsibility for the past becomes our democratic and ethical relationship with Others of the present time. This chapter, however, also critically engages with the presence of the persistent nationalism in the narratives of both official history textbooks in the three countries and in *Future*. It illustrates how each nation's desire to maintain their ideal 'imagined community' becomes an obstacle to elicit the intersubjectivity of history – the critical task of writing a transnational history. This then proceeds to a discussion of the concept of 'intergenerational responsibility' for the past and raises a question of what kind of historical consciousness is required to assume responsibility for the past. This idea of responsibility for the past is the crucial question that brings with it the imperative of rewriting or creating a (common) history textbook contributing towards historical reconciliation between the three nations; it is a relevant concept for other post-conflict/war societies.

Collective Memory, Collective Identity and Imagined Communities

The invention of the past and the future through common historical narratives has been crucial for the formation of the idea of the 'nation' living within the confines of the modern state, or of an 'imagined community', as Benedict Anderson (1991) calls it. A nation is politically imagined, Anderson claims, because the members of the nation will never meet or hear of most of their fellow-members, yet a nation *does* exist in the minds of the people who behave as if they are part of it. In an imagined community, Anderson writes, 'regardless of the actual inequality and exploitation that may prevail in each, the nation is always conceived as a deep, horizontal comradeship' (p. 7). Over the past two centuries, this sense of 'fraternity' drove millions of people to 'willingly to die for such limited imaginings' (p. 7). Writing a national history serves to form an imagined community by creating and cultivating national heroes and shared symbols that restore or confirm a national dignity and identity.

Kim Chul (2008) argues that ethnic nationalism and its associated national history also function to fulfil one's desire to be dignified and to confirm one's greatness by distributing the image of the ideal 'I' that one wants to see within oneself. Kim continues to argue, however, that such an ideal 'I' is a fiction. Therefore, to erase the gap between the ideal and reality, national history and collective memory are constantly modified to 'purify' undesirable history into redemptive narratives in order to construct an ideal historical subjectivity. Thus, national history is constructed by the image of an 'ideal' nation and 'self' through constant adaptation, (re)interpretation, mobilization, erasure, oppression, and exclusion of memories of particular historical contexts (Kim, 2008). Through this process, multiple memories are filtered, selected and modified into a single unified historical narrative within a nation-state. The teaching of literature and history becomes the important medium through which such unified narratives are distributed, fostering ethnic consciousness and nationalism. Anderson's 'imagined community' and Kim's insight illustrate the essential problem between China, South Korea and Japan vis-à-vis their attempt to create a common transnational history textbook and to overcome their enmity: the presence of firm narratives of 'us' and 'them' in each nation that ascribe particular roles and memories to the citizens of neighbouring nations, as will be discussed.

'Historical Dispute' in East Asia

East Asia's historical dispute was sparked in 1982 when a Japanese newspaper reported that the Japanese Ministry of Education required revisions to Japanese textbooks that changed the description of Japan's aggression in China from 'invasion' to 'advancement' (Nozaki, 2002). Since then, the issue of Japanese history textbooks has remained a catalyst of the anti-Japanese movement and of the war over history between Japan, China and South Korea, which reached an apex in 2001.

In early 2001, a group of Japanese revisionists published a history textbook called the *New History Textbook (Atarashii Rekishi Kyokasho)*, which characterized the Asia-Pacific War as the 'liberation of Asia' from Western imperialism. It grossly undermined, if not completely omitted, the brutality of Japanese aggression while simultaneously honouring Japanese soldiers who courageously sacrificed their lives for their country. In April, while a number of Japanese scholars, teachers and civil society members expressed their concern that such revisionist views would damage Japan's relations with its neighbours, the Japanese Ministry of Education, Culture, Sports, Science and Technology (MEXT) approved the *New History Textbook* for use in junior high schools. Although the *New History Textbook* only achieved 0.4% of the market share of official history textbooks in Japan, the MEXT's approval of the revisionists' textbook heightened both international and domestic concerns over a possible remilitarization of Japan as well as an escalation of anti-Japanese sentiment in China and South Korea.

In August 2001, Japanese Prime Minister Jyunichiro Koizumi visited the Yasukuni shrine to honour the war dead. The Yasukuni, a shrine of Shinto (Japan's indigenous religion), served to form the Japanese national identity and imagined community of Imperial Japan as the subject of the divine figure, *Kami*: the Emperor.[2] During the Asia-Pacific War, the Japanese were taught that dying in battle for the Emperor was the most noble act, which in turn promised the war dead to be worshipped as children of *Kami* at the Yasukuni – the highest virtue for many Japanese soldiers (Takahashi, 2005). The Yasukuni still remains in the heart of Tokyo as a memorial to the war dead, including 14 Class A war criminals, convicted of crimes against peace by the International Military Tribunal for the Far East (hereafter the Tokyo Trial). Consequently, Koizumi's visit to the Yasukuni shrine was perceived by concerned Japanese and Japan's neighbours as neglect of Japan's war responsibility, and fomented diplomatic tensions between Japan and its neighbouring countries. To ease the diplomatic tension over the past, the Japanese Government made efforts to establish the two respective official bilateral history commissions mentioned above – one with South Korea in 2001 and another with China in 2006 – with the mandate of authoring collaborative historical study reports. Both commissions were to cover history from ancient times to the present.

China–Japan Official History Commission

The Japanese representatives in the Chinese–Japanese official history commission are scholars from various universities and the National Institute for Defence Studies (NIDS). The Chinese members are drawn exclusively from the Chinese Academy of Social Science and Beijing National University. Shinichi Kitaoka, the chief commissioner of the Japanese group in this bilateral commission, stated that the Japanese group does not aim to establish a common historical recognition, but rather to identify the divergent historical interpretations between China and Japan in order to minimize the gap in their understanding of each other's perspectives (cited in Shoji, 2008). On the other hand, according to Jyunichiro Shoji (2008), chief researcher of the centre of war history at the NIDS and a member of the Chinese–Japanese official history commission, the Chinese members assume that there is only one correct history to recognize and hold that the goal of the bilateral commission is the achievement of a common, 'correct' historical understanding.

The major disagreements between the two groups included: (1) the evaluation of the 1946-48 Tokyo Trial; (2) the number of victims of the 1937 Nanjing Massacre; and (3) the self-aggrandizing nationalist nature of China's patriotic education. The Japanese group insists that the Tokyo Trial lacked impartiality with respect to its legal procedure and its accusation against Japan for crimes against peace while neglecting the US use of the atomic bomb and the indiscriminate air raids conducted during the war (*Mainichi*

Press, 2010a). Conversely, the Chinese group emphasized China's contribution to the Tokyo Trial, which established the notion that invasion and the waging of war are violations of international law and therefore punishable offences (*Mainichi Press*, 2010a). As for the Nanjing Massacre, the Japanese group wrote that the number of the victims differs depending on, for instance, how one defines genocide and illegal killing; it also mentioned that, among Japanese scholars, 200,000 is the maximum estimated number of the casualties (*Sankei Press*, 2010). On the other hand, the Chinese group presented two different figures: that of 200,000 as used during the Tokyo Trial, and 300,000 as reported by the Nanjing War Crime Military Court (*Sankei Press*, 2010) and insisted the latter number is China's official view (*Yomiuri Press*, 2010).

The Japanese authors directed criticism towards China's patriotic education system, alleging that it is a primary source of contemporary anti-Japanese sentiment (*Mainichi Press*, 2010a). In response, the Chinese group insisted that the Chinese education system clearly distinguishes between Japanese military leaders and ordinary Japanese people. They argued that since the patriotic education system aims at fostering Chinese national pride and confidence, it enables students to contribute to the further development of China, thereby promoting a view that is qualitatively different from a narrow-minded ethnic nationalism (*Mainichi Press*, 2010a).

Kitaoka, the Japanese team's leader, commented that the history project is a sort of political 'insurance' that would enable policy makers from both countries to collaborate on other security issues (cited in Shoji, 2008). On the other hand, Bu Ping, the chief commissioner of the official Chinese–Japanese history commission, said that the primary responsibility of both the Chinese and Japanese intellectuals is 'to serve the national interest' (*Mainichi Press*, 2010a).[3] How each group comes to define 'insurance' or 'national interest' remains unanswered. So far, only these disagreements have been publicized by the media, while the fruits of the commission's task of minimizing discrepancies in historical recognition have failed to materialize.[4]

Japan–South Korea Official History Commission

The Japanese and South Korean history commission issued reports in 2005 and in 2010 [5], but, as with the Chinese–Japanese commission, the reports only served to present the continuing disagreements in historical interpretation between the two groups. This commission also established a subgroup for 'history textbook studies', which examines official history textbooks in both countries. The commissioners consist of scholars from various universities throughout Japan and South Korea. The major continuing source of disagreement concerns how each country's official history textbooks describe the history of the twentieth century. The South Korean group complained that none of the Japanese history textbooks have ever referred to the 1910 Japanese annexation of Korea as illegal. In response, the Japanese group asserted that Korea's claim is not yet well supported by scholars of international law (*Asahi Press*, 2010a).

The Japanese group has also pointed out that Korean history textbooks do not refer to: (1) the agreement reached by the Japanese people for a Peace Constitution as a result of their national remorse and reflection following the war; (2) the 1995 public acknowledgement and apology by Japanese Prime Minister Tomiichi Murayama for the suffering inflicted by the Japanese on their Asian neighbours; and (3) the 1998 *Heisei* Emperor's (Hirohito's son) official apology for past wrongdoing. Rather, the Japanese group asserted, South Koreans depict the revisionist *New History Textbook* as though it represents the content of the majority of Japanese official history textbooks (*Mainichi Press*, 2010b). Finally, while the Japanese commissioners claimed that it would be more liberal to acknowledge and co-exist with the multiple interpretations of history, their counterparts asserted that the core issue is whether or not the Japanese people acknowledge and regret their past wrongs (*Mainichi Press*, 2010b). One Japanese member commented that the fundamental problem with the Korean side is their inability to overcome ethnic nationalism (*Asahi Press*, 2010b), while another Japanese commissioner claimed that the project was 'barren' due to the starkly different historiography between the two groups (*Nikkei Press*, 2010).

A Transnational Trilateral History Textbook: *History that Opens to the Future*

Future is to date the only published history textbook jointly written and distributed in China, South Korea and Japan. *Future* differs from the official bilateral history commissions in four primary ways. First and foremost, *Future* is the first trilateral, rather than bilateral, history textbook effort between the three countries. Second, it is a quasi-official/private project as only the Chinese authors/editors are state-employed scholars and museum curators [6]; the South Korean and Japanese members are non-state officials and those commissions are made up of scholars, schoolteachers and civil society members. Third, the official commissions cover the entire gamut of history from ancient to present times, whereas *Future* focuses exclusively on the interactions between China, Korea and Japan from the late sixteenth century to the twentieth century. Finally, while the official commissions endeavour to present parallel narratives of the periods in question, *Future* created a shared narrative to cover its time period. Because of its limited time period and the exclusive focus on the three nations, *Future* cannot be used as a primary textbook and is therefore a supplemental textbook in the three countries.

All the participants of *Future* were concerned about the emergence of the Japanese revisionists' history textbook and intended to create a transnational history textbook to counter the distorted historical views of the

Japanese revisionists who insisted that writing a common history textbook between the three nations is *impossible*.

Historical Narratives in *Future*

Each country's history within *Future* was written and edited by its national team to a shared narrative that all groups agreed upon. Each national team also chose the illustrations and references for their individual section. *Future* received considerable public attention in the three countries upon its release. The official Chinese newspaper, the *People's Daily*, hailed *Future* as the best book of the year in 2005 for its contribution to education.[7] *Future* also received the 2005 Special Award from the Japanese Journalist Association. It was in South Korea, however, where *Future* was most widely received, being distributed to every middle school throughout the country. Subsequently, some six thousand practicum reports on using *Future* in a history class setting have been published in South Korea (Saito, 2008).

Future strongly delineates the correlations between modernization, colonialism and imperialism and describes Japan as having appropriated its colonial subjects as human resources to be consumed for its own benefit. *Future* also depicts the dynamism of the colonial resistance movements against Japanese imperialism in China, Korea and also in South-East Asia, rendering colonial subjects as agents instead of merely depicting them as the objects of Japanese policy. Such narratives inevitably refute Japanese revisionists' claim of 'liberating Asia from the Western powers', and discredit their argument that the clash between the Japanese and their colonial subjects was an 'unfortunate' outcome in the process of Japan's 'good will' in modernizing Asia (*New History Textbook*, 2005) by revealing Japan's sole intention to exploit those living in occupied areas as a resource.

Future allocates 20 pages to the description of Japanese atrocities in China and Korea, such as the Nanjing Massacre, rapes, indiscriminate bombings, biological warfare and human experiments. The joint textbook states that all of these crimes were in violation of international law and describes comfort women used by the Japanese as 'sex slaves' (*Future*, 2006, p. 133). It also includes witness testimony of a former Japanese soldier, Hajime Kondo, recorded in the Tokyo District Higher Court in November 2003 (p. 135). Kondo's account provides detailed depictions of the crimes the Japanese soldiers had committed against Chinese civilians. Kondo also admits that he suffers from a sense of guilt that could be relieved if the Japanese Government sincerely offered an apology and compensation to Asian victims.

Future also discusses the politics of the Tokyo Trial in far more detail than any other official textbook in the three countries, demonstrating the lingering legacy of the Tokyo Trial's failure to bring justice to Asian victims. It illustrates that the Tokyo Trial introduced the Nanjing Massacre to the Japanese public who had, otherwise, little idea about the atrocities against the civilians committed in the name of their country. *Future* also describes how the issue of the Japanese Emperor's responsibility for the war crimes was exempted from the trial, while indicating the Emperor's political responsibility for the policy decisions as the head of the Japanese imperial state. It then continues to claim that since the primary interest of the tribunal was Japan's crimes against the Allies, Japanese crimes against Asian victims were not prosecuted, despite the Allies' knowledge of the Japanese use of comfort women and the human experiments the Japanese conducted. As for the unsettled legacies, *Future* describes how the issue of Japan's responsibility to Asian victims remains ambiguous, still in search of resolution. As a result, unlike the official history commissions, *Future* prevented itself from being trapped by ideological debates around whether or not the Tokyo Trial represented victor's justice. Instead, it showed how the 'historical dispute' is in fact about those who were betrayed by the politicized legal system as practised more than sixty years ago while reminding readers of the *incompleteness* of past justice and of their duty to revisit what law has left out in order to pursue historical justice.

Another section within the textbook presents three war memorial museums, one from each country: the Chinese People's Anti-Japanese Resistance Museum, the Korean Independence Museum and the Hiroshima Peace Memorial Museum. It states that the exhibition at the Chinese Anti-Japanese Resistance Museum aims to convey the message that one should never forget the suffering of the Chinese victims and the courage of the communist comrades who fought against Japanese imperialism. Similarly, the Korean Independence Museum is shown as housing the archives of the Japanese atrocities, which are displayed in order to pass on to future generations the memory of Korean agony, resistance and patriotism. Finally, *Future* notes that the Hiroshima Peace Memorial displays artefacts that demonstrate the power of the atomic bomb to annihilate and calls for the total abolition of nuclear weapons and for perpetual world peace. In depicting these three memorials, *Future* illustrates the different ways of remembering victimhood and raises the question of what ought to be remembered. For the Chinese and the Koreans, their 'historical lesson' can be learned from the memory of the national humiliation and heroism that encouraged youth to fight for their countries, whereas the memory of the atomic bomb teaches the Japanese that a nuclear war can destroy the whole world and thus that 'eternal world peace' must be sought. The text encourages students to compare the different exhibition practices of the war memorials of each country and asks how East Asian youth should remember the war in order to build a peaceful East Asia.

Struggles towards a 'Point of Connection' and 'Responsible Community'

Kazuharu Saito (2008), one of the Japanese authors of *Future*, provides detailed accounts of the complexity of writing the joint textbook, acknowledging that it was extremely difficult for each author/editor to see history from other perspectives. One of the debates between the Japanese authors on the one hand, and the Korean and Chinese authors on the other, concerned the responsibility that Japanese individuals might hold for the war. The Chinese and Korean members objected to the Japanese authors' suggestion to include not only crimes committed by the Japanese state but also to highlight the responsibility of ordinary Japanese people. The Chinese and Korean authors argued that this would obscure the responsibility of the Japanese state (Saito, 2008). From the Chinese perspective, the effort made by the central government to distinguish between the Japanese state and ordinary people in Chinese textbooks, for instance, should be appreciated. By so doing, the Chinese officials attempt to diminish anti-Japanese sentiment, which has the potential to damage relations between China and Japan. For the Koreans, an official acknowledgement and apology by the Japanese state for its crimes in Korea – and not an ambiguous notion of the 'metaphysical guilt' of the individual Japanese person – has been demanded for decades. This particular chasm between the three national groups demonstrates some of the complexity that lies within the domestic politics of each nation. The debate also indicates the possibility of a transnational historical narrative since the contentious issue of individual responsibility is being explored, rather than silenced or contained within separate bounded narratives.

Another contentious debate concerned the issue of whether or not Japanese victimhood should be described. According to Saito (2008), the Chinese and Korean authors argued that references to Japanese victimhood would undermine Japan's responsibility for the war and the popular view, widely held in China and South Korea, that the use of the atomic bomb precipitated the end of the war and liberated them from Japanese aggression. In fact, until recently, none of the South Korean official history textbooks had referred to Japanese victimhood from the atomic bomb. In 2002, some privately written Korean history textbooks published as alternatives to the official ones mention the devastation of Hiroshima, but not Nagasaki (Saito, 2008).

Likewise, in the 1990s, Chinese official textbooks began to mention the US use of the atomic bomb in Japan with the simple statement: 'two atomic bombs were dropped in Hiroshima and Nagasaki' (Saito, 2008). No reference to the annihilative power of the A-bomb or the suffering of the victims was made. As a result, not only are the memories of the Japanese atomic bomb victims excluded from the official historical narratives of the Second World War in China and South Korea, but also the memories of the Chinese and Korean atomic bomb victims. The Japanese authors argued that articulating both Japan's aggression and victimhood would give a more complete account of the war. Moreover, the historical view of the atomic bomb as the singular agent that brought the war to an end is itself an over simplified narrative. Yet, the Chinese and Korean authors argued that even though it was not necessarily true that the use of atomic bombs ended the war, it was true that many of the Asian victims of Japanese aggression did feel that the bomb saved them from further suffering (Saito, 2008), revealing the multiplicity of 'truth(s)' around one historical event. Ultimately, *Future* includes detailed accounts of how the bombs devastated Hiroshima and Nagasaki as well as the emotive testimony of a survivor. Furthermore, *Future* describes the presence of non-Japanese atomic bomb victims (Allied prisoners of war, Koreans and Chinese) and notes that most of the colonial atomic bomb victims never received any medical aid or compensation from the Japanese Government, implying that the lingering war legacy of Japan vis-à-vis the Koreans and Chinese continued into the post-war period.

Disagreements were not, however, always between the Japanese authors and their Chinese and Korean counterparts. The Korean group, for example, argued that the Chinese authors hardly recognized Korea's victimhood. For instance, Chinese history textbooks describe the Chinese as victims of the 1894-95 Sino-Japanese war, usually failing to make any reference to Korea despite the fact that the war was provoked by a dispute over the control of Korea between China and Japan. As a result, the Korean authors strongly insisted that the Sino-Japanese war be described as having taken place in Korea, and that the textbook acknowledge how Korea had been forced to agree to an unfair diplomatic treaty with the Qing Dynasty (Saito, 2008). In response, the Chinese authors revised the narratives repeatedly. In this process, Saito observed how the Chinese authors struggled with freeing themselves from a China-centric historical view – especially in their status as state-employed historians – in order to respond to the Other's call. Furthermore, the Chinese authors dropped their insistence on including a reference to the 300,000 casualties of the Nanjing Massacre as the sole correct figure. *Future* therefore presents different figures for Nanjing's death toll without asserting which one is correct. The Chinese authors ultimately prioritized conveying the overall historical background and the victims' suffering to the readers (Saito, 2008). This is also one of the remarkable contrasts between *Future* and the official Chinese–Japanese bilateral history commission, which all but ground to a halt over this debate about numbers.

Saito (2008) claims that the historical dialogue within *Future* aimed to respond to the Other's calls and engage with the Other's historical memory. It is difficult to face the Other's painful memory and attend to the radically different historical views of the Other. But, Saito notes that this is a *sine qua non* in order to develop a dialogue with the Other. He also notes that it was not only the Japanese who faced difficulties in engaging with the Other's memory, but also their counterparts, who themselves were posed difficult questions and had to make efforts to engage with the memory of the victimizer's victimhood. Authors of *Future* from China and South Korea acknowledged that writing *Future* required each of them to struggle with freeing themselves from their own historical view in order to respond to the Other's call. For instance, Ha Jung-Moon (2005), one of the Korean authors of *Future*, noted that the Korean members found their own nationalism in their dominant historical narratives by learning *from* the Other's struggle.

These authors' attentiveness to the Other recalls Todd's notion of 'responsible community'. The notion of this community is not a fixed or consolidated social or political entity. Rather, it is an inspiration, a pedagogical praxis of encountering the differences of the Other in order to transform the relation between the self and the Other into a more just and democratic one. Todd (2001) notes that learning *from* the Other, instead of leaning *about* them, 'allows us an engagement with difference across space and time ... It is only when we learn *from* the stories the Others have to tell that we can respond with humility and assume responsibility' (p. 73). Attentiveness to the radical difference of the Other is the critical component of a responsible community. Todd (2004) argues:

> [Others' alterity] constantly threatens to break in upon and dissolve the communal bond. Yet, equally paradoxically, it is precisely in attending to this difference, to others as others, that enables formations of community, formations that take seriously the burden of justice ... This view of community is hence incomplete, dependent as it is on the changing quality of relationality and interaction that shapes social togetherness. (pp. 342-343)

Future was not developed in an environment free of tension. Ha Jung-Moon (2005) commented that the members of *Future* came close to giving up their project many times as they confronted radically different historical views of the Other. Yet, the contention was that tension is necessary for the process in order to identify the self–Other relation from which one can seek a way of engaging, negotiating and reconciling with the difference of the Other, building a bridge across the gulf. To resist the Japanese revisionists' attempt to efface the memories of victims and to seek historical justice, the authors/editors of *Future* shared the responsibility for the past, and ultimately formed a point of connection – the crucial foundation of a responsible community. This point of connection indicated a way of exchanging dialogues with the Other, a way of relating one's present with the memory of the Other, and a way of furthering the project of justice, and opened up possibilities for historical reconciliation in the future.

Pending Tasks for *Future*

While *Future* does elucidate new approaches to certain critical historical events, and new connections between Others, one may rightly wonder to what degree the core themes of *Future*'s narratives actually differ from the state-approved textbooks of the three countries. Wang Zheng (2009) favourably evaluates *Future* by noting that: 'unlike other Japanese textbooks, the Nanjing Massacre section is fairly straightforward' while 'Japan's colonial rule of Korea is described as illegal and compulsory' (p. 8). However, Alexander Bukh's (2007) extensive research on Japanese state-approved history textbooks demonstrates that the majority of official Japanese textbooks published after 2002 present the Nanjing Massacre as involving the killing of not only Chinese soldiers but also of many Chinese women and children.[8] As for Japanese colonial policy, Bukh finds that '[some of the textbooks] note ... drafting of Koreans and Chinese into the Imperial Army, attempts to forcibly spread the Shinto religion to Korea ...'(p. 697). Bukh's close examination indicates that 'there have been a number of instances when the narrative has transcended national borders by including other Asian peoples in the depictions of victimhood' (p. 702). However, Bukh also notes that such narratives of Japan's aggression are presented in the context of a clear separation between the Japanese people and the state. This distinction has played the key role in Japan's post-war 'healthy nationalism' from which 'the nation came to be perceived in generally positive terms as a source of opposition against the state's interests, whereas the state came to represent the negative past of imperialism, authoritarianism, and barbarism' (p. 690).[9]

In fact, since the end of the Second World War, peace education has proliferated throughout Japan. However, Japan's peace education, which is often integrated into the literature and social science curricula, mostly focuses on the issues of nuclear disarmament and militarism. To teach the brutality of the war, Japanese schoolteachers have usually employed the stories of ordinary Japanese people's ordeal as a result of the war and graphic post-atomic images. The stories of Japanese suffering are then followed by the teaching of the Peace Constitution that contains the notions of universal human rights, democracy and the culture of peace. This kind of post-war Japanese education has created a highly critical view of militarism and wars among the Japanese public. But, it has failed to lead to a critical enquiry into Japanese individuals' responsibility for supporting the imperial government that committed atrocities in their name. Rather, Japanese anti-militarism and post-war Japanese identity as a 'peace-loving nation' (Orr, 2001, p. 2) have served as a national redemption – which seems to have absolved guilt and responsibility for war crimes. As a result, the Japanese still fail to resolve, or are not even aware of, war legacies. Bukh (2007) points out that post-2000 textbooks generate 'a certain sense of commonality and solidarity between the Japanese people and the Chinese and Koreans' (p. 697) by describing them all as victims of the war. Therefore, if the Japanese authors' suggestion to explore Japanese individual culpability and complicity had been incorporated, *Future* might have opened up new possibilities for engaging with the notion of responsibility. In turn, this could have disrupted the

Japanese readers' position of comfort and prompted a reconsideration of their historical view.

Future maintained the official Chinese government view of post-war history. The textbook depicts the establishment of the People's Republic of China as the great hope for the Chinese people since it returned land to the peasants and secured education and cultural rights for minority groups. The maintenance of such narratives can easily invite criticism not only from Japanese revisionists but also from historians in general. Had the textbook included the continuous suffering of Chinese people even after the war – such as during the 1958-62 Great Leap Forward, which aimed to resuscitate China's war-exhausted economy in order to compete with industrialized countries through aggressive modernization but resulted in famine on a massive scale – *Future* could have revealed the lingering scars of the war and helped readers to critically reflect upon the violent nature of modernization. Such narratives of ordinary people's pain might have interrupted the notion of history as a necessary sacrifice for a brighter future, and evoked within readers the recognition that history is never naturally moving towards a better future and instead requires a commitment to take responsibility for the present by reflecting upon the past.

Future also fails to question the notion of Korean ethnic consciousness. Kim Chul (2008) notes that Japan functions as a mirror that shows the 'I' that Koreans want to see as true of themselves. Japan's persecution of the Koreans highlights not only their national pain, but also their patriotism, glory and honour, and enables the forgetting of memories that would disrupt Koreans' historical consciousness. Just like the official history textbooks in South Korea, *Future* failed, despite the gradual awareness of Korean nationalism embedded in their national history, as mentioned above, to overcome the Korean desire to clean national history of its disruptive remnants. The fact is that not everyone can be categorized either as patriotic or traitorous, even under colonialism.

Kim refers to a South Korean documentary film about 26,000 young Korean *tokkotai* pilots (commonly referred to as *Kamikaze* in the West) who volunteered to serve in the Japanese Army and died as suicide attackers on Japan's side rather than by fighting against Japanese imperialism. The documentary appeared in South Korea in the midst of an anti-Japanese collaboration campaign of 2005. Nonetheless, as Kim points out, the Korean public – even those who had been crying out for the political purging of Japanese collaborators – remained silent towards the memories of those Korean *tokkotai.* Why? Kim suggested that it was because the memory of Korean *tokkotai* disrupted a monolithic collective narrative that renders Koreans as both victims of the Japanese Imperial Army and resistant to Japanese aggression. These Korean *tokkotai* sang *Arirang*, the most popular Korean folk song, but pledged allegiance to the Japanese Emperor before their final take-off, just like Japanese *tokkotai* pilots. Furthermore, the documentary disclosed that these Korean pilots were commemorated in the

Yasukuni shrine (Kim, 2008). The Korean *tokkotai* illustrate the multiple subjectivities even within oneself: each embodied a subjectivity of strong attachment towards the motherland, of colonial subject and of one who has chosen fight and die as Japanese imperial subject. In the South Korean imagined community, there is no place for these 26,000 Korean *tokkotai* to be remembered. To remember the Korean *tokkotai*, one is required to deconstruct attachment to a particular dominant historical narrative in order to acknowledge other multiple historical subjectivities. *Future* does refer to the existence of Korean and Taiwanese *tokkotai* when it mentions the Japanese suicide pilot who renounced Japanese militarism in his will. These Japanese, Korean and Taiwanese *tokkotai* cannot be homogenized as victims of Japanese imperialism, however, because they were never the same kind of the victims.

In sum, all the history projects between the three countries, whether official or unofficial, have yet to elicit the intersubjectivity of history by means of introspection around their own nationalism. Moreover, *Future* and the official history commissions remain ambiguous regarding the question of why we in the present are called upon to take responsibility for things we have not done (in the past), despite the fact that this question can signify the grounds for collaborative works like *Future* and the commissions. Attention to this area also raises a question of the subjectivity that is called upon to take responsibility for the past.

Intergenerational Responsibility

Jonna Thompson (2009), reflecting on the responsibility for the past, develops the notion of 'intergenerational' responsibility. Thompson notes that 'political institutions cannot be built from scratch in each generation. They have to be adapted to changing conditions, to be corrected for failing, to respond to changing conceptions of justice' (p. 205). This recalls Jacques Derrida's notion of inheriting the future-to-come. Derrida (2001) claims:

> We inherit a language, conditions of life, a culture ... which carries the memory of what has been done, and the responsibility, so then, we are responsible for things we have not done ourselves and that is part of the concept of heritage. (p. 102)

We are bequeathed institutions from our predecessors and are responsible for maintaining, reforming and rebuilding them towards *just* institutions (Derrida, 2001; Thompson, 2009). For instance, the contemporary Japanese have inherited a Peace Constitution that calls on the Japanese to strive for the banishment of oppression and intolerance from the Earth (see the preface of the Constitution, 1947). To inherit this constitution means that the Japanese must take intergenerational responsibility not only for undoing the wrongs of their predecessors, but also for fighting against any oppressive acts against individuals who cry for justice regardless of nationality.

As for the question of the 'I' who is called upon to take the intergenerational responsibility for the past, it is true that one's identity is constituted by multiple elements, such as gender, ethnicity and religion. Nationality only represents one aspect. However, it is also true that when one collectivity commits atrocities against another group in the name of a nation-state, and when the victims cry out, 'you take responsibility for that past violence', they reinforce the accountability of the constituted members of the nation. A constituted member of a nation is an individual who makes rational judgements and is responsible for shaping the political culture by voting, participating in public discourse and criticizing/supporting policies. In the East Asian context, the Japanese today, including the author, are not directly responsible for wrongdoings of the past, but are accountable for war legacies that still maintain certain power relations and Japanese privileges over the Other.

In December 2009, seven South Korean women, who had worked in the Mitsubishi factory (they were all between the ages of 13 and 14 at the time) as colonial subjects during the war finally received a 'pension' from the Japanese Government. After sixty-four years of struggle, each woman received only ninety-nine yen (less than US$1.00). This incident is one of the numerous cases that illustrate lingering war legacies and injustice in the present time. The Japanese still partake in the oppressive colonial legacy, and practise privilege over the Other; this is what we are summoned to take intergenerational responsibility for, repairing and transforming our relation with the Other into an ethical and just one. The former colonial Mitsubishi workers demand the Japanese to *intervene* into the ongoing practice of injustice in the present time to end the colonial legacy of injustice. Therefore, historical reconciliation requires not merely sharing common historical recognition of 'how it really was' between the former adversaries. Rather, it calls upon us to be touched by the past and to be awakened by the recognition of the incompleteness of past justice as well as the continuing power relation and structure that reproduce injustice to the Other in the present time. Historical reconciliation thus requires the development of historical consciousness that enables one to question the notion of historical 'progress' that assumes the past as the cost of a brighter future. Instead the possibility of the present to repair and retry what was failed and betrayed in the past must be grasped in order to create a democratic relationship between us and the Other in the *present* time.

Conclusion

This chapter indicates that approaching the development of a transnational history textbook with the intention of finding a 'point of connection' in order to form a 'responsible community' may open up new discussions over how the traumatic memories of Others can be encountered, how transnational history can be represented, and how a democratic social relationship with

Others in the present can be established. *Future* outlines not only for those producing common history textbooks but also for those whose historical memories, emotions and political backgrounds vary significantly, the possibility to come together and bridge the gulf that separates the one from the Other. I argue that through their struggle to free themselves from their own dominant narratives in order to encounter and respond to the Other's call, the members of *Future* showed how the practice of remembrance can serve as a pedagogical praxis that engages historical memories as a critical communicative force to generate a democratic relationship with the Others in the present. *Future* is not a completed work, as the authors freely admit, but its incompleteness is still ethical, embracing the futurity that calls us to continue the dialogue.

At the same time, however, this chapter reveals two crucial problems in the transnational history projects between the three countries. First, both *Future* and the official commissions have failed to critically question the nationalism of their contributors. As a result, *Future* too appears to display the core elements of the three dominant historical narratives and thus fails to reveal the illusion of the imagined community of each of the three countries. An imagined community is a political product that shows the ideal 'nation' and the 'self' through constant modification and purification of history into redemptive narratives, while oppressing and excluding undesired memories. By critically engaging with the presence of nationalism in both official history textbooks and *Future*, this chapter intends to interrupt the notion of homogeneous 'national' or 'ethnic' subjectivity and calls for eliciting the intersubjectivity and multiple memories of history.

Second, none of the history project initiatives seem to have engaged in a discussion about the notion of responsibility for the past in substantive ways. The reform of textbooks and curriculum for a societal transformation requires not merely inserting the idea of democratic citizenship or the notions of a culture of peace or human rights, but substantive discussion of individual responsibility for the past, the present and the future. By exploring the notion of intergenerational responsibility and lingering war legacies, I hope that this chapter can open up new discussions between the three nations over what responsibility we are called upon to take in order to signify the imperative of the collaborative work undertaken by the authors of *Future*. I also hope that this study raises the pedagogical question of how we can foster historical consciousness that treats history not merely as a 'past event' that should 'never again' occur, but as a promise of hope from the past that calls upon us to inherit intergenerational responsibility for the possibility of the present to break the course of unjust legacies to create a democratic future-to-come.

Notes

[1] In October 2009, the Foreign Ministers from Japan and South Korea respectively publicly stated the possibility of producing an official common

history textbook between China, Japan and South Korea (Park & Nagano, 2009).

[2] The concept of *Kami* in Japanese tradition refers to a spirit that eternally remains pure and respected. The Emperor was deified by the Meiji Constitution in 1889; the head of the Empire that was sacred and inviolable. Takahashi (2005) provides detailed accounts of the politics of war memory and Japanese national identity constructed around the Yasukuni.

[3] All the translations in the text are the author's own.

[4] Two respective historical narratives written by the Chinese and the Japanese commissioners are available at: http://www.mofa.go.jp/mofaj/area/china/rekishi_kk.html (the official website of the Ministry of Foreign Affairs of Japan).

[5] Both reports (2002-2005 and 2007-2010) are available at: http://www.jkcf.or.jp/history/ (the website of Japan and South Korea Cultural Exchange Foundation).

[6] Bu Ping, the head of the Chinese Academy of Social Science as well as the chief commissioner of the official Chinese–Japanese bilateral joint history project, is also the principal leader of *Future*'s Chinese contingent. One interesting note is that the Chinese group also includes researchers from the Chinese People's Anti-Japanese Resistance Museum and the chief curator of the Nanjing Massacre Memorial Museum (Wang, 2009). Also, unlike the official bilateral commission, the Chinese *Future* group includes scholars from Shanghai as well.

[7] *Future* was introduced as a compulsory textbook along with China's official one in the Shanghai junior high school in 2005 (Liu Ying, 2005).

[8] However, Nozaki (2002) points out that the reference of the 'comfort women' was completely removed from seven junior high school history textbooks in their new drafts for 2002.

[9] See also Orr (2001). Orr discusses that the Japanese ideology as a 'peace loving nation' recognizes the victimhood of other Asians, but points out that the 'central element of war responsibility and war victimhood' in Japanese selective remembrance is 'the [Japanese] desire to identify with Asian victimhood rather than deny it' (p. 175).

References

Anderson, B. (1991) *Imagined Communities: reflections on the origin and spread of nationalism*. London and New York: Verso.

Asahi Press (2010a) Japan-South Korea Joint History Commission: think beyond 'national history', March 26. (In Japanese)

Asahi Press (2010b) The Second Term Report of the Japan-South Korea Joint History Commission: Criticizing the History Textbook of the Other, 23 March. (In Japanese)

Bukh, A. (2007) Japan's History Textbooks Debate: national identity in narratives of victimhood and victimization, *Asian Survey*, 47 (5), 683-704.

China-Japan Joint History Commission, Ministry of Foreign Affairs of Japan (2010) http://www.mofa.go.jp/mofaj/area/china/rekishi_kk.html

Derrida, J. (2001) Justice, Colonisation, Translation, in Paul Patton & Terry Smith (Eds) *Jacques Derrida: deconstruction engaged: the Sydney seminars*. Sydney: Power Publications.

Ha J. (2005) What Does it Mean 'Sharing Common Historical Recognition'?, in the symposium 'Japan-South Korea History 2005: To Construct the Future of East Asia', hosted by the Hiroshima Citizen Network, June 25. (In Japanese)

Japan and South Korea Cultural Exchange Foundation. A Report of the Japan-South Korea Joint History Commission (2010) http://www.jkcf.or.jp/history/ (In Japanese)

Japan-China-South Korea Joint History Textbook Commission (2006) A History that Opens to the Future: Japan, China and South Korea = Joint Editing: contemporary and modern history of the three nations. Tokyo: Koubunken. (In Japanese)

Kim C. (2008) Resistance and Despair, in Yoichi Komori, Che Wonshik, Park Yuha & Kim Chol (Eds) *Meta-history of East Asia's Controversy over Historical Recognition: a joint attempt of 'the South Korea and Japan Solidarity 21'*. Tokyo: Seikyu-Sha. (In Japanese)

Liu, Y. (2005) A Joint History Textbook among China, South Korea and Japan introduced in Shanghai's junior-high school. JP.eastday.com. http://jp.eastday.com/node2/node3/node13/userobject1ai17946.html (In Japanese)

Mainichi Press (2010a) China-Japan Joint History Commission: disparity of the historical recognition over 'Tienanmen Incident' between China and Japan, 10 February. (In Japanese)

Mainichi Press (2010b) Japan-South Korea Joint History Commission: strive for overcoming the confrontation, 24 March. (In Japanese)

New History Textbook [*Atarashii Rekisho Kyokasho*], Chapters 4 and 5. Translated by Japanese Society for History Textbook Reform from *Atarashii Rekishi Kyokasho* (2005 version). http://www.tsukurukai.com/05_rekisi_text/rekishi_English/English.pdf

Nikkei Press (2010) Japan-South Korea Joint History Commission is 'Barren': too far to achieve the common historical recognition, 23 March. (In Japanese)

Nozaki Y. (2002) Japanese Politics and the History Textbook Controversy 1982-2001, *International Journal of Educational Research*, 37, 603-622.

Orr, J.J. (2001) *The Victims as Hero: ideologies of peace and national identity in postwar Japan*. Honolulu: University of Hawaii Press.

Park, J. & Nagano, Y. (2009) South Korea and Japan Consider History Textbook with China, *Los Angeles Times*, 30 October.

Saito K. (2008) *The Chinese History Textbook and East Asia's Historical Dialogue: a report from the joint history textbook writing between China, South Korea and Japan.* Tokyo: Kadensha. (In Japanese)

Sankei Press (2010) Problem of Reconciling the [Conflicting] Historical Recognition of the 'Nanjing Massacre', 1 February. (In Japanese)

Shoji J. (December 2008) Prospects of China-Japan Joint History Commission. Briefing Memo. *The National Institute for Defence Studies Commentary* no. 127, 1-5. (In Japanese)

Simon, R.I. (2000) The Paradoxical Practice of *Zakar*: memories of 'What has never been my fault or my deed', in Roger I. Simon, Sharon Rosenberg & Claudia Eppert (Eds) *Between Hope & Despair: pedagogy and the remembrance of historical trauma.* Lanham: Rowman & Littlefield.

Takahashi T. (2005) *The Issue of Yasukuni Shrine.* Tokyo: Satsuma-Shinho. (In Japanese)

Thompson, J. (2009) Apology, Historical Obligations and the Ethics of Memory, *Memory Studies*, 2(2), 195-210.

Todd, S. (2001) On Not Knowing the Other, or Learning from Levinas, *Philosophy of Education*, 68-74.

Todd, S. (2004) Teaching with Ignorance: questions of social justice, ethics and responsibility community, *Interchange*, 35(3), 337-352.

Wang, Z. (2009) Old Wounds, New Narratives: joint history textbook writing and peacebuilding in East Asia, *History and Memory: Studies in Representation of the Past*, 101(26), 1-16.

Yomiuri Press (2010) China-Japan Joint History Commission: [starkly] different historical recognitions exposed, February 2. (In Japanese)

PART 3

Education, Conflict and Development in Northern Uganda

CHAPTER 7

Fortifying Barriers: sexual violence as an obstacle to girls' school participation in Northern Uganda

MAUREEN MURPHY, LINDSAY STARK, MICHAEL WESSELLS, NEIL BOOTHBY & ALASTAIR AGER

SUMMARY Despite considerable research on barriers to girls' participation in education, little is understood about the experiences of female survivors of sexual violence as they interact with the school system. Using data from a 2007-08 longitudinal qualitative data set, the barriers to school enrolment were explored for survivors of sexual violence as well as other conflict-affected girls in Lira District, Northern Uganda. The results of the analysis suggest that all girls, regardless of their status as sexual violence survivors, face similar barriers to accessing education that need to be addressed in a holistic and comprehensive manner. Financial constraints, the quality of schools, and cultural barriers that do not prioritize girls' education, as well as the prevalence of early marriage and pregnancy, were common experiences for all girls enrolled in the study. Additionally, girls faced self-doubt and a lack of self-efficacy about their ability to achieve in school, which was compounded by bullying from peers and stigma from the community. For survivors of sexual violence these barriers were strengthened by virtue of their 'doubly disadvantaged' status. Additional support and targeted interventions are needed to empower this particularly vulnerable group to overcome the barriers impeding school enrolment.

Like for the young girls who have dropped studies,
I used to think that I was the only one but we are many.
(Sharon [1], survivor of sexual violence)

Introduction

Great progress has been made in the decade since the Dakar World Education Forum's pledge to achieve universal primary education by 2015. Overall, more students are now enrolling in school and, of these new enrolments, a rising percentage are female. However, despite a considerable reduction in the gender gap in primary education, school still remains out of reach for millions of girls in the developing world. While the total number of primary school aged children not enrolled has been reduced by more than 30 million since 1999, 54% of out-of-school children still are girls. Girls also remain much more likely than out-of-school boys to never attend school at all (UNESCO, 2010).

Research has emphasized time after time the importance of girls' education for development. Education has proven to be associated with economic growth (Klasen, 1999), lower fertility (Subbarao & Raney, 1995) and reduced rates of domestic violence (Sen, 1999). However, despite the almost universal acknowledgement of the importance of girls' education, many barriers to their full participation still remain. Researchers have found that these obstacles exist on a multitude of levels, including entrenched societal beliefs that do not prioritize female education, practices that create incentives for early marriage, and financial constraints such as school and supply fees (LeVine, 2006; Roby et al, 2008; Sutherland-Addy, 2008).

While in general there are numerous barriers to girls' participation in school, some circumstances have been seen to increase the likelihood that girls prematurely drop out of formal education. For example, early pregnancy has been associated with increased drop-out rates for girls (Eloundou-Enyegue, 2004; Grant & Hallman, 2009). Similarly, girls in conflict-affected settings are less likely to be enrolled in the formal education system for reasons that range from a lack of appropriate school facilities and qualified teachers to concerns regarding the safety of girls travelling to and from the school itself (Kirk, 2003).

However, despite considerable research on barriers to girls' participation in education, we do not yet fully understand the experiences of specific, vulnerable populations of girls as they interact with the school system. One such group is survivors of sexual violence, particularly those in armed conflict settings. Research on the intersection of gender-based violence and education has focused primarily on the immediate school environment. Researchers have concentrated on the unequal power dynamics between male teachers and female students, and male and female pupils as well as the vulnerability of students on their routes to and from school (Bisika et al, 2009; Leach & Machakanja, 2000). Despite the plethora of research on obstacles to achieving gender parity in education and on school-based violence, our understanding of the experiences of survivors of sexual violence and their decisions to participate in the formal school system remain underdeveloped. By drawing from the results of a 2007-08 longitudinal, qualitative research study undertaken by Columbia University's Care and Protection of Children (CPC) Learning Network and the non-governmental organization Christian Children's Fund – Uganda (now known as ChildFund International), this chapter examines the unique experiences and challenges faced by survivors of sexual violence in one context and provides a better understanding of their interactions with the formal education system.

Sexual Violence and the 'Doubly Disadvantaged'

Sexual violence is recognized as one of the foremost challenges facing women and girls around the world. Acts of sexual violence permeate societies from the most developed countries to the most impoverished nations and affect individuals regardless of race, ethnicity and class. A World Health Organization multi-country study (2005) on the prevalence of lifetime experiences of sexual violence estimated the range of those who experience some form of sexual violence to be between 6% (a city in Japan) and 59% (an Ethiopian province) among the 15 sites studied. Given the reticence of many survivors of sexual violence to speak about their experiences, research regarding the prevalence of sexual violence has been imprecise. However, this under-reporting of incidents only serves to make available estimates more alarming for their conservative nature. Additionally, adolescents and children may face unique and increased risks of sexual violence due to their limited ability to protect themselves against aggressors. One study, which reviewed justice system and rape crisis centre statistics in seven countries, found that between one-third and two-thirds of reported sexual assault victims were aged 15 years or younger (Heise et al, 1994). Also, studies of adolescents have found that peers and intimate partners are among the most common sources of sexual violence (Erulkar, 2004; Jewkes, 2005).

Situations of armed conflict have also been shown to increase the prevalence of sexual violence. The use of rape as a weapon of war has affected large numbers of young women (Milillo, 2006), and many adolescent women have been abducted into rebel groups (McKay & Mazurana, 2004; Wessells, 2006). In addition, conflict-affected populations are often displaced and forced to live in chaotic settings such as camps that have high levels of alcoholism and gender-based violence (Annan & Brier, 2009), including sexual exploitation and violence towards young women.

Survivors of gender-based violence experience many consequences, including higher risks for poor mental and physical health (Coker et al, 2000; McNutt et al, 2002). Survivors might experience post-traumatic stress disorder (Thompson, et al., 1999; Johnson et al, 2008), suicidal thoughts and attempts (Ellsberg et al, 2008), sexually transmitted diseases, eating disorders and chemical dependency (Koss & Heslet, 1992). Beyond the immediate physical and mental consequences, sexual violence survivors often experience negative reactions from their families and the community and their extreme social isolation (Sideris, 2003; Milillio, 2006). Social isolation itself is profoundly painful, and it creates even greater distress by blocking access to desired activities and making it difficult to fill the social roles that are expected of young women in their social context.

In addition, unmarried survivors of sexual violence who face pregnancy alone can encounter discrimination within the community and rejection from their families. For example, formerly recruited teenagers are often called 'rebel wives' and held at arm's length by the community (Wessells, 2006). These consequences can have long-term effects, as girls may face obstacles to achieving important milestones such as marriage due to their status as survivors of sexual violence. A study in Wakiso District, Uganda found that pregnant adolescents faced family and community rejection, violence and stigma. These girls were turned out from their homes, beaten by their parents, and faced economic struggles to provide for their children (Atuyambe et al, 2005).

As described above, girls are a disadvantaged group who face discrimination and heightened challenges when interacting with the formal education system. The term 'doubly disadvantaged' has been used to describe the experiences of socially excluded groups when interacting with the school system (Lewis & Lockheed, 2008). The same concept of overlapping challenges has relevance for the experiences of survivors of sexual violence. As the following research will describe, barriers that block girls' participation in school are significant. Experiences such as sexual violence, which serves to further stigmatize and isolate girls, can in fact strengthen and fortify these barriers to education.

The Study and Its Context

For roughly 20 years, Northern Uganda was engulfed in a civil war between Joseph Kony's Lord's Resistance Army (LRA) and the Government of Uganda. The conflict was characterized by its brutality and by the abduction of children from their homes. These children were frequently used as porters, conscripted into fighting units or made 'bush wives' for commanders. The years of conflict left few, if any, areas of Northern Uganda untouched by violence.

The circumstances in Northern Uganda reflect many of the difficulties of educating girls in conflict-affected situations today. Many researchers have posited that chronic exposure to violence can 'normalize' violent acts in the community, perpetuating instability even after a conflict has reached an official end (Hume, 2004). Lending support to this theory, rates of sexual and gender-based violence have proven to be particularly high in the conflict-affected areas of Northern Uganda. One recent study found that 51.7% of respondents experienced intimate partner violence in the previous year while 41% had been forced by their husbands to have sex in the same period (Stark et al, 2010). The same study found that 5% of respondents reported an incident of rape by a non-domestic partner in the previous year. While this study reflects violence rates experienced by adults as opposed to adolescents, it indicates the pervasiveness of violence within these communities.

In addition to the continued culture of violence, Northern Uganda has also struggled to maintain girls' enrolment in school. One major barrier to school enrolment was eliminated in 1997 with the advent of universal primary education (UPE). This legislation removed formal primary school fees, thereby reducing financial barriers and greatly increasing school enrolment throughout Uganda. However, while the elimination of formal fees reduced financial barriers overall, informal fees such as parent–teacher association fees, uniform fees and other hidden costs still hinder school enrolment, particularly for the poorest segments of Ugandan society (Women's Commission for Refugee Women and Children, 2005).

Since the advent of UPE, the gender gap in primary enrolment across Uganda has effectively been eliminated, as the gross gender parity index for primary school enrolment improved from 0.80 in 1990 to 1.01 in 2007 (UNESCO, 2010). However, inequalities still persist, with only 20% of girls enrolled in secondary education (compared to 25% of boys) and a large percentage of over-aged girls still enrolled at the primary level (UNESCO, 2010). There are also marked gender disparities in achievement, with girls scoring lower than their male counterparts on Primary School Leaving exams (Murphy, 2003). The gender gap in education is also greater in war-affected Northern Uganda when compared with the rest of the country. The most recent Demographic and Health Survey (2006) reported that 35% of females and 17% of males in Northern Uganda had no education. These numbers show a considerable difference when compared to the overall percentage of Ugandans with no education (overall in Uganda 23% of females and 12% of men have never attended school) (Uganda Bureau of Statistics and Macro International Inc., 2007).

The Study

From June 2007 to August 2008, Columbia University's CPC Learning Network and ChildFund International undertook a longitudinal, qualitative study to explore the experiences and understandings of girls affected by sexual violence in Lira, Northern Uganda. This study provides valuable insight into the experiences of girls, half of whom were admitted survivors of sexual violence, and their challenges accessing the formal education system. The goals of the Columbia–ChildFund study were purposefully broad and varied in an attempt to capture information on different facets of these girls' lives. Overall, the research aimed to explore the experiences of girls after an incident of sexual violence, and to learn about what support they had received and what support they believed would improve their situation. For the purposes of this chapter, we will focus specifically on the theme most relevant to our area of interest: the experiences of survivors of sexual violence when re-entering or continuing within the education system.

The study consisted of a series of four semi-structured, open-ended interviews, each 20 minutes to 1 hour in length. The first and second interviews were administered within a few weeks of one another from January through August 2007. There was a period of approximately six months between each of the subsequent interviews, with the third interviews conducted between January and March 2008 and the fourth interviews between June and August of the same year. While the overall length of the study was short, this period was a time of immense change for the participants, which the study sought to capture through its longitudinal design. The study included 30 participants, aged 13-17, who were initially drawn from one of four Internally Displaced Persons' (IDP) camps (Agweng, Ayami, Barr and Ogur) in Lira District, Northern Uganda. During the course of the study, most respondents returned to their home villages from these camps. During this process two respondents were lost to follow up.

Survivors of sexual violence were initially identified through IDP camp records. Subsequently, snowball sampling was utilized to further identify survivors through those already engaged in the study. The second half of the sample, composed of girls from the general camp population, was selected using random sampling in each camp. This half of the sample was not a comparison group but rather a source of information about how other girls who were not known survivors viewed issues of sexual violence and about community and peer attitudes toward survivors. Participants in the research received in-kind compensation (pots, school uniforms, etc.) at the conclusion of the study.

Interviewers utilized a semi-structured interview guide that focused broadly on the girl's life story and how circumstances changed after she was displaced. In addition, survivors of sexual violence were asked about their experiences *after* the incident while girls selected from the general population were asked about their attitudes and perceptions of gender-based violence. Since the girls selected from the general population were not directly asked if they had experienced sexual violence, it is possible they had experienced incidents that went undiscovered during the course of the study.

Effects of the War on Girl Survivors

The 2007-08 Columbia–ChildFund study occurred amidst a time of tremendous change for Northern Uganda, which was reflected in the narratives of the participants' lives. All study participants had been raised during the 20-year conflict between the LRA and the Government of Uganda. All were displaced from their home villages due to the war and were residing in IDP camps in Lira District, Northern Uganda at the time of the initial interview. While these camps were rife with gender-based violence, alcoholism, poverty and disease (Médicins Sans Frontières, 2004), Lira District overall was not as severely affected by the war as Gulu or other districts in the North. A 2006 truce between warring parties increased hopes for peace in the region and consequently most of the study participants had returned to their home villages by the time the final interview occurred during the summer of 2008.

During the course of this study not only was the environment of Northern Uganda rapidly transforming but the circumstances of the participants' lives also underwent numerous changes. When the first and second interviews took place between January and August 2007, only two of the participants were married. One participant had a child and two were pregnant. Approximately half the participants (16 girls) were enrolled in school though many were over age for their class. By the time of the final interview 12 to 18 months later, in which 28 of the original 30 participants agreed to be interviewed, 10 girls were married, five had children and four were pregnant. Only eight girls were enrolled in school.

Effects of the war were widespread. Almost all the girls spoke of increasing poverty caused by the loss of land and destruction of crops due to the war. Struggles for food and basic necessities such as clothes, school supplies and medicines were typical. Many of the study participants were direct witnesses to violent attacks on their villages and four were abducted by the LRA. Violence within their communities was pervasive. Beyond rebel attacks, most girls also spoke of violence within the camps or in their homes. For example, Vivian spoke of violence she had witnessed: 'One day my mother started to quarrel and later it reached up to the level of fighting and [my father] fought my mother seriously to the extent of vomiting blood'. Similar themes of intimate partner violence, among the girls' husbands, fathers and uncles, were seen throughout the girls' narratives.

Additionally, continued displacement affected the ability of the participants to remain in school. Many schools were closed due to instability and attacks on communities. Even when schools remained open, many teachers fled to larger towns to escape the violence. Children were particular targets of the LRA and many were unable to walk to school due to the risk of abduction on the roads. Annie describes the situation: 'It was very difficult to live because there were no schools. The teachers had also fled and the school pupils were just there like that!' This lack of schools and teachers, and the continued instability, contributed to patterns of drop-out and re-enrolment evident in the girls' narratives.

Barriers to Education

While many of the life experiences of the participants were negative, a feeling of hope was central to many of their stories. Vital to this conviction was a sense of possibility for the future, particularly through participation in the education system. Education and the opportunities it provides were prominent themes throughout the interviews, with many girls emphasizing the importance of staying in school both for future financial security as well as for their own feelings of self-worth. Of the 14 girls who were not enrolled in school during the initial interviews, nearly half spoke explicitly of their disappointment at not being in school or their desire to be enrolled. Vivian, who was not enrolled in school, explains her feelings: 'For me I always think that I should study because now that I do not study I feel bad'. Staying in school is seen by many of the girls as a means to a better, more secure future. For example, Kizza stated, 'if you have not studied you are as good as useless' and Lucy explained, 'I live better in a way that when I finish my education maybe, by good luck, I will get a job, it will make my life easy'. However, the high hopes these girls had for their education did not translate into school enrolment. Participation in the education system declined throughout the year with only 8 of the 28 girls who participated in the final interview enrolled in school by the end of the study, a dramatic decline of a fifth of the sample in the space of one year. While the participants were vocal about their desire to remain in school, it appears that other factors overshadowed this hope and prevented them from continuing with their education.

All of the girls enrolled in the study spoke of barriers to school enrolment. Both survivors of sexual violence as well as those girls drawn from the general population encountered many of the same struggles as a consequence of living in poor, displaced, rural Ugandan communities. Lack of funds for schooling, lack of proper supplies, and cultural hurdles that do not prioritize girls' education were all barriers to school enrolment. Beyond those widespread challenges, the perceived frequency of sexual violence created additional barriers for girls. Families often decided to remove their daughters from school or encouraged early marriage as a way to protect the girls' future prospects in light of potential sexual violence. Girls who had encountered sexual violence prior to marriage were often referred to as 'spoilt'. While this term was not reserved exclusively for survivors of violence, as any girl who 'started to make love at an early age' (Annie) could be considered 'spoilt', this term was primarily used when describing the experiences of survivors.

At the time of the initial interview, survivors of sexual violence had a slightly worse record of school enrolment, with 7 of 15 enrolled compared to 9 of 15 of girls who were not known survivors of sexual violence. However, by the time of the final interview only 5 of 14 survivors and 3 of 14 girls from the general population were enrolled in school.

Financial Constraints

One of the most common barriers to school enrolment for the entire sample, cited by 22 out of the 30 participants, was financial. Wartime displacement and fear of LRA raids limited freedom of movement and subsequently decreased access to land for agriculture. This insecurity hampered the ability of communities to engage in their typical means of income generation – agriculture – and appreciably reduced financial stability. Sarah explains:

> My life was difficult ... when violent things are surrounding your life it makes life hard. Like people even used not to dig because every time you have to flee and you have to be in the bush and people don't go to the garden, so life was hard on my side and there were no girls studying.

For those citing financial concerns as a barrier to school enrolment, many spoke of the lack of sufficient funds to pay the school or examination fees required for enrolment and to advance to the next class level.[2] Lucy describes her experience: 'For me ... if there was somebody to pay for my school fees, I would be now in senior one but since there is nobody I am still repeating primary seven'. In addition to the lack of funding for school fees, girls also lacked basic items required for school enrolment such as school uniforms or supplies. As Sharon states, '[people] make it very easy to leave studies because money for buying all the items for studies is not there – things like 96 page book, pens, mathematical set and others'. Similarly, the lack of ability to buy underwear or sanitary pads presented another significant struggle for girls who had reached the age of menstruation. Jendyose explained the consequences for girls who did not have the proper supplies during menstruation: 'They have a hard time in school to the extent that they may even stop their studies because whenever they are at school they are always teased'.

It is not only the direct costs that are associated with education that cause challenges to school enrolment, but also the loss of income associated with a child who is in school and therefore not generating agricultural or other income while they are in school. For some families, the immediate needs of the household supersede the desire to keep a child in school. Vivian explains her situation: 'My father had a cough and whenever they tested they never found anything so they told me to come back home and help the other children with digging'. In some cases, the decision to keep a child out of school may simply be a necessary choice to ensure the survival of the household.

Financial concerns were slightly more prevalent in the concerns of survivors of sexual violence, with more than half of these respondents specifically citing this as a barrier to school enrolment while slightly fewer than half of non-victims mentioned finances as a challenge to school participation. Families are sometimes less willing to provide financing for girls who are viewed as 'spoilt' as a result of sexual violence. Juliet, who was a survivor of sexual violence, explains, 'Sometimes I think that people have refused to pay my school fees and yet if the incident had not happened they were going to pay my school fees. My friends are going to school and I'm just seated at home, I'm useless'. Thus sexual violence imposed burdens of stigma and raised significant barriers to school participation.

School Quality

The quality of education and the availability of supplies as well as teachers were identified as barriers by many of the study participants. In particular, these concerns were emphasized as part of the effect of the war and the girls' displacement from their homes. During the conflict, insecurity affected the ability of teachers to regularly attend class. Martha described: 'That time when I came to the camp there was no education because the teachers had also run away'. Even when schools were available the lack of quality of the education was a concern of girls. As Helen describes: 'They studied but the teaching was weak because there were few teachers in the school and even we used to not to do examination. If there were to be exams we were not going to pass because of poor teaching and studies of no value'.

Similarly, the lack of certification or higher-level education of the teachers themselves who taught the girls during their time in the camps was mentioned. For example, Esther explains, 'Now the teachers teaching people in the camps – some of them have just sat P.7 (primary seven)'. Overcrowding due to a lack of sufficient teachers and infrastructure was also a problem during the girls' time in the camp. Laura explains, 'nowadays there are not even enough desks and pupils sit on the floor'.

Cultural Barriers

It is evident from their narratives that girls in Northern Uganda face many challenges as they strive to continue their education. Financial, social and cultural barriers collide to limit the enrolment of girls. Cultural judgements still persist that do not value a girl's education and conclude that the costs incurred to send a daughter to school are not worthwhile. Annie describes her experience: 'I really had problems with my parents in that they refused to pay for my school fees while they were paying for my brothers', the reason being that girls are not meant to study'. Likewise Jane details her father's view on schooling: 'He said we are now old girls and girls are not supposed to study for long'. The idea that it is a waste of money for girls to be enrolled in school is prevalent within these communities. As girls who marry take the investment in education along with them to their husband's family, many parents choose to not educate girls.

Girls' education is not only seen as an inefficient use of resources but is also hampered by cultural stereotypes that reinforce the view that girls are not intelligent or are unable to learn. The girls commonly related stories where they or girls in the community were referred to as 'useless'. As Juliet describes: 'The parents say that, whether or not she wants, she has to get married. Even if you go to school it will not help anyone, girls are useless'. Similarly, Esther explains: 'They [my parents] used to tell me that there are problems and that I should just get married, because there was nothing. I was going to sit around at home doing [nothing] since I was even very stupid'. This perceived lack of ability, along with the belief that educating a girl is a poor financial investment, creates considerable barriers for girls' enrolment in the education system.

Early Marriage

Associated with the pervasive financial difficulties described above is the pressure for young girls to leave school and enter into marriage at an early age. At the time of the initial interview, two study participants were married. While both were survivors of sexual violence, one was actually married to her perpetrator. Neither of these girls had continued with schooling after their marriage. By the final interview one year later, 10 girls were married and, similarly, none remained in school.

Reasons given for marriage were typically financial. Marriage can be used as a mechanism to alleviate financial pressures on a girl's household by reducing the costs required to support a daughter. Not only do families save money by reducing their costs but the family typically also gains from the transaction due to the common practice of paying a dowry to the family of the girl upon marriage. Ruth explains: 'because of the dowry they force their daughters to get married while others just because of a misconception that girls are nothing'. Marrying off a daughter is an important economic engine for families in resource-poor settings. Many families do not view the benefits of further study to outweigh their immediate economic needs. Annie details:

> They can easily say that this girl even if we take good care of and we send her to school, she will not even help us. She will help a different clan. She is just wasting our money for nothing. So it is better if she gets married, so that the money received from her marriage her brother can use for going to school or getting married.

The problem of early marriage is also linked to the problem of sexual violence. Early marriage is seen by many in the community as a preventative act to keep girls from becoming 'spoilt'. Pearl describes: 'They force us saying we would get spoilt if we don't get married'. In this way, early marriage is thought of as protection of a girl's virtue and value. Sandra details an experience she observed: 'Like recently at the end of the school term, there is a man who came to marry a school girl and the father also accepted that the girl may receive the money for marriage. After all girls have no future in education because you might get spoilt for nothing'. When attending school, girls are outside the realm of parental protection and control. They are exposed to boys and men in the community and, in the eyes of the family, are increasing their likelihood of being 'spoilt'.

Cultural pressures for girls to marry also influence the girls' attitudes regarding their own futures. Beliefs that girls 'should' leave school and get married are reinforced by these family and community views. Annie noted an example of a girl in her community who conceded to the pressures and discontinued her schooling. She explains:

> And on her side she begins to think that she has grown and the breast has grown big too. So she begins to see herself as somebody fully grown because she cannot continue with studies and because she is dull and cannot pass exams in class and the pupils laugh at her at school. So this brings the idea of marriage and she gets married when she is under age.

Pregnancy

Another important factor that causes girls to drop out of school is pregnancy. Support systems for pregnant girls in low resource settings are limited, and negative community responses towards pregnant, unmarried girls are common. Sandra explains: 'If you get pregnant and leave school, people take you as someone of no value'. In addition, the responsibilities of girls with children are different from those without. Juggling these priorities can be demanding and makes it difficult, if not impossible, to remain in the school system. Mary states: 'you know sometimes I think that if there was any way I could remove the baby, I could have gone back to school to study and be free from all this marital stress'. Ultimately, of the nine girls in this study who were pregnant or had already given birth by the final interview, none were enrolled in school.

In addition to leaving the school system, unmarried pregnancy can also result in increasingly isolating social consequences. Community members sometimes encourage their daughters to avoid associating with survivors of sexual violence in order to protect the reputation of their daughters or out of fear that bad behaviour may spread. Laura details her experience: 'Not studying has made my life so hard, the mothers of my friends complain that I have spoilt their daughter and made them to produce early since I don't study any more'.

Stigma and Bullying

Devaluing the education of girls is another significant barrier towards enrolment. This is particularly true for survivors of sexual violence who not only have the cultural stigmatization of being female but also are viewed by the community as 'spoilt' due to their early sexual experiences. Following exposure to sexual violence, community acceptance and reintegration are important markers of the ability of the victim to return to her normal daily life. Ten out of fifteen survivors of sexual violence in this study mentioned community reactions or peer bullying as barriers towards school enrolment. The willingness of the community at large to accept the victim as a fully functioning member of the community is essential in the rehabilitation process (Wessells, 2006; Stark, 2006; Betancourt et al, 2010).

Community reactions can also influence the parents' willingness to fully accept the return of their daughters after a rape event. Cultural norms that necessitate turning out such girls are reinforced through negative community pressures. For example, Juliet examines the reaction of her community to a girl who had experienced a rape: 'They say this girl is a prostitute, useless. If they were my parent they would chase me away from home, and not send me to school'. Similarly, Sharon describes:

> There are some people who support that training and they are fond of encouraging those girls to read/struggle very hard, while there are others who say once a girl is impregnated, she must definitely go to her husband and not go back to school again. Because they normally say that once a girl is impregnated, that girl is a spoiled girl and she would just be wasting money if she is to be taken back to school again.

These negative community attitudes can be a powerful barrier for survivors of sexual violence who wish to remain in school.

Support from family, community and peers before and after an incident of sexual violence can be different, and may affect school enrolment. For example, Juliet details her experience: 'Before [the rape] happened people used to encourage me to go to school but now I'm always worried because people always remind [me] of what happened'. The idea that the community 'knows' what has happened to these girls emerged as an important theme in their interviews. Lucy detailed her experience in the following way: 'For me I just decided to start absenting myself because the moment I could go to school pupils could abuse me and say you see that girl who was raped and I feel ashamed. So the best I could do was to stop going to school'. Having to contend with bullying from peers at school further contributed to the survivors' sense of isolation and was a factor in some girls' decisions to withdraw from school.

Internal Barriers

To read these accounts, it is impossible not to notice the frequent descriptions of the girls as 'useless', 'worthless', etc. The idea that girls are not as smart as, or do not have as much potential as boys is a prevalent cultural stereotype. These cultural views have influenced girls' beliefs in themselves both in regard to their experiences in general as well as their success in the education system. For example, Sarah explains, 'For me I see that God did not give me the gift of that one [being bright], and it has made me have less interest in it [school]'.

These feelings of low self-efficacy and self-worth are only exacerbated by experiences of sexual violence. These experiences not only change the way a girl is perceived by her parents, community and peers but also the way she perceives herself. Self-esteem and self-efficacy towards completing school can be greatly affected by an incident of sexual violence. Faith describes her experience: 'The incident that happened has changed my life in the sense that for me I used to worry and think of anything but now that it has happened to me, whenever I am alone I begin to think about it and I cry then I think that I may not go back to school'.

Conclusion and Recommendations

Prior to and during the course of this study, a majority of both survivors of sexual violence and girls from the general population dropped out of school, with approximately one-third of the sample remaining enrolled by the end of the study. The experiences of these 30 girls show that achieving gender parity in education still faces many challenges, particularly in post-conflict settings where systems and resources are overstretched and violence commonplace. Furthermore, these results suggest that all girls, regardless of their status as sexual violence survivors, face similar barriers to accessing education that need to be addressed in a holistic and comprehensive manner. For survivors of sexual violence these barriers are strengthened by virtue of their 'doubly disadvantaged' status. Additional support and targeted interventions are needed to empower this particularly vulnerable group to overcome the barriers impeding school enrolment.

These results demonstrate the importance of the social environment and social networks in influencing girls' participation in the education system. As detailed in the girls' narratives, it is the interaction of multiple influences – culture, family, peers, the school and the community – that ultimately affect their ability to remain engaged in the education system. For example, culturally preconceived beliefs that regard females as mothers and wives rather than educated professionals frame the reactions and support of community members when girls are enrolled in school. Lack of community support can influence parental decisions to enrol their daughters, and negative family and community beliefs may affect girls' self-efficacy and self-assurance to succeed within the education system.

Understanding the interactions of these social networks and their contributions to girls' educational outcomes can best be realized by utilizing a social ecological framework for analysis (Boothby et al, 2006). Seen through this lens, it is the dynamic interaction of girls with family, peer and community networks and the interactions of these networks with each other in cultural context that uniquely shapes each girl's educational outcome. For survivors of sexual violence, this means girls face barriers and constraints on a multitude of levels and it is not only their status as survivors of sexual violence that hinders their participation in the education system. This viewpoint suggests that interventions to reduce gender disparities in educational enrolment and attainment should be grounded in an understanding of the interrelated nature of factors that affect girls' participation in the education system.

At the societal level, any change in the status of girls within the education system needs to begin with a change in family, community and cultural views of girls. As both sexual violence and unequal school participation have their roots in harmful values and norms towards women, programmes need to help establish new perspectives on women and girls. Engaging with local leadership, providing community education, and ensuring legal referral mechanisms are in place, so that when sexual violence occurs there are consequences, are all essential steps to improve the status of women in these communities.

To promote community ownership and reduce the trepidation men sometimes feel when programmes promoting new gender norms begin, both women and men must be engaged equally in the planning and implementation process of any programme. Additionally, underlying causes of violent acts, such as consuming poverty and powerlessness, must be addressed in the community for lasting change to occur.

In addition to these wide-ranging reforms, efforts to achieve universal primary education and full gender parity require disaggregating views of 'the child'. The overarching classification of girls as one homogeneous group is insufficient to characterize the range of experiences and challenges young women face when growing up in the developing world. While the challenges and barriers to education are similar for all girls, incidents of sexual violence can lead to further isolation, which can fortify barriers to the education system. Particularly vulnerable groups, such as survivors of sexual violence, require interventions that acknowledge the special concerns relevant to this group and the provision of extra supports.

Stigma and a lack of community acceptance for victims of sexual violence are considerable obstacles for this 'doubly disadvantaged group' to fully engage in the education system. The results of this study reinforce the findings of other researchers (Wessells, 2006; Stark, 2006; Betancourt et al, 2010) who have shown the power of stigma in creating barriers to community reintegration. These studies have also shown that community and family acceptance can act as a mediating factor and can improve reintegration outcomes for victims of sexual violence. These mechanisms for acceptance and reintegration already exist in communities around the world and interventions should strive to identify and bolster these community-originated processes as opposed to imposing outsider-driven methodologies for reintegration.

To improve the experiences of survivors of sexual violence within the school systems, educators need to work with social workers and other service providers to enhance the protective environment of the school so that it is a safe place for survivors. Teachers need training to understand the unique needs of vulnerable groups such as survivors of sexual violence. In addition, social workers need to be cognisant of educational opportunities and increased barriers for survivors and be ready to assist them in navigating the system.

Gender-based violence and the gender gap in education are intrinsically related, as both challenges have their basis in the unequal power dynamics between women and men. Ultimately gender-based violence and the lack of gender parity in education reflect the low status of girls in many developing world communities. This lack of status is reflected again and again in the prevalence of certain obstacles – lack of empowerment, forced early marriage, financial constraints, etc. – seen in a variety of communities around the global south. While these barriers affect all girls in the developing world, these challenges are exacerbated for survivors of sexual violence because of their increased isolation from the community and the physical and psychological consequences they encounter due their status as survivors of sexual violence. Comprehensive programming that addresses the unique needs of these vulnerable subgroups, while also tackling the larger barriers that all girls face, is needed if educational access and opportunity are to become realities for all girls.

Notes

[1] All names have been changed to protect the identity of study participants.

[2] Although formal school fees were abolished at the time of the study, many participants noted the continuation of informal charging.

References

Annan, J. & Brier, M. (2009) The Risk of Return: intimate partner violence in Northern Uganda's armed conflict, *Social Science and Medicine*, 70, 152-159.

Atuyambe, L., Mirembe, F., Johansson, A., Kirumira, E.K. & Faxelid, E. (2005) Experiences of Pregnant Adolescents: voices from Wakiso district, Uganda, *African Health Sciences*, 5(4), 304-309.

Betancourt, T.S., Agnew-Blais, J., Gilman, S.E., Williams, D.R. & Ellise, B.H. (2010) Past Horrors, Present Struggles: the role of stigma in the association between war experiences and psychosocial adjustment among former child soldiers in Sierra Leone, *Social Science and Medicine*, 70(1), 17-26.

Bisika, T., Ntata, P. & Konyani, S. (2009) Gender-Violence and Education in Malawi: a study of violence against girls as an obstruction to universal primary school education, *Journal of Gender Studies*, 18(3), 287-294.

Boothby, N., Strang, A. & Wessells, M.G. (2006) *A World Turned Upside Down: social ecological approaches to children in war zones*. Bloomfield: Kumarian Press.

Coker, A.L., Smith, P.H., Bethea, L., King, M.R. & McKeown, R.E. (2000) Physical Health Consequences of Physical and Psychological Intimate Partner Violence, *Archives of Family Medicine*, 9(5), 451-457.

Ellsberg, M., Jansen, H.A., Heise, L., Watts, C.H. & Garcia-Moreno, C. (2008) Intimate Partner Violence and Women's Physical and Mental Health, *The Lancet*, 371 (9619), 1165-1172.

Eloundou-Enyegue, P.M. (2004) Pregnancy-Related Dropouts and Gender Inequality in Education: a life-table approach and application to Cameroon, *Demography*, 41(3), 509-528.

Erulkar, A.S. (2004) The Experience of Sexual Coercion among Young People in Kenya, *International Family Planning Perspectives*, 30, 182-189.

Grant, M.J. & Hallman, K.K. (2009) Pregnancy-Related School Dropout and Prior School Performance in KwaZulu-Natal, South Africa, *Studies in Family Planning*, 39(4), 369-382.

Heise, L., Pitanguy, J. & Germain, A. (1994) Violence against Women: the hidden health burden. Discussion Paper. Washington, DC: World Bank.

Hume, M. (2004) 'It's as if you don't know, because you don't do anything about it': gender and violence in El Salvador, *Environment and Urbanization*, 16(2), 63-72.

Jejeebhoy, S.J., Shah, I.H. & Thapa, S. (2005) *Sex without Consent: young people in developing countries*. London: Zed Books.

Jewkes, R. (2005) Non-consensual Sex among South African Youth: prevalence of coerced sex and discourses of control and desire, in S.J. Jejeebhoy, I.H. Shah & S. Thapa (Eds) *Sex without Consent: young people in developing countries*, 86-95. London: Zed Books.

Johnson, K., Asher, J., Rosborough, S., et al (2008) Association of Combatant Status and Sexual Violence with Health and Mental Health Outcomes in Postconflict Liberia, *JAMA*, 300(6), 676-690.

Kirk, J. (2003) Women in Contexts of Crisis: gender and conflict. http://portal.unesco.org/education/en/file_download.php/5a4d022ff7d20aaa539c844566a718a7Women+in+contexts+of+crisis.+Gender+and+conflict.doc (accessed 10 February 2010).

Klasen, S. (1999) *Does Gender Inequality Reduce Growth and Development? Evidence from Cross Country Regressions*. Washington, DC: World Bank.

Koss, M.P. & Heslet, L. (1992) Somatic Consequences of Violence against Women, *Archives of Family Medicine*, 1(1), 53-59.

Leach, F. & Machakanja, P. (2000) *Preliminary Investigation of the Abuse of Girls in Zimbabwean Junior Secondary Schools*. London: Department for International Development.

LeVine, S. (2006) Getting in, Dropping out, and Staying On: determinants of girls' school attendance in the Kathmandu valley in Nepal, *Anthropology and Education Quarterly*, 37(1), 21-41.

Lewis, M. & Lockheed, M. (2008) *Social Exclusion and the Gender Gap*. Washington, DC: World Bank.

McKay, S. & Mazurana, D. (2004) *Where are the Girls? Girls' Fighting Forces in Northern Uganda, Sierra Leone and Mozambique: their lives during and after the war*. Montreal: Rights and Democracy: International Center for Human Rights and Democratic Development.

McNutt, L.A., Carlson, B.E., Persaud, M. & Postmus, J. (2002) Cumulative Abuse Experiences, Physical Health and Health Behaviors, *Annals of Epidemiology*, 12(2), 123-130.

Médicins Sans Frontières (2004) *Internally Displaced Camps in Lira and Pader, Northern Uganda.* Kampala: MSF – Holland.

Milillo, D. (2006) Rape as a Tactic of War: social and psychological perspectives, *Affilia: Journal of Women and Social Work*, 21(2), 196-205.

Murphy, L. (2003) Does Increasing Access Mean Decreasing Quality? An Assessment of Uganda's Progress towards Reaching EFA Goals. Background paper for EFA Monitoring Report 2003. Paris: UNESCO.

Roby, J.L., Lambert, M.J. & Lambert, J. (2008) Barriers to Girls' Education in Mozambique at Household and Community Levels: an exploratory study, *International Journal of Social Welfare*, 18(4), 342-353.

Sen, P. (1999) Enhancing Women's Choices in Responding to Domestic Violence in Calcutta: a comparison of employment and education, *European Journal of Development Research*, 11(2), 65-86.

Sideris, T. (2003) War, Gender and Culture: Mozambican women refugees, *Social Science and Medicine*, 56(4), 713-724.

Stark, L. (2006) Cleansing the Wounds of War: an examination of traditional healing, psychosocial health and reintegration in Sierra Leone, *Intervention*, 6(4), 206-218.

Stark, L., Roberts, L., Wheaton, W., et al (2010) Measuring Violence against Women amidst War and Displacement in Northern Uganda Using the 'Neighborhood Method', *Journal of Epidemiology and Community Health*, 64(12), 1056-1061.

Subbarao, K. & Raney, L. (1995) Social Gains from Female Education, *Economic Development and Cultural Change*, 44(1), 105-128.

Sutherland-Addy, E. (2008) *Gender Equity in Junior and Senior Secondary Education in Sub-Saharan Africa.* Washington, DC: World Bank.

Thompson, M., Kaslow, N., Kingree, J., et al (1999) Partner Abuse and Posttraumatic Stress Disorder as Risk Factors for Suicide Attempts in a Sample of Low-Income, Inner-City Women, *Journal of Traumatic Stress*, 12(1), 59-72.

Uganda Bureau of Statistics (UBOS) and Macro International Inc. (2007) *Uganda Demographic and Health Survey 2006.* Calverton, MD: UBOS and Macro International Inc.

UNESCO (2010) *EFA Global Monitoring Report 2010: Reaching the Marginalized.* Paris: UNESCO and Oxford University Press.

Wessells, M.G. (2006) *Child Soldiers: from violence to protection.* Cambridge, MA: Harvard University Press.

Women's Commission for Refugee Women and Children (2005) *Learning in a War Zone: education in Northern Uganda.* New York: Women's Commission for Refugee Women and Children.

World Health Organization (WHO) (2005) *WHO Multi Country Study on Women's Health and Domestic Violence against Women.* Geneva: WHO.

CHAPTER 8

Teachers' Perceptions of the Effects of Young People's War Experiences on Teaching and Learning in Northern Uganda

BETTY AKULLU EZATI,
CORNELIUS SSEMPALA & PETER SSENKUSU

SUMMARY Worldwide education has been heralded as one of the ways of instilling values such as respect for differences, mutual tolerance in post-conflict situations and peaceful coexistence. Hence both governments and non-governmental organizations have focused on the promotion of education as part of peacebuilding efforts. Yet, long-running conflicts and wars affect schools and classroom experiences in ways that have not yet been fully understood. Using data from an ongoing research project, this chapter explores how experiences of conflict continue to affect teachers and young people's relations and possibilities in the classroom. This chapter shows that increased aggressiveness, indiscipline and low academic ambition among learners, and low morale and motivation among teachers are common characteristics of post-war teaching and learning. The main lesson from this chapter is that war-related experiences continue to affect teachers and learners and to influence classroom dynamics in particular ways; these affect the possibilities for education to contribute towards peacebuilding and call for interventions that address teachers' and learners' post-conflict needs.

Introduction

Literature on post-conflict reconstruction highlights the role of education in peacebuilding. It illustrates the importance of schools as sources of intervention and as instruments to overcome violence and improve respect for humanity (Boyden & Ryder, 1996). Many suggestions are put forward for the ways in which education might contribute towards peacebuilding; for instance, the curriculum, textbooks and teachers might be used to mitigate conflict in school settings (Smith & Vaux, 2003); schools might teach children to be peace makers (Harris, 2000); integrating students previously schooled separately might break down barriers between groups (Smith & Neill, 2006); and skills of literacy, numeracy and critical thinking provided by basic education might be important for sustainable development and social equity (Miller & Affolter, 2002). Moreover, basic education might go a long way in instilling values of respect for difference, mutual tolerance, sharing, participation and cooperation. Despite this emerging research and many normative statements concerning education's crucial role in promoting peace, little empirical evidence exists to throw light on how teachers and learners engage with each other in post-conflict contexts.

It is clear that for effective peacebuilding to take place through schools, a better understanding of the processes at play within post-conflict classrooms is required. Since they are the 'life blood' of the education system (Buckland, 2005), many have suggested that peacebuilding education requires well-prepared teachers. Likewise, children and young people and their well-being and ability to learn are certainly critical to any peacebuilding effects that education might have. Yet, research on the challenges teachers face in catering for students' needs during and after conflict is scarce, as is research that illuminates the ways in which the conflict experiences of teachers and learners affect their classroom interaction. Thus, empirically based, situated knowledge around learners' needs in the post-conflict context and the kind of preparation that teachers need to address them is limited. It is pertinent, therefore, to further explore the effects of war on education – to understand the ways in which war experience affects teaching and learning and the relationships of teachers and learners in classrooms – if schools are to effectively contribute to peacebuilding.

This chapter explores how experiences of conflict remain with teachers, children and young people, and affect their experiences, relationships and possibilities in the classroom by focusing on the post-conflict situation in Northern Uganda. In particular, this chapter highlights how the effects of the region's conflict translate into classroom experiences of teachers and learners. Before outlining the research findings and exploring their relevance in regard to peacebuilding education, however, it is necessary to introduce the research context: the post-conflict situation in Northern Uganda.

War in Northern Uganda

Describing the effects of the 20 years (1986-2007) of war in Northern Uganda between the Lord's Resistance Army (LRA) and the Ugandan armed forces, researchers assert that it eroded security, kept people in perpetual fear of torture, mutilation and rape, displaced about 1.5 million people, and led to loss of lives, destruction of property and the abduction of 25,000 children

(Emry & Heninger, 2005; Erenreich, 2005; Global Child Report, 2004). The number of children involved in conflict in Northern Uganda is greater still as others have been recruited into the fighting forces. In addition to soldiering roles, children were also used as spies, porters, sex slaves, domestic workers and miners. At present, children and young people in Northern Uganda aged 4-22 years were born during and have lived through war. As one child in Northern Uganda describes: 'If you are under 20 and living here, you have known virtually nothing else your whole life but what it is like to live in a community enduring armed conflict – conflict in which you are the prime target' (cited by Singer, 2005, p. 41).

As a result of the war, a quarter of a million children over the age of 10 have lost one or both parents (Ministry of Education and Sports [MoES], 2008). About 70% of the people in Northern Uganda survive thanks to non-governmental organization (NGO) assistance and 95% live in absolute poverty (Higgins, 2009), many of them in internally displaced people's (IDP) camps where families live in harsh conditions characterized by shortage of basic necessities and social services. About two million Northern Ugandans moved to IDP camps as the conflict escalated; they nonetheless lived in constant fear of being attacked by the rebels, as the security even within the camps was unpredictable. According to Gulu District statistics (2005), there were 24 camps in Gulu District – one of the four districts that make up the region of Northern Uganda – 10 of which were situated in areas with no health care at all.

Another form of displacement typical in Northern Uganda during the war was euphemistically called 'night commuting'. This was a term used to refer to people who travelled daily to town centres in search of safer places to sleep than their rural homes where the threat of kidnap by the LRA was high. A report by Médicins Sans Frontières (2004) indicates that a large number of people, mostly children, left their homes each evening in search of a safe place to sleep. Some walked as many as 15 kilometres, starting the journey just as night fell and coming all the way back in the morning. Between 40,000 and 50,000 people travelled daily to town centres in the Acholi districts of Gulu, Pader and Kitgum.

Sexual violence was also a major problem throughout the war and in IDP camps. Emry (2004), in a UNICEF commissioned study on sexual and gender-based violence, reports that adolescent girls and women night commuters were often sexually assaulted or raped as they travelled to their sleeping spaces at night. The same study revealed that rape and child sexual abuse had become 'normal' in Pabbo IDP camp. The study revealed that six out of every 10 women have suffered sexual violence and that 70% of the girls below 18 years of age are survivors of sexual violence (Emry, 2004). Murphy and colleagues, in this volume, explore the ways in which experiences of sexual violence present a barrier to education for girls in Northern Uganda. The increased number of rape cases could be, among other things, attributed to the breakdown in social order and traditional customs in the region. The war environment may have resulted in more aggressive behaviour on the part of boys in their interactions with girls, at times harassing, abusing or raping them.

As observed by Humanitarian Update (2003) and Gifty, (1995), the brunt of the war in Northern Uganda was borne by the civilian population, in terms of destruction of homes and property, abduction and rape of mainly youth, children and women, and looting – all of which reduced the inhabitants of Northern Uganda to a state of frustration and despair. Alerotek (2005) states that the situation rendered people idle. Men resorted to drinking, and anti-social behaviour became rampant in IDP camps. Similarly, the Northern Uganda Psycho-Social Needs Assessment (NUPSNA; 1998) also found that alcohol abuse has increased in the region, due to frustration and idleness as well as worries and fear mainly related to insecurity. Many children have dropped out of school and become involved in criminal activities (Harris, 2000).

Education during the War

During the war, schools were relocated to the more than 200 IDP camps in Northern Uganda where there was some degree of security. There, pupils had to study from learning centres (MoES, 2008). These learning centres were overloaded, since one learning centre comprised three to five former rural schools. For instance, in Kitgum district, about 140 primary schools (86% of the total number of primary schools in Kitgum) serving 10,600 pupils were displaced into 34 learning centres. Hence, the learning environment in most IDP camp schools was overcrowded, with no effective partitioning between classrooms, the noise level was high, and there were minimal toilet facilities. In some schools, facilities such as pit latrines and water were shared with the communities around the school. Such working conditions negatively affected teachers' ability to facilitate learning (Machel, 1996; Sommers, 2002; Higgins, 2009).

In a study by Save the Children, Uganda (2007), on average enrolment was at 6901 primary school pupils per district in Northern Uganda, 742 pupils per school and 109 pupils per class, although there are variations in enrolment in different schools and classes. The teacher–pupil ratio in all the districts in the region was at about 1:62. Compared to the national class size figure of between 46 and 53 pupils (already high according to international standards), the average class sizes in Northern Uganda were very high, particularly in Oyam (1:81) and Pader (1:103) districts. The MoES (2008) also reports that some classrooms had as many as 300 students per teacher. As in many conflict-affected situations, the education of many children was disrupted and others had no educational opportunity; a needs-assessment carried out by the MoES (2008), reported that 250,000 children received no education at all.

As the Northern Ugandan case demonstrates, war has a devastating impact on education. It causes extensive physical and psychological damage to communities, teachers and pupils and limits opportunities for quality education (Buckland, 2005). Clearly, conflict prevents children from realizing their right to education. It affects not only access and retention of learners but also their ability to concentrate on schoolwork.

With cessation of war in Northern Uganda in late 2007, relocation of schools to their original sites began. However, many of the original schools were ruined and furniture looted. Hence there is currently an acute shortage of furniture, with only a minority of children sitting on chairs and benches. Due partly to fear, and lack of classrooms and furniture, some schools were physically split, with few pupils and teachers returning to their original sites while sections remained in the learning centres; this created problems as the two centres were managed by one head teacher. In addition, some teachers handling more than one class had to move to and from the learning centres and original sites.

Lack of requisite teaching skills on the part of teachers is another serious challenge, particularly since teachers do not generally receive support or additional training in how to cope with the realities of the post-conflict context from the MoES. Authoritarian teaching methods, still pervasive in many war-torn countries (and still in use in Northern Uganda), often reinforce the sense of powerlessness that students already feel (Rudenberg et al, 2001; Johannessen, 2002).

A report by the African Network for the Prevention and Protection against Child Abuse and Neglect(ANPPCAN) (1993) on the effects of war on children shows that war situations created new learning needs for children, some of whom are physically disabled and/or psychologically troubled, or have experiences as ex-combatants. According to the report, these children, above all, need a trusting and caring environment where healing can start to take place. Beyond this, the report does not spell out the new learning needs of conflict-affected children. While existing research from Uganda and elsewhere indicates that experiences of conflict can have significant and lasting psychosocial consequences for young people (Cairns & Dawes, 1996; Farver & Frosch, 1996; Ladd & Cairns, 1996; Amnesty International, 1997; Castelli et al, 2005; Apio, 2005; Sommers, 2006; Human Rights Watch, 2007; Lai & Thyne, 2007), research has yet to explore the ways in which these in turn affect young people's educational possibilities, their relationships with teachers and other students, and teaching and learning processes in the classroom. Hence there is a need to better understand learning needs and the teaching and learning relationship itself through analysis of the challenges the experiences of war present in a classroom setting. This need is especially pressing in Northern Uganda, where our research reveals that almost all the children in the region have witnessed the burning of villages, the killing of a relative or friend, and direct torture, meaning that it is safe to assume that nearly all children have experienced armed conflict, at least to a degree.

Research Methodology

This chapter analyses challenges that war presents to education, specifically focusing on teachers' and learners' experiences in Northern Uganda. So far the existing research outlined in this chapter, though providing some information on effects of war and violent conflict on children and young people, does not focus on understanding exactly what happens in classrooms in the post-conflict context and how these processes affect teachers and students.

In designing this study, we discovered that in many teacher education institutions in Uganda, no specific training is provided for teachers to enable them to cope with working in conflict or post-conflict situations. This is despite the fact that as key persons involved in the provision of formal education, reconstruction and reorganization of educational institutions in war areas will depend greatly on teachers (Bickmore, 2005). Teachers are the key agents in ensuring effective learning and in determining the quality of education that children receive (Smith & Neill, 2006). Teachers play a role in motivating learners to attend school, they are the ones to select content and methods to be used, they shape the environment, select and assemble teaching materials. However, for teachers' efforts to translate into effective learning, they do not only require appropriate working conditions, professional rewards, prospects for promotion and career growth, and tangible institutional support in the form of resources, personnel and funds (Smith & Neill, 2006), but also learners who are motivated. Since experiences of conflict affect learners' motivation, psychosocial well-being and perceptions of schooling and its relevance, it is important to understand how these experiences affect teaching and learning possibilities. Effective peacebuilding through school is dependent on effectively trained teachers and on the learners with whom they interact on a daily basis. Thus, an understanding of teachers' perceptions of learners' needs is important in planning for post-conflict educational reconstruction. It is also important to understand how learners interpret their war experiences (and those of their communities, peers and teachers) and how they bring these into their classrooms.

With these goals in mind, we (a team of researchers from Makerere University, Uganda) undertook a field study in the Northern Uganda districts of Amuru, Gulu, Lira and Apac from November 2007 to May 2008. We chose these districts because in the Acholi sub-region, the effects of war were felt most strongly in Gulu and Amuru districts while in the Lango sub-region, Lira and Apach were the worst affected. It is in Amuru district that the infamous Atiak massacre took place. Apach and Lira witnessed horrid episodes such as the cooking of people in pots and the well-known Aboke girls' kidnapping.

The study relied heavily on qualitative approaches, namely, interviews and focus group discussions. However, questionnaires were also used to enable the researchers to gather perceptions and experiences of the war from the vast population of the IDP camps. Data was collected both from primary and secondary schools. The respondents were district education officials, community leaders, head teachers, teachers and learners. Since the research was conducted at the time when movement into the rural areas was still risky, mainly schools located in the urban and trading centres and in IDP camps were selected. Altogether data was collected from 42 primary and 11 secondary schools in the four districts. In Acholi sub-region, schools located in Gulu town, and in the IDP camps Unyama, Koro-Abili, Alokolum, Tegot Latoro and Koro-Tetugu were selected. In Lango sub-region data was collected from Lira Town, and the IDP camps of Aloi, Alito, Obim, Apalla and Aboke. These camps were selected purposely based on security in the location at the time of data collection.

The findings that we present here draw on the survey and interview responses of adults (primarily teachers and head teachers, but also community leaders) and present their understandings of the challenges to the teaching and learning process in the post-conflict context. Teachers describe here the ways in which they see the legacies of conflict-related experiences manifest in the classroom practices and behaviours of the children that they work with. Likewise, head teachers and community leaders reflect upon the implications of conflict on teachers, schools and society, demonstrating the ways in which classroom processes and the individuals who enact them are affected by the conflict and post-conflict situation. Further research should endeavour to situate and relate learners' own perspectives to these findings.

Research Findings

This section presents findings from our study in Northern Uganda. A question posed to teachers on challenges experienced when dealing with learners in post-conflict situations showed that learners demonstrated a range of challenging behaviours and attitudes. Teachers' responses included such descriptions of their students as: 'very chaotic'; 'stubborn and disrespectful'; 'like bullying and fighting'; 'show military behaviours'; 'hostile'; 'destructive and disorderly'; 'short tempered and rude'; 'prone to emotional outbursts'; 'lack of interest in education'; 'less competitive and sometimes withdrawn'; 'less innovative'; 'aggressive'; 'violent'; 'irritable'; 'disrespectful and lack discipline'; etc. In addition to challenges related to students' behaviours, head teachers also identified 'low morale and lack of motivation' as teacher-related challenges that affected students' learning. Low morale and lack of motivation reportedly affected teacher cooperation and also led to alcoholism.

Table I summarizes thematically teachers' and head teachers' responses to the challenges that affect teaching and learning in their schools. The three themes are explored in more detail below.

	Teachers		Head teachers	
	Frequency	%	Frequency	%
Aggressive and undisciplined learners	40	45.5	28	52.8
Low academic ambition of learners	28	31.8	20	37.7
Low teachers' motivation and low morale	15	17.1	31	58.5

Table I. Teachers' and head teachers' responses with regard to challenges affecting teaching and learning in the post-conflict situation.

The majority of the teachers and more than half of the head teachers perceived the learners as aggressive, lacking discipline, and not valuing education. The teachers explained that they were facing greater discipline problems in schools than they had before the war. They linked this to the wartime experiences of young people. One teacher explained: 'We are dealing with learners who have practically had nothing but a violent and insecure past – learners with unique needs'. Among the majority of the head teachers, challenges related to teachers that affect student learning were also reported. These challenges that teachers and head teachers perceived are discussed below as per the three themes introduced in Table I.

Aggressive and Undisciplined Learners

Findings from teachers in Northern Uganda showed that they perceived children to be emotionally unstable. Learners who had suffered abduction were generally described as follows: 'particularly militaristic'; 'wild'; 'violent'; 'hostile and uncooperative'; 'very stubborn'; 'destructive and disorderly'; 'problematic'.

However, there was considerable difference between the ways that teachers described boys and girls who had been abducted. Abducted boys were seen as particularly aggressive and hard to control. Reports about the boys state: 'They exhibit military behaviours, always carrying a stick, saying it is a gun'; 'They tend to shout at each other and at the teachers when they want to put across a point'; 'They are prone to fighting each other and to stealing/theft'; 'They are hard to talk to, restless, unnecessarily quarrelsome'; 'They envy each other and enjoy rumour mongering'; 'They have no respect for elders and teachers'; 'They like stories that have to do with war'. On the other hand, teachers had the following to say about girls who were captured by the LRA: 'Not social to other pupils, reserved, lonely, very careful in what they do'; 'They do not talk freely to people'; 'They tend to be isolated and do not like school'; 'They are abusive, react immediately and talk vigorously and emotionally when provoked'; 'They are security conscious and tend to sit at the class entrance ready to flee in case of any emergency'. Girls were reported by teachers to be very emotional and to cry for no 'justifiable' reason. Teachers said that it was very hard to manage girls. Some girls preferred to be alone and this in turn limited their ability to participate in team/group work. One teacher explained, 'the girls are extremely difficult. One day, I asked a girl to give an answer to a question I had posed to the class, but she just kept quiet. When I insisted on getting an answer from her, she started crying'. Another teacher from a girls' only school also reported:

> I had a student who cried a lot. She was very bright but came to school without anything. When you asked her about what is troubling her, she would say 'nothing', when you insist she would scream. One day, I asked her to write her problems for me, she tore the paper into pieces, and then she started squeezing the toy that was in the classroom.

Though teachers did hint at aggression in girls who had been abducted, what they tended to emphasize most was the withdrawn, quiet and isolated nature of these girls.

In addition, other deeper issues related to indiscipline are pointed out in statements like the ones below, which are surprisingly included in answers to questions related to discipline: 'Some pupils are often sad, withdrawn from work, lack seriousness at work'; 'They hate rules and regulations, and are not time conscious!'; 'They are not quite smart'; 'They lust for food'; 'They suffer stigmatisation'. As these statements make clear, teachers have to deal with deep psychological, emotional and immediate needs behind pupils' indiscipline. One teacher said:

> The violence experience seems to flow in the blood of many pupils today. A number of students get involved in vandalizing school property, excessive aggression towards one another and quarrelling, defiance of school authority and lack of respect for teachers, drug abuse, rampant use of abusive language and threatening language and all sorts of antisocial behaviour you can imagine… . This is not the way young people used to live before the war.

At secondary level, undisciplined students can be a great danger not only within the school but also to surrounding communities. A teacher from one of the boys' schools reported that indiscipline at the school has made it almost impossible for the school administration to restore the school to its former glory. He added:

> Students of this boarding school are generally stubborn, hostile, disorderly, aggressive, arrogant, militaristic and violent. They have come to constitute the same threat to neighbouring communities

> as the rebels formerly had. ... When they invade the villages and the pubs, the locals are on edge, fearing the crime and deviant behaviours of the unruly boys.

Teachers reported a tendency of pupils running away or exhibiting a lot of fear. Constant fear of imminent attacks from rebels to exact brutal punishment on a non-cooperative local population had, after all, taken its toll. Describing the situation in his school, one of the head teachers noted how the pupils 'are difficult to handle, they do not respond to the administration positively. They are hostile and they like forming cliques'. A teacher in another school also reported that 'some students are quiet, but when provoked, they fight'.

In addition, officials of the Ministry of Education and Sports have witnessed indiscipline in Northern Uganda's schools and attempted to address its consequences. One of the officials from the education office reported, 'The classrooms and compound are shabby and littered. The students are not interested in their bodily hygiene. They do not want to use the official school language [English]. They do not like school uniforms'. The officials have taken seriously the issue of handling discipline by introducing workshops for student leaders, teachers and Board of Governors and Parent Teacher Association members. Issues relating to psychological and emotional maturity, teacher–pupil relationships, parental responsibility, peer counselling, adolescence and sexual maturity, etc. are openly discussed at these workshops. Problems related to indiscipline cause a lot of frustration among teachers and parents/guardians and lead to unwillingness among many teachers to work in Northern Uganda.

It appears, therefore, that the issue of indisciplinc is not only related to abduction, but in a wider sense, to the experience of life in the IDP camps. For instance, abducted children were reported to adjust faster to school regulations than those not abducted. Although several reasons could explain this behaviour, one of them could be the clash between a rigid framework of discipline in the rebel forces as compared to the near-total absence of a cultural/moral frame in the social setting of the IDP camps. In line with this, an elderly female head teacher of one of the primary schools in Gulu stated:

> People stayed in IDP camps where the moral fabric of the community was severely eroded. Young children use abusive and crude words/language. Our tribal moral code has gone. Children have been exposed to so much indecent language and behaviour in the IDP camps where the sort of parenting which could have provided the required moral/linguistic background was almost inexistent. [pause] Our Acholi culture is gone!!

Religious leaders also felt that war and the concentration of people in IDP camps had annihilated the cultural and moral norms that once would have been enhanced by formal education. For these leaders, the breakdown of the family institution has to be given special attention if one can hope to appreciate the emotional and moral needs of young people in the region. In the IDP camp setting, religious leaders felt there was no moral anchor on which teachers could rely. In the words of one Catholic bishop in the study area: 'War has not only killed our people, it has dehumanized them and reduced them to wild beasts with no morals. The school may in the short and long run do little to bring them back to true humanity. We all have to get involved if the human dignity of the Acholis and Langis is to be restored'.

The conditions in camps exacerbated the situation of social and moral collapse that these respondents describe. One of the local leaders reported that a family of five or more would often share a small hut, with no privacy at all in such an environment. The homes were described by the respondents as congested and as not providing a friendly environment for school-going children. People lived on hand-outs from NGOs. Parents and guardians were unable to provide scholastic materials and to meet other educational needs. With the demise of parental economic power came the consequent failure of the parent to claim any control over the child. The disintegration of culture and family, as well as, in many cases, the death of parents and caregivers resulted in populations of children without a moral compass to empower them in navigating the post-conflict world. In line with the NUPSNA (1998) study, we found that insecurity has contributed to a widespread breakdown of the normal social support system, leading to poor parenting, indiscipline, failure to be educated, failure to marry and marital break-ups. In this context, enforcing discipline takes up a lot of the teachers' energies and time, which they would otherwise spend on classroom teaching and instruction.

The collapse of cultural and moral norms also enabled the resurrection of older cultural trends that discourage education for girls. A local leader pointed out that during the war and the life of poverty in IDP camps, girls came to be increasingly seen as a source of wealth (bride price) for their parents or relatives, a trend that resulted in increased vulnerability for young girls. Cases of early pregnancy and marriage for girls have come to be seen as part of the normal way of life and what was once a relatively common pattern of seeing girls' futures in terms of secondary and higher education has gradually faded. Girls' drop-out rate is high, and interest in schooling among girls themselves and their families is quite low. An informant from one of the communities stated: 'At the age of 14, my daughter told me that she wanted to get married to a rich man who will save her from all this suffering. She is not enthusiastic about going back to school any more'. This change of mindset partly explains why there is a general moral licentiousness around early sex and pregnancy among school-going girls, often resulting in early school drop-out.

There was an ambivalent attitude towards corporal punishment among teachers. Some teachers are in favour of corporal punishment and others are totally against it. The ambivalence is perhaps related to a deep awareness of the need to include otherness (e.g. the formerly abducted) in the new post-war community on the one hand, and a lack of skills in handling cases of indiscipline on the other. Indiscipline brings to the fore the difficult issue of psychological reconstruction. The implications of lack of discipline are many but the most outstanding one is the realization that psychological reconstruction is going to require a lot more time and effort than the reconstruction of physical infrastructure through rebuilding the schools.

Low Academic Ambition

Interestingly, our study finds that although war is expected to affect performance negatively, students performed better at the height of war than they did after. This was reported by five of the head teachers of secondary schools in Gulu. One of the head teachers reported that performance had been going down since the cessation of war. Another teacher observed that more students passed in first grade before the war than after. Explaining these results, one of the teachers asserted that during the war people were confined to one place, hence students were able to read. The period after war, however, is characterized by freedom of movement, which seems to have some negative effects on young people's lifestyles (discussed in relation to early sex and pregnancy above) and on learning outcomes. This might be especially the case since some parents can no longer effectively fulfil their parenting roles, thus giving children unusual amounts of freedom. Children have also taken on more responsibilities in the post-conflict context in order to meet basic needs for themselves and their families. For instance, many were moving back and forth between the IDP camps and their original homes to tend their gardens. It was also noted by some teachers that some children, particularly orphans and children who head households, are forced to work before and after school. Food is often limited, making it difficult for children to concentrate. The post-conflict context, therefore, accounts for the decline in performance, suggesting an interesting nuance to the assumption that war itself negatively affects learning outcomes.

Findings from both teachers and head teachers showed that learners had 'low academic ambition', which was exhibited through 'absent mindedness in class', 'lack of interest in education', 'lack of concentration', 'lack of competitiveness', and many had 'low self-esteem'. In fact this study showed that for children, long-term interests associated with success in academic work are viewed as secondary to short-term survival interests such as developing the ability to recognize warning signs of impending trouble. The survival instinct gradually overtook the competitive one for social mobility. Indeed many children became accustomed to the survival routine (Harris, 2000).

War and violent conflict causes a sense of hopelessness and disinterest in education among the learners such that many lose sight of any future prospects. This disinterest in education was obvious in the carefree attitudes of learners. Many cared less about completing homework while others preferred staying outside class but within the school compound. As Machel

(2001) explains, when young people lack the opportunity for recreation and learning, often without hope for the future, the stress and boredom of the camp life make them prone to high-risk behaviours. In one educational institution, the school management revealed that over 46% of the girls between the ages of 15 and 20 are proven HIV/AIDS cases. Out of the sampled female pupils 40% of them aged between 15 and 25 were child mothers. Teachers reported that the child mothers complained that it is hard to concentrate on schoolwork when their own children are left unattended to at home.

Decline in competitiveness and willingness to participate in class activities such as group work by the learners was another problem observed by the teachers. As Vygotsky (1978) asserted, learning takes place through interaction with others, and failure to work in groups affects students' ability to learn.

Although as the findings from teachers showed, in many cases students had a negative attitude towards education, many wanted to be at school. One primary school boy explained his reasons for wanting to be at school:

> I lived in Otti's camp for one month but later joined Kony in Sudan for two months. I was assigned to carry luggage like sugar, beans and other things. I am at school because when in school I can easily forget about the problems I have. At school I have friends and they give us food. At home we go without food and eat in the evening. Home condition is not good.

In a similar vein a girl also reported that 'I like being in school because it is safer than home. I particularly like the games which I cannot play while at home'. The learners from primary schools wanted to be in school because of the pastoral care they received from teachers. As one learner reiterated, 'even the orphans are comforted'.

As the above excerpts suggest, many children experienced more acceptance and well-being at school than they did at home. One of the district leaders explained how children's ambivalent feelings about their community and stigmatization by the community led to a view of the school as a sanctuary. He stated: 'many times children are abducted from home, so they felt that the family and the local community had failed to protect them. Moreover when a child is abducted, he or she is a child but on return they are given names such as "rebels", "returnees", "child soldiers"'. This means that children, in spite of 'coming back home', still experienced rejection from home; in many ways these returnees are 'not at home' due to stigma and labels. At school, teachers and children themselves reported a more accepting environment that resisted stigmatization of 'returnee' children.

Despite the fact that many children wanted to be at school, they were not seen to be learning well or achieving the desired outcomes. Low academic achievements are caused by many factors, including irregularity of school attendance, negative attitudes towards learning, lack of concentration, absenteeism, and the low quality of many lessons due to class size and teachers' inability to manage students. School records in the disturbed area revealed high absenteeism. One female teacher explained: 'It is only during the examination time when almost all students attend class, but even then they don't attend subjects they consider hard. There are no mechanisms to entice or force them to attend classes regularly'.

It is important to note that many of these reasons that can explain low achievement in Northern Uganda are intimately linked to the conflict experiences of young people and teachers in the region. As one teacher from Gulu observed:

> The painful experiences, memories and feelings preoccupy their minds and that is why probably they cannot perform well. All students who experienced catastrophic situations display symptoms of psychological distress and inability to concentrate on their class work. Such students may leave school without achieving a lot for themselves.

Young people's poor performance could also be due in part to a loss of any hope among young people of getting jobs. A boy from a secondary school suggested that 'qualified graduates from Northern Uganda should have equal opportunities for employment. They should stop segregation'. From the very inception of nation-state politics in Uganda, education was seen as a major tool to break down class barriers and to achieve a more inclusive society where anyone from any social status or group could overcome marginalization. According to this rhetoric, everyone (not only the well born) was free not only to share in national growth, but also to access and be accepted in higher social and economic groups since one had a right to function at higher levels of specialization by virtue of educational merit alone. Students are keenly aware of the decline in meritocracy in their society. Responses suggest that learners liked schooling not only because of short-term interests of security and the company of peers, but also for the long-term sense of a brighter future where they can enjoy equal opportunity for employment in a democratic social political environment. That learners no longer see the possibilities of employment or the opportunities for meritocratic assent once offered by schooling is likely to be connected to the disinterest in education that teachers and community members reported witnessing in students.

Researchers have also attributed low academic achievement to low parental involvement in the lives of their children. Similar findings were reported in the proceedings of a conference in Northern Ireland where it was reported that in the aftermath of conflict parents experienced difficulties re-establishing protection for children and rituals or traditions for the transition to adulthood (Conference Proceedings Summary, 2005). The Palestinian participants in the same conference similarly noted a drop in patience of parents to explain things to their children, to answer questions, and to spend time with their offspring, although some of the change may be due in part to increasing family size.

Our approach points to numerous factors to account for poor academic performance in war and post-war regions. It is important to stress that poor academic achievement can partly be blamed on the immense poverty that is experienced, for example, in Northern Uganda. As one head teacher noted: 'The government policies of UPE [universal primary education] and USE [universal secondary education] give opportunity to students to attend school without paying school fees. But all the same, many parents cannot provide their children with books, pens and pencils which in turn curtails the enrolment and attendance of many young people'.

In relation to low self-esteem, many learners expressed preferences for professions such as secretary, nursing, military and police. In fact the majority of the boys preferred professions that would enable them to take revenge for their wartime experiences. One learner had this to say about his future profession: 'I want to become an army man so as to teach Kony and Museveni a lesson for keeping us in misery for long'. Such unresolved anger and resentment among young people calls for serious training in anger management for both teachers and learners. This study confirms Harris's (2000) findings that in many cases, children affected by violence are unable to sit still in class because they are depressed or afraid. Such behaviours lead to poor relationships between teachers and students.

Characteristics exhibited by the learners imply teachers needed a lot of tact to keep them awake, attentive, focused and interested, which the teachers did not have or were unable to provide. Though teachers are aware that a good (loving and caring) learning environment is an essential factor in creating confident and interested learners, and generally they do their best, they do not quite know how to properly go about creating such an environment. They clearly point out that they are in dire need of external support in terms of refresher courses and training workshops on how they can handle psychosocial issues and peacebuilding.

In primary schools 81% and in secondary schools all the teachers wanted more training on ways of addressing children's needs. They clearly stated that there are gaps in their training in handling traumatized and problematic pupils. They pointed out that they need: 'More seminars, radio talk shows and TV on post-war experience; and how to create a good school and classroom environment'; 'How to create a good teacher–learner relationship'; 'how to generate interest in education'; 'how to create active and engaging learning situations'; 'how to counsel disturbed pupils, and how to monitor and follow them up'. Teachers' inability to handle learners appropriately and skilfully undoubtedly affected children's performance, and many underachieved.

Low academic ambition highlights the crucial issue of ideological reconstruction. First, creating an integrative environment devoid of stigmatization is vital in post-war contexts. Creating an environment where children feel safe is crucially related to this issue, especially in cases such as Northern Uganda, where the line between victims and perpetrators is very difficult to draw. Second, it is imperative that young people unlearn vocabularies that feed on an ideology of segregation between northerners and southerners. This ideology, as authors have argued (Hansen & Twaddle, 1990; Mamdani, 1991), dates to colonial times where tribes in the north of the country were relegated to the margins of the nascent nation-state.

Low Morale and Lack of Motivation among Teachers

It is generally accepted today that the emotional engagement of teachers is an important key to boosting the teaching and learning process. Nonetheless, much of government and donor agency intervention is geared towards having all children finish primary school, and towards meeting the Millennium Development Goals. This is a genuine concern, since hundreds of thousands of war-affected children are still out of school, yet there are equally pressing issues around what happens in the classrooms of those children who are in school. Teachers in post-conflict zones, in particular, merit further attention. Looking at our research results, there are five contentious issues that arise from the data about these teachers, namely, low morale, absenteeism, lack of concentration, poor relations with students and alcoholism. However, since data on low morale was often illustrated by the respondents in terms of the other four issues (absenteeism, lack of concentration, poor relations with students, alcoholism) only low morale has been discussed in this chapter.

Like everyone else, teachers underwent the stresses and pains of the long conflict. Many of them are what one could call 'wounded healers' who have themselves suffered the effects of war (e.g. abduction, loss of loved ones, physical maiming) and are struggling amidst abject poverty. They shared the pervasive sense of helplessness, pessimism, negative thinking, guilt, shame, depression and the general sense of hopelessness and despair that a long-running war imposes on its victims. Many of them were trained, graduated and/or worked during the war. They readily offer vivid narrations of how they survived during the war; for example, one teacher explained that 'I narrowly survived more than one ambush on my way to and from teacher training schools. Then one day, I was abducted and managed to escape from the rebel fronts'.

Not surprisingly, head teachers described their teachers in these words: 'Poor time management', 'absenteeism', 'latecoming', 'dodging lessons', 'lack of commitment to work', 'lack of concentration' and 'care free'. These behaviours were pointed out as a source of poor performance since they rendered the completion of the syllabus impossible. As one of the district officials pointed out, 'teachers' work method have become mechanical, their output capacity is very low. They are no longer part of the teaching system. I have always asked myself if teacher one-to-one relations with the learners still exist'. It is this issue that made one of the teachers reflect thus: 'What should a teacher accept to deal with; their learners, themselves, their families or the environment?'

Latecoming was another problem cited by head teachers which affected completion of syllabi and in turn the performance of learners. Latecoming was due to the fact that some teachers started the day by digging. In addition, a number of them stayed far away from school and had to walk or use bicycles. One of the teachers reported that he has to 'walk 14 km [to and from school] daily. So if I do not have classes, I do not go to school'. The distance from their homes to school sometimes made teachers dodge lessons, abstain from school and fail to pay attention to the needs of the learners. General absenteeism from duties was reported by all the head teachers as very common.

Teachers were described as having carefree attitudes and lacking commitment to work. In fact, one head teacher intimated that some teachers wanted to be forced to teach. Many did not prepare lessons or mark the exercises they gave to learners. Some were even reported to come to school drunk. As one of the parents explained, 'one day a teacher came to school drunk. Some of them even drink together with the students. How do you expect children to respect such teachers?' One of the community leaders also reported that it is common to find teachers in bars taking alcohol during class hours.

Moreover, there is poor cooperation among teachers. Teachers' behaviours have in turn resulted in poor relationships with parents and learners. Thanks to lack of training in alternative approaches to teaching and on how to handle learners (especially those exhibiting the behaviours described above), many teachers are unable to deal with learners' problems. Consequently, when confronted or annoyed by students some teachers ignored them; others quarrelled violently or fought with pupils. Some teachers sent disruptive children away from class; others punished them by making them dig. Another teacher noted that 'students seemed to present many psychological problems at school but could not easily be met because of their overwhelming numbers in the classes'.

The head teachers and district officials also reported that teachers suffered low self-esteem, which in turn affected their relationship with learners. In one of the schools, a teacher was reported to have removed his shirt to fight a pupil. It was also reported by some head teachers that teachers feared the learners. Elaborating on this assertion, one head teacher described a scenario where a student pointed at a teacher and said, 'I have killed 82 people and you will be the eighty third'. Other teachers intervened and rescued the teacher.

Teachers' problems are aggravated by the prevailing negative social image of teachers in the region. One of the head teachers described the situation in these words:

> The school environment used to be a centre of standard setting.
> Only teachers had radios, every teacher at least had a bicycle ... all

> these helped promote the status of the teacher. This has changed; they do not even own bicycles. That is why any cheap thing, for example, the cheapest phone credit [locally called airtime], beer with the highest alcohol level, poor houses are associated with teachers.

In one school where teachers' houses are available, the teachers said: 'Look at our houses; they have not been renovated for a long time. How would you expect children to respect teachers who live in such conditions?' The social image of teachers is not a source of encouragement. Parents cannot do much to supplement income for the teachers since they themselves are still very poor, and only beginning to pick their lives up.

Teacher-exchange programmes by, for example, Invisible Children, where local and foreign teachers work together and share expertise and encouragement, go a long way in boosting the morale of local teachers. Seeking home-grown solutions to the problem of motivation, many teachers expressed the urgency of the need for training in self-management and self-development skills. Such training might awaken individual teachers to their professional and personal potentials and skills, and make teachers confident about themselves and their contribution to the region. In particular, respondents referred to the re-establishment of teacher unions, and through them, the engagement of savings and credit schemes to improve their financial conditions.

A number of teachers abandoned ship and opted for 'better jobs with the NGOs' in terms of pay and amount of stress. Teachers who remained in the education sector are poorly motivated due to poverty and stress. They often have to look after big families (their own children and the children of their deceased relatives), and have to endure stressful working conditions, handling big classes of up to 100 pupils. Little wonder then that young people in the region do not want to become teachers, and teachers from the rest of the country do not want to work in Northern Uganda. A report by the Women's Refugee Commission quoted in ANPPCAN (1993) stated that: 'One of the great difficulties of attracting young people to teaching is the rate of pay and long hours. In some areas, teachers make 59,000 Ugandan Shillings a month (about USD 34) and work 8-10 hours per day, six days a week'. Recently the Government has promised to increase the salaries of teachers in war-affected areas, but still, the salaries remain at a level lower than what one would need to survive and look after a family.

Perhaps nowhere have teachers' needs been more neglected in efforts of educational reconstruction than in Northern Uganda. Problems related to teacher esteem may be a worldwide phenomenon, but here, they pose a serious problem since teachers live in unimaginably poor conditions. At school, they are entrusted with responsibilities that normally belong to parents or guardians and they have to handle large classrooms filled with troubled students; outside school they are looked down upon. The crucial implication here is that apart from the need for training in classroom management and counselling of pupils, as many researchers have suggested, teachers' financial plight needs to be considered a priority in post-war educational reconstruction efforts.

Conclusions and Recommendations

This chapter shows that teachers experience several challenges as they teach learners affected by war, yet they are not able to effectively handle these challenges due to inadequate training and empowerment. This in turn affects the schools' ability to effectively provide healing for the learners and to ensure quality teaching and learning, compromising the potential of education to contribute towards peacebuilding more broadly. In a study in Rwanda, teachers who had received training were able to create a good learning atmosphere in the classroom, identify learners' problems and give assistance according to their problems, encourage learners to like studies, involve learners in co-curricular activities, and shape the social and moral behaviour of the pupils (Harris, 2000). The study demonstrates the potential that specialized training for teachers in the post-conflict context offers as a successful intervention to address many of the challenges described in Northern Uganda.

As already mentioned, many scholars have emphasized the importance of education as an instrument in the reduction of societal violence in post-conflict situations (Woolman, 2001; Davies, 2004). Indeed this study confirmed education as an avenue for providing a sense of hope and stability to war returnees, and the wider community, through provision of knowledge, values, competencies, attitudes and behaviours that encourage respect for human dignity and diversity. Education has the capacity to help young generations to build a better future and also learn new ways of thinking in order to live together. This is demonstrated by the fact that when learners in Northern Uganda were asked about their 'happiest moment', 90% said it was the day they went back to school. As Bird (2003) explains, schooling is one of the best methods of helping in the healing of psychosocial trauma for children and can play a critical role in their return to normal life.

Likewise education can give children the opportunity to develop life-saving skills, bring shape and structure to their lives, and provide protection against exploitation and harm (Bush & Saltarelli, 2000; Inter-agency Network on Education in Emergencies [INEE], 2004). It is due to these potentials that governments, together with NGOs, focus on education in post-conflict situations. However, for potential to be enacted, as Machel (2001) emphasizes, educational development must be dedicated to addressing the traumatic impact of war on children in order to establish a sustainable future. A promising way forward lies in supporting and training teachers to do this based on a firm understanding of the challenges that they face and of the needs of the learners with whom they interact.

In particular ways, education is already playing an important role in supporting peacebuilding in Northern Uganda, and this can only be strengthened with increased attention to supporting the teaching and learning process. For instance, regarding the issue of formerly abducted pupils, most informants from Northern Uganda saw integration into the existing school system as the best solution for rehabilitation. They suggested the following: 'avoid stigmatization – treat all children equally'; 'Teach good manners and motivate them'; 'Provide guidance and counselling'; 'Organise face-to-face talks with resource persons'; 'Encourage all pupils to join football clubs, drama, and other social activities'; 'Provide love, acceptance and care to the learners'; 'Provide learning materials and meals at school'; 'Encourage peace talk'; 'Encourage talking compounds with messages that help learners'; 'Organise parent days and improve parents' involvement in ensuring discipline at school'; 'Visiting children at home and sensitizing parents about their responsibilities and the importance of education (especially for girls)'. There was a general mindset of inclusiveness among the informants, which is an important resource in forging a future of peaceful school environments. It is a mindset that reflects a more general willingness to forgive and reconcile with former rebel fighters who have come back to live within local communities. The issue of community stigmatization retards the steady progress already made in this area and our findings demonstrate that returnees appreciate schools' efforts to resist stigmatization within their premises.

In the particular environment of the school, however, post-conflict realities demand a lot of new skills in handling discipline on the part of teachers. That is why the issue of corporal punishment needs to be candidly rejected and teachers need to be trained in other more constructive and dialogical methods of disciplining. In addition to the clear need for further, tailored teacher training, we suggest that the metaphor of 'problems', regularly used to describe the challenges of post-conflict education in Northern Uganda, be increasingly replaced by the metaphor of 'needs'. It is possible that when children's needs are not taken care of, they become unruly or aggressive, in order to compel people around them to 'pay attention' to their needs. When the world around them does not pay attention, levels of indiscipline, emotional instability and low academic achievement thrive. Indiscipline and the rest, accordingly, are the expression of the pain and frustration that many learners in Northern Uganda hold within them as a result of their conflict-related experiences. In the end, the most pressing challenge on the part of educators, parents, guardians and communities is the identification of children's and young people's needs and the development of appropriate responses to meet these needs. While students who bring conflict-related experiences to the classroom do pose educational challenges for teachers, as this research shows, the most pressing issue is that school systems, especially in post-conflict situations, are themselves failing needy children. The failure to address conflict experiences in the classroom by training and supporting teachers to do so limits the possibilities of education to contribute towards peacebuilding.

References

African Network for the Prevention and Protection against Child Abuse and Neglect (ANPPCAN) (1993) *Uganda Chapter Report of the Regional Workshop on the Impact of Armed Conflict on Women and Children.* Unpublished workshop report. ANPPCAN office, Kampala.

Alerotek, M.A. (2005) *Exposing the Violence of IDP Camps: a report from the ground,* World Vision, Gulu.

Amnesty International (1997) The Destruction of Childhood by the Lord's Resistance Army in Uganda. Unpublished report.

Apio, E. (2005) Born of War in Uganda: the real cost of Uganda's civil war. Paper presented to the 4th world conference on family laws and children's rights, 20-23 March, in Cape Town.

Bickmore, K. (2005) Teacher Development for Conflict Participation: facilitating learning for difficult citizenship education, *International Journal of Citizenship and Teacher Education,* 1(2), 1-16.

Bird, L. (2003) Surviving School: education for refugee children from Rwanda 1994-1996. UNESCO International Institute for Educational Planning. http://unesdoc.unesco.org/images/0013/001330/133047e.pdf

Boyden, J. & Ryder, P. (1996) The Provision of Education to Children Affected by Armed Conflict. Oxford: Oxford Refugee Studies Centre, University of Oxford.

Buckland, P. (2005) *Reshaping the Future: education and post conflict reconstruction.* Washington, DC: World Bank.

Bush, K.D. & Saltarelli, D. (2000) *The Two Faces of Education in Ethnic Conflict: towards a peace building education for children.* Florence: UNICEF Innocenti Research Centre.

Cairns, E. & Dawes, A. (1996) Children: ethnic and political violence – a commentary, *Child Development,* 67(1), 129-139.

Castelli L., Locatelli, E. & Canavera, M. (2005) Psychosocial Support for War Affected Children in Northern Uganda: lessons learned. Coalition to Stop the Use of Child Soldiers. London.

Conference Proceedings (2005) Northern Ireland Conference Report on Reducing the Effects of Violence on Young People in Divided Societies. Northern Ireland, June.

Davies, L. (2004) *Education and Conflict: complexity and chaos.* London: RoutledgeFalmer.

Education Department, Gulu (2005) Gulu District Statistics, Unpublished.

Emry, M. (2004) *No Safe Place to Call Home. Child and Adolescence Night Commuters in Northern Uganda.* New York: Women's Commission for Refugee Women and Children.

Emry, M. & Heninger, L. (2005) *Learning in a War Zone: education in northern Uganda.* New York: Women's Commission for Refugee Women and Children.

Ehrenreich, R. (2005) *The Scars of Death: children abducted by the LRA in Uganda.* Human Rights Watch/Africa. Human Rights Watch Project, New York.

Farver, J.A.M. & Frosch, D.L. (1996) L.A. Stories: aggression in pre-schoolers' spontaneous narratives after the riots of 1992, *Child Development*, 67, 19-32.

Gifty, Q. (1995) *Traumatized Children of the War in Northern Uganda.* Unpublished survey report, World Vision, Kampala.

Global Child Report (2004) Child Soldiers. Coalition to Stop the Use of Child Soldiers, pp. 105-107. London.

Hansen, H.G. & Twaddle, M. (Eds) (1990) *Uganda Now: between decay and development.* Basingstoke: Macmillan.

Harris, I. (2000) Peacebuilding Responses to School Violence, *NASSP Bulletin*, 84, 5-24.

Higgins, K. (2009) Regional Inequality and Primary Education in Northern Uganda. Briefing paper - Background Papers for the World Development Report 2009, 2. http://www.odi.org.uk/resources/details.asp?id=2504&title=regional-inequality-primary-education-northern-uganda

Humanitarian Update - Uganda (2003) Vol. V, Issue 4. United Nations Office for Coordination of Humanitarian Affairs (UN OCHA). http://wwwreliefweb.int/rw/rwb.nf/AllDocsByUNID

Inter-Agency Network on Education in Emergencies (INEE) (2004) *Minimum Standards for Education in Emergencies, Chronic Crises and Early Reconstruction.* Paris: UNESCO.

Johannessen, Eva Marion (2002) *Evaluation of Human Rights Education in Southern Caucausus.* Oslo: Norwegian Refugee Council.

Ladd, G.W. & Cairns, E. (1996) Children: ethnic and political violence, *Child Development*, 67, 14-18.

Lai, Brian & Thyne, Claytone (2007) The Effects of War on Education, *Journal of Peace Research*, 44(3), 277-292.

Machel, G. (1996) *Promotion and Protection of the Rights of Children: the impact of armed conflicts on children.* Report of the Expert of the Secretary General. New York. http://www.un.org/children/conflict/english/themachelstudy.html

Machel, G. (2001) *The Impact of War on Children.* London: Hurst & Company.

Mamdani, M. (1991) *Politics and Class Formation in Uganda.* Kampala: Fountain Publishers.

Médecins Sans Frontiers (2004) Life in Northern Uganda. All Shades of Grief and Fear. Unpublished Report.

Miller, V.W. & Affolter, F.W. (2002) Helping Children Outgrow War. Technical Paper no. 116. Washington, DC: Agency for International Development (IDCA).

Ministry of Education and Sports (2008) Final Report on Education Needs Assessment for Northern Uganda (Adjumani, Amolatar, Amuria, Apac, Dokolo, Gulu, Gulu Municipal Council, Kitgum, Lira, Lira Municipal Council, Oyam and Pader.) Kampala: Education Planning Department.

Northern Uganda Psycho-Social Needs Assessment (NUPSNA) (1998) Executive Summary. Kampala: Unicef.

Rudenberg, S.L., Jansen, P. & Fridjhon, P. (2001) *Living and Coping with Ongoing Violence: a cross-national analysis of children's drawings using structured rating indices.* London: Sage.

Save the Children, Uganda (2007) *Baseline Survey of Education in Post Conflict Areas in Uganda.* Save the Children Uganda.

Singer, P.W. (2005) *Children at War.* New York: Pantheon.

Sommer, M. (2006). Fearing Africa's Young Men. The Case of Rwanda. Conflict Prevention and Reconstruction Unit, Working Paper 2 No. 32. Washington DC: World Bank.

Ssekamwa, J.C. (1997) *History and the Development of Uganda.* Kampala: Fountain Publishers.

Smith, A. & Vaux, T. (2003) *Education, Conflict and International Development.* London: Department for International Development.

Smith, R. & Neill, J. (2006) Developing Frameworks for School Self Evaluation to Improve Schools Effectiveness for Peace in Northern Ireland, *Improving Schools*, 9(2), 153-174.

Sommers, M. (2002) Children, Education and War: reaching Education for All (EFA) objectives in countries affected by war. CPR Working Paper, no. 1. Uppsala University. http://www.prio.no/CSCW/Dataset/Armed

Vygotsky, L.S. (1978) *Mind in Society.* Cambridge MA: Harvard University Press.

Woolman, D. (2001) Educational Reconstruction and Post Colonial Curriculum Development: a comparative study of four African Countries, *International Education Journal*, 2(5), 27-46.

CHAPTER 9

Schools and Peacebuilding in Northern Uganda: young people's perspectives

JEREMY CUNNINGHAM

SUMMARY The impact of armed conflict on education is devastating. Although education may be a cause of armed conflict, it can play an important role in recovery and peacebuilding. What are the attributes of good-quality peacebuilding education? Although infrastructure, funding and access are vital elements, so is the nature of school practice. A framework is proposed for understanding peacebuilding education, based on a synthesis of knowledge, values and actions for skills. Schools in a district of Northern Uganda are examined for their contribution to peacebuilding education, using empirical evidence from young people in seven schools, as well as observation, documentary study and interviews with teachers and officials. The formal curriculum, extra-curricular activities and school culture are the contexts investigated. The findings are that knowledge important for peacebuilding, such as human rights, is being taught largely by non-governmental organizations and with little support from the curriculum. Values of forgiveness and fairness are fairly well developed, but that of equal dignity appears much weaker. Some students are building skills through participation in authority structures, and some experience of problem solving and sensitization. However, the lack of democratic participation and the failure of some teachers to adhere to the code of conduct reduce the potential of school culture to contribute to peace. Suggestions are made for improvements.

Introduction

The impact of conflict on development is devastating: of more than 100 million children out of school around the world, half are in conflict-affected countries, above all in Africa (Tomlinson & Benefield, 2005). The international community is deeply concerned with the prevention of conflict, but equally important is the process of peacebuilding.

Preventing the outbreak of armed conflict may be referred to as *peace-keeping*. This may be achieved by autocratic government and the suppression of minorities intent on securing their rights (Gurr, 2000); it neither implies nor requires emancipation. On the other hand, *peacebuilding*, as defined by Hanlon (2006, p. 32), means 'promoting a just and stable peace by helping to end the war and by helping to create the conditions that reduce the likelihood of the war starting again'. Galtung (1985) defined 'positive peace' as the opposite of structural violence, occurring when people are socially dominated, politically oppressed, or economically exploited (Galtung, 1969). Since the injustices of structural violence can contribute towards violent conflict, peacebuilding actions must address underlying inequalities and grievances.

Education is implicated in reinforcing and perpetuating inequalities; for example, through the distorted curricula in Rwanda (Mamdani, 2001) and in the ready recruitment of under-educated young men (and women, though to a lesser degree) into armed forces, as in Sierra Leone (Bush & Saltarelli, 2000). Not all believe that education has a role to play in dealing with the legacies of conflict; for example, education is barely mentioned in Ali & Matthews' study of peacebuilding in Africa (2004). However others, such as David (2002), claim a role for education as a significant element in successful peacebuilding. Non-governmental organizations (NGOs) are increasingly engaged in educational activities in the post-conflict context. These activities may take place in communities, truth commissions and historical enquiries, as well as in the formal institutions of schools and colleges. Academic, theoretical and empirical research in this area has grown in recent years (Davies, 2004; Harber, 2004; Buckland, 2005; Lederach, 2005), but the contribution of education to peacebuilding is still poorly understood.

A social learning approach sees humans as having potential for both war and peace. It is how people are socialized that determines how peaceable society is (Boulding, 2000). A response to structural violence may be armed conflict, but initiators of insurgencies seldom foresee the long-term costs; the alternative is peaceful collective political action. Values of a peaceful political culture are learned socially and schools play an important though not a unique role (Harber, 1998). The provision of good general schooling is fundamental. Responsive to local, regional and global contexts, such schooling should improve social mobility, access to employment and responsiveness to economic and technological change.

Educated individuals are better able than the uneducated to negotiate, compromise, and navigate the social and political terrain in order to achieve their goals. These skills may reduce the likelihood of armed conflict (Wessells, 2005). In their efforts to improve society, individuals rarely act alone, but usually collectively and often in civil society: unions, religious groups, traders' associations and advocacy organizations. Frequently, civil society institutions are rapidly created after violent conflict, with hope of increasing democratization – empowering the dispossessed, farmers, teachers, students and factory workers (Jeong 2005). Empirical evidence from Kenya (Obura, 2002) and South Africa (Jones, 2005) shows that schooling can contribute to mediation and peacebuilding skills, but that is it important to maintain good links with the local community and civil society so as to avoid isolation and misunderstanding.

Provision and access are basic requirements, but they should not be set against educational reform aimed specifically at developing peaceful political values. Quality must be demanded as well as quantity. Of course, curriculum reform and school development after different types of armed conflict will depend on some consensus between central government, local government and communities on the roots of the conflict. Little change can be expected if the analysis is highly contested. Oberschall (2007) shows that after ethnic conflicts, parents do not want the school curriculum to be biased against their ethnic group in history, civics and literature. They want the school administration to treat all ethnic groups fairly, and to protect them against harassment by other children. However not all armed conflicts are ethnically based; many have complex socio-economic elements.

Reform, then, is not simply a matter of curriculum content. Harber (1998) argues that the organization of classrooms and schools must be more congruent with democratic aims, and that participative teaching methods develop respect for human rights. School can be a valuable training ground for peacebuilding through civil society, or it may unconsciously teach violence. For example, school students with a grievance may destroy their own school if they are incapable of using appropriate skills to address the issue; those who are more skilled can engage with the authorities and peacefully achieve their 'political ends'. Knowledge of legal, political and rights systems should increase individual and community agency; values of fairness, equal dignity, forgiveness and tolerance may motivate people to deploy civil and political means to obtain positive peace.

The key question is 'What are the attributes of good-quality peacebuilding education?' Although infrastructure, funding and access are vital elements, my own background and expertise lead me to focus on the quality of school practice. First, I discuss a framework for understanding peacebuilding education, based on a synthesis of knowledge, values and actions for skills. Then I examine how schools in a district of Northern Uganda may be contributing to peacebuilding education, mainly using empirical evidence from young people in seven schools, but also including observation, documentary study and interviews with teachers and officials. The formal curriculum, extra-curricular activities and school culture are the contexts investigated in this study. Implications are drawn out for peacebuilding education in the district, and (with some qualification), more generally. I conclude with suggestions for improvement.

Synthesis: knowledge, values and actions for skills

By its title *peace education* proposes an appropriate education for peacebuilding. It is defined by the United Nations High Commission for Refugees (UNHCR) as:

> The process of promoting the knowledge, skills, attitudes and values needed to bring about behavior changes that will enable children, youth and adults to prevent conflict and violence, both overt and structural; to resolve conflict peacefully; and to create the conditions conducive to peace, whether at an intrapersonal, interpersonal, inter-group, national or international level. (Baxter, 2000, p. 2)

Peace education is used around the world in post-conflict contexts (Reardon, 2000). Its proponents claim it to be more than a school subject: it is a 'process' – a whole approach to education to be conveyed through a variety of subjects across the curriculum, and its broad approach allows for adaptation to local needs. Only rarely does peace education appear in schools as a subject in its own right, and few programmes define the necessary knowledge content. Some include human rights and humanitarian law; others, though clearly based on such concepts and values, avoid their direct mention (International Network for Education in Emergencies [INEE], 2007).

Human rights ought to provide an important foundation for any peacebuilding education. They are aimed at the prevention of war, the tolerance of different ideas and beliefs, the participation of citizens in governance, the establishment of procedural justice, and the promotion of economic and social well-being of all (United Nations [UN], 1945). Ratified by the great majority of states, they are both 'settled norms' (Frost, 1996) and international legal instruments enshrined in the UN conventions.[1] Education appears not only as a specified right in Article 26 of the United Nations Universal Declaration of Human Rights, but also in the requirement that it should be used to strengthen respect for human rights. The preamble to the Universal Declaration of Human Rights makes clear the educational obligation of governments and individuals:

> that every individual and every organ of society, keeping this Declaration constantly in mind, shall strive by teaching and education to promote respect for these rights and freedoms.(UN, 1945)[2]

Human rights education is based on the main global human rights instruments and articles (Osler & Starkey, 1996). Omission of human rights from school curricula in many countries has generated advocacy by the UN and NGOs. The UN General Assembly has proclaimed a World Programme for Human Rights Education 'to promote a common understanding of the basic principles and methodologies ... to provide a concrete framework for action

... and to strengthen partnerships and cooperation from the international level down to the grass roots' (UN, 2005 p. 1). Young people learn about human rights by example as well as in theory, and therefore consideration of the impact of human rights education should encompass the values and action skills developed by young people (Cunningham, 1991, 2000). A weakness of human rights education is that human rights themselves are contested in a number of different cultures.[3] Human rights education does not generally appear as a school subject with guaranteed curriculum time, and by itself it is not capable of covering the range of knowledge and skills that young people need to be actively involved in their own community and nation. For example, it generally does not address national political, legal and social institutions and their operation.

Peace and/or human rights topics often appear in *civic, social* and/or *political education*, designed to teach young people the knowledge and values they need as loyal members of the state (Kerr, 2000). Such courses, which assume a passive role for the general population (Lockyer et al, 2003), tend to be theoretical, and take place at secondary level only. They often lack any participation or action to develop skills, and are perhaps conceived to keep subordinate groups 'in their place' (Osler et al, 1995). *Citizenship education* has developed to emphasize (a) a more active participative approach (Lord & Flowers, 2006), and (b) a more internationalist or cosmopolitan dimension (Crick, 2000; Motani, 2007). Participation and action are usually key elements. This approach has its roots in developed countries, and it is not uncontested. For example Gamarnikov & Green (2000) criticize what they consider to be its neo-liberal and individual consumerist stance. Unlike peace education, both civic and citizenship education have a clear body of knowledge, including key subjects like human rights, and often have specific allocated curriculum time.

Of the four 'educations' described, it seems that 'citizenship education' provides the approach that embraces most comprehensively the requirements for good-quality education for peacebuilding: it covers local, national and global institutions; it also includes personal capacities and actions; and finally, through adaptation of the more commonly found 'civic education', it can be inserted into the curriculum as a named subject.

Reardon (2000), drawing on a wide range of sources, distinguishes between educating '*about*' peace – the study of institutions, causes of violent conflict, political and economic structures – and educating '*for*' peace – the development of peace-making capacities. The former implies some body of knowledge, and the latter demands values and skills. Some citizenship education scholars also argue for the need for a *synthesis,* in which *knowledge, values* and *skills* are all given importance, and where school students address issues in their own lives, at the local, national and global levels (Osler et al, 1995; Arthur & Wright, 2001). Education is not synonymous with 'schooling'; there are many ways in which people become educated: through conversations in the community, through the media, and through personal study, for example. However, I find this synthesis of knowledge, values and skills to be a useful framework through which to examine *schooling* for peacebuilding. Schooling is taken to include both the formal taught curriculum, the non-formal elements such as clubs and extra-curricular activities, and the rituals and processes of the school, such as assemblies, discipline and disputes procedures; so-called 'school culture'.

Elements under Investigation

This section discusses the three parts of the 'synthesis' framework, and the elements to be investigated in Northern Uganda using this framework.

Knowledge means an understanding and recall of definite facts, articles, events and institutions. It is relatively straightforward to plan for and to test simple factual recall, and much of the world's educational assessment is based on this approach. However, it also consists of the ability to make connections and cross-references, capabilities that are less easy to assess. What is the required knowledge for peacebuilding? It may be the history of the recent conflict, human rights articles, or local and contextual knowledge such as community systems for discussion and redress, but I am unqualified to investigate those areas.

I decided to focus on knowledge of human rights, which assists peacebuilding because people need a secure foundation for their claims, advocacy and actions. Being able to refer to global standards strengthens the position of the otherwise relatively powerless (Gibney 2003; Blau & Moncada 2005). The UN demands that every state should ensure that its citizens be taught their rights (Article 26 quoted above), and although not all education is schooling, school is the one place where a large share of the population can be exposed to knowledge deemed desirable. The school context for such learning should be the organized taught curriculum, supported by the examination system. Investigation was made into what rights students easily recalled, whether they knew about any conventions or constitutional provisions, and the sources of any knowledge.

It is possible to learn human rights or recent history parrot-fashion, but yet have no understanding or commitment to peace: '*knowledge without values*'. *Values* are beliefs about what is desirable, applied as normative standards to choose among alternative modes of behaviour. Families and communities contribute to values development, and schooling is where a large share of the population can be subject to values teaching (Carlton, 1995). Programmes of study, moral teaching in assemblies, daily problem solving and dispute resolution represent the conscious approach. However, the everyday culture of the school has an impact, for young people learn not just from what is said, but also from what they experience.

A variety of frameworks for understanding values have been proposed (Schwartz, 1992; Hofstede, 2001). As values are often unacknowledged by the individual, there is considerable debate about whether their development can be objectively assessed (Carlton, 1995). I follow those scholars who argue that values can be uncovered; for example, Inglehart & Welzel (2005), who have analysed over eighty national surveys of values to explain links between social and economic change.

Can peacebuilding values be identified and purposefully fostered in schools, and if so, which ones? In view of the lack of scholarly consensus, it seems reasonable to propose a limited values framework relevant to the specific context. In Northern Uganda, reconciliation between those who were abducted by the Lord's Resistance Army (LRA) and those who directly and indirectly suffered from the war (Baines, 2007) has been promoted by local religious leaders. Reconciliation is considered to be a necessary but insufficient element of peacebuilding (Borer, 2006). Lederach (1997) proposes that the process of reconciliation can take place when acknowledgement and forgiveness meet justice and peace. More general processes of mediation and counselling also require the values of forgiveness and fairness, and a school is one arena where such values can be taught and experienced. The presence of two values – 'forgiveness' and 'fairness' – will therefore be investigated in Northern Uganda. The fairness to be explored is that of 'due process' and 'proportionality' in the resolution of problems or the handling of offences against rules.

The third value to be explored is 'equal dignity'. This is chosen over the term 'equality', which can be interpreted to mean either 'the same' or 'fair treatment' in terms of distributive justice (Sen, 2009). 'Equal dignity' is about regarding other human beings as equal to oneself, and treating them accordingly. It is the value that lies behind the first article of the Universal Declaration of Human Rights (UN, 1945).

In this study, questions were asked about the best ways of solving problems in schools, or what makes a good prefect, and inference has been made about the values underlying the answers. The evidence must be treated with due caution, because in interviews people often say what they believe they are expected to say and because value inference is inevitably a subjective process. This was mediated to an extent by approaching the matter of values expression indirectly.

It is possible to care deeply about peace or human rights but have no *skills* of, for instance, discussion, negotiation, cooperation or advocacy that will help secure favourable outcomes with respect to peacebuilding: '*values without efficacy*'. Saying what you ought to do or plan to do is evidence of values, but does not necessarily lead to any action. The development of peacebuilding *skills* requires participation, action and practice (Benn, 2000). Arguably these concur with various tabulations of 'citizenship skills' (Griffiths, 1998; Duerr et al, 2000; Osler & Starkey, 2005. I suggest that a minimum skill level is needed to take any action, and repeated actions lead to skill development (Halpern, 1998). Thus, action and skills are in a linked relationship: a skill can only be observed or assessed in operation. For example, it is not enough to tell someone that you are a skilled musician or manager – the evidence is in the practice. This link is expressed by the term '*actions for skills*'. In this study, actions that may develop peacebuilding skills include keeping good order, fair problem solving, sensitization and democratic participation for improvement. Due account must be taken of people's tendency to cast themselves in a good light when reporting past actions, and opportunities are few for a short-term observer to evaluate skills in action.

Context

Northern Uganda provides a suitable setting for a case study into post-conflict schooling and possibilities for peacebuilding education, as it has suffered twenty years of violent conflict, arising from the turbulent history of the country since independence in 1962. Following an exploratory visit to Gulu district in Northern Uganda in 2006, I have been engaged in doctoral research for which I made a three-month visit to Gulu town and district in late 2009.

The war in Northern Uganda started in 1986 as an insurgency aimed at the capture of state power (Behrend, 1999). The Lord's Resistance Army (LRA), led by Joseph Kony, lost the support of the local population and resorted to kidnapping children for its forces and supply columns. Some 25,000 young people were abducted, and became victims and perpetrators of violence and atrocities (Civil Society Organizations for Peace in Northern Uganda [CSOPNU], 2006). Government efforts to defeat the LRA were ineffective for many years. An estimated 35,000 people were killed and 90% of the population forcibly moved into internally displaced people's (IDP) camps. This created terrible conditions with high death rates, total loss of farming livelihoods, and the loss of confidence and self-esteem among many of the survivors of conflict and displacement. The districts of Northern Uganda have lost decades of development and feel marginalized compared to other regions of Uganda. Since 2007, the immediate violence has stopped; Kony and his forces are in Sudan and the Central African Republic. People are returning to their villages.

Large numbers of rural schools were displaced from their home sites during the war, and moved onto urban temporary sites. Urban schools themselves suffered attacks, destruction and abductions. The results for educational standards were devastating. Schools are now moving back to their original sites, but face great challenges. There is no overall 'peacebuilding education' plan. However, the Government has formulated a comprehensive development framework, the 'Peace, Recovery and Development Plan for Northern Uganda' (Government of Uganda, 2007), as a strategy to eradicate poverty and improve the welfare of the populace in Northern Uganda. Within this, the main educational problems are defined as lack of classrooms, insufficient teachers (exacerbated by high absenteeism), and high pupil drop-out. The plan focuses on classroom construction and expansion, teacher training, provision of scholastic materials, and support for alternative education such as skills training. 'Improving the quality of services' is referred to, but with no detail or attached strategy. The current President of Uganda is trying to reinforce national unity and reduce ethnic rivalry though 'patriotic clubs' and presidential officials' speeches in school. This has a worrying militaristic element [4] and seems to equate peace with order. Some suspect the ruling party of using these patriotic clubs as a tactic in the forthcoming 2011 presidential elections.

Education in Uganda is largely decentralized, but there are unifying elements: the national curriculum and examinations system and the national standards for teacher training and professional development. Additionally, development partners and international NGOs are in a close relationship with government. The United States Agency for International Development (USAID) funded programme 'Revitalising Education, Participation and Learning in Conflict Areas' (REPLICA) has trained teachers and provided peace education texts for schools in Northern Uganda and is run from an office in the Ministry of Education.[5]

Many abducted young people have been captured by government forces or have escaped from the bush. They are known as 'abductees' or 'returnees'. There are large needs for trauma recovery and psychosocial support for these young people (Kostelny, 2008), remedial general education to compensate them for the educational years lost, and life-skills and vocational training to help them back into agriculture and other work (Robinson, 2007). Interviews with teachers have revealed that there have been tensions and problems between returnees and non-abductees who suffered displacement and bereavement. At the local level, other local, national and international NGOs have also been involved in peacebuilding education, providing psychosocial training and therapy, introducing guidance and counselling to schools, and addressing the deficit in girls' education. Interviews with district and municipal officials showed that the concept of peace education is well understood. NGO support is welcome but there are problems with the amount of time teachers are taken out for training, and with overlap and confusion between the different NGO programmes.

Method

A week was spent in each of seven schools, selected on advice from a local NGO and from the District Education Officer as broadly representative of the district: all were government schools, and none was at the top or the bottom of the examination league tables. The rural schools were necessarily within reasonable commuting distance from Gulu town. The sample includes:

- two urban primary schools, and one urban secondary school, itself in temporary accommodation having been displaced from its home village 40 km away. These are described as 'Urban Primary 1', 'Urban Primary

2' and 'Urban Secondary'. Urban Primary 1 has an annexe for visually disabled children who are integrated into the school.
- two rural primary schools serving the emptying IDP camp Coo Pe, and a rural secondary school. In the analysis they are described as 'Rural Primary 1', 'Rural Primary 2' and 'Rural Secondary'. Rural schools face bigger challenges than urban schools: they have very poor infrastructure and their distance from town leads to staff lateness and absenteeism. They have higher female drop-out figures and achieve lower primary examination results than urban schools. All three schools had been displaced from their original sites (more than once) and had only recently returned 'home'.
- a special primary school for 'war affected children', either 'returnees' or orphaned children. It is described as 'Special School'. It is the only such special school in Uganda.

The schools' sites and facilities vary considerably. The special school was built recently with funds from a European country and although showing signs of wear and tear, it was the best state school site I have seen in Uganda. The urban primaries still showed signs of the damage done in the war, but there was evidence of rebuilding and repair. The rural secondary had just moved to refurbished buildings. The two rural primaries had very basic classrooms, built with the help of NGOs. The urban secondary was on a very cramped site, with wooden walls, and papyrus mats dividing each class. In all the mainstream schools the class sizes were high: between 60 and 100.

In each school, semi-structured interviews were carried out with the head, and four other teachers, including a deputy head and a senior woman teacher. Much of the time in each school was spent in informal observation in the compound, classrooms and staffroom. I taught several lessons in each school too, and listened to teachers solving problems or running clubs. I studied curriculum documents, examination papers, textbooks, and school and classroom rules.

The main focus for this chapter is the view of students. At least two interviews with groups of students were carried out in each school. As the aim was to investigate knowledge, values and actions relating to peacebuilding, in each school I chose to talk with one group whose goal was to contribute to management and good order – the prefects – and with a 'sensitization' club that was intended to contribute to a peaceful culture. The clubs were variously named 'World Vision Club', 'Peace Club', 'Girls Education Movement', 'Music, Dance and Drama Club'. For comparison, one further interview was conducted with the student council from the primary teachers' training college.

The total number of young people involved was 186. I spoke with 16 groups of young people; the groups ranged in size from 4 to 22 young people, with an average group size of 11. My previous experience of interviewing young people in cross-sectional focus groups was that just one or two more confident speakers dominated the discussion, with the majority of the group rather overcome by the novelty of the situation. I decided to work with groups that knew each other and were presumably used to discussion. These groups were the most likely to be familiar with the ideas under examination, but this would be compensated for by a wider range of voices within the groups. It meant that I could not rule out other young people being equally familiar with the ideas, but I considered it probable that they would not. Usually the teacher 'patrons' of the groups had received some training which they were supposed to pass on to the young people in a cascade model. While, I did not know whether prefects had any training, I expected most of them to have good academic performance and general knowledge.

The people of Gulu district are mainly from the Acholi tribe. With the help of an Acholi research assistant, these interviews were mainly in their mother tongue, Luo. While all schoolchildren learn English, the level of oral skills is very variable, especially in the primary schools. I wanted to be sure that the young people were able to say what they thought without obstruction or fear. One early interview was carried out in English in order to test out the schedule. The research assistant has been involved in youth work and workshops on peacebuilding so he is familiar with the concepts of the study as well as the local culture. The interview schedule was jointly constructed. It was my habit to meet the group at the beginning and end of the interview and to allow the research assistant to conduct the interview in my absence. Inevitably there is some loss of character and individuality in the transcription and translation process. Luo is a simpler language than English and some of the rights and peace concepts have nuances in English that cannot be expressed in a Luo vocabulary.

Findings

Knowledge

Familiarity with rights. Groups were asked if they had come across the terms 'human rights', 'children's rights', 'women's rights', and what the terms meant to them. The terms were easily recognized: the English word 'rights' can be often seen on banners and t-shirts in the town, and there is a Luo translation, 'twero', which also means 'power'. Needs-related socio-economic rights were recalled twice as often as civil and political rights, with 60 references. Children have learned about their rights to food, shelter, medical attention, education, and freedom from abuse and exploitation. The right to education was the single right most often referred to. The issue of child labour is controversial in Uganda. In article 32 of the Convention of the Rights of the Child, it is defined as dangerous work or work that interferes with education (UNICEF, 2010), but teachers informed me that children refer to their right to be free from child labour to try to avoid normal domestic tasks or school sanctions.

Freedom of movement, opinion and expression, worship, and those answers that included the word 'freedom' were mentioned only five times in all 10 of the primary groups. Rights concerned with democratic participation and due process; for example, the right to be charged, to be tried in public, and not to be imprisoned without due cause, were not recalled or mentioned at all.

Knowledge of human rights conventions or Uganda constitution. The young people who participated in my research did not know about the UN or African Union human rights instruments, or the 1995 Uganda constitution. In response to direct and indirect questions, there were only two references to 'a list of all the rights we have'. Although the original documents are complex, simply worded versions of the Declaration and the Convention on the Rights of the Child have been produced for children (UNICEF, 2010), but they are not available in this district. Some young people have seen leaflets from NGOs explaining what rights they have.

> With me, I have learnt about rights from workshop which was organized by diocese of Northern Uganda. We were distributed a book which was entitled 'All People have Rights', this book contains all the rights of human beings. (Urban Secondary focus group)

Sources of knowledge about rights. When asked where and how they learned about rights, the largest proportion of young people reported that it was the result of activity by local NGOs. The most popular local radio station, Mega FM, is used to reach a wide audience and it has a policy of making its airwaves available to NGOs at low cost.[6] The local group Human Rights Focus has bought many weekend morning slots for community sensitization. Mega FM was set up with a grant from the British Government.

Many young people have been taught about human rights in workshops. The training has been aimed specifically at school clubs, and at the wider community. Some local government officials are teaching rights mainly to secondary students, through the briefing of Uganda National Students' Association (UNSA) leaders and prefects. There is some family and community learning as well. For instance, young people said the following:

> We attended the workshop which was organized by Invisible Children and a lot was discussed about human rights and education in schools. (Urban Secondary focus group)

> Ugandan National Student Association plays a key role in promoting human rights. We have been trained at District level that is the role of the UNSA to coordinate and protect students' rights. (Urban Secondary focus group)

> In several occasions from home with my uncle who works like a paralegal in the community, he has tried to tell me about some

> rights which whole human being are entitled to, e.g. right to live, freedom of speech and expression etc. (Urban Secondary focus group)
>
> From local song and poems. (Rural Primary focus group)

Three times as many responses referred to out-of-school learning about rights than to in-school learning. There is a very small section on human rights at the end of primary year 7, which is often missed as preference is given to examination preparation. Secondary schools have optional subjects, 'Political education' [7] and 'Christian religious education', which carry some reference to human rights. There is also a small amount of rights learning in science, related to HIV, reproductive health or child protection. Any other teaching is at the discretion and motivation of the teacher, which was confirmed by teacher interviews.

> I have learnt about human rights from school because I am a prefect ... where normally we learn human rights issues as a group. The group organizes ... meetings at the end of each month and ... we share our experiences and opinions on peace, human rights and securities. (Urban Secondary focus group)
>
> Heard from one of our teacher(s) during lesson hour. (Rural Primary focus group)

Implications. Young people are mainly learning about rights directly or indirectly from NGOs and not from the mainstream curriculum. The process of NGOs teaching people about human rights began during the war, when allegations of atrocities by both sides led first to the collection of evidence about human rights abuses, and then to the employment of the language of rights in the efforts to bring the war to an end through negotiation. The use of local radio was not primarily aimed at young people, but interventions by international organizations like the Norwegian Refugee Council, UNICEF and others led to the training of hundreds of primary and secondary teachers. They were encouraged to set up school clubs, and teach human and children's rights in the non-formal curriculum.

My argument is that for peacebuilding, young people ought to learn about human rights, not just children's rights and women's rights. They ought to learn about the indivisibility of rights, not just one element. The rights that are being taught are largely socio-economic rights, such as the right to education and health. This tends to marginalize the importance of rights of due process and participation that can lead to individuals and communities taking more control over their own lives.

While NGOs responded to the urgencies of the conflict and post-conflict situation, and have been successful in sensitizing people to the idea of rights, this approach is not sustainable in the long term. Indeed there is evidence that the pressure on time and resources has resulted in a superficial approach that is in danger of creating a backlash. If the NGO presence in Northern Uganda is reduced in future, the impact of their work may fade over time. It is necessary for comprehensive human rights knowledge to be firmly built into the taught curriculum.

Values

Forgiveness. There was evidence of the value of forgiveness from all interviews, with 58 references from 14 groups. Ideas about counselling, dispute resolution and mediation are well established, and were mentioned by many groups, and it seems likely that school policy in this area is at least supporting this value. This was confirmed by almost universal reports from teachers about their work in counselling and guidance, and their resolution of problems and dilemmas.

> Practice policy of love for one another between teachers and students (Special School focus group)
>
> In case of physical harms created on somebody you have to provide medical treatment to buy heart of forgiveness from the victims. (Urban Secondary focus group)
>
> Importance of safe school to children, e.g. safe schools normally have halls counselling and guidance. (Urban Primary 1 focus group)
>
> [Prefects] should act as a mediator between teachers and students. (Rural primary 2 focus group)

Fairness. Young people found it easy to recall incidents of *un*fairness in school, with 53 comments from all 15 school groups.[8] The ways in which these incidents are related reveal their underlying values or expectations about fair treatment. References to unfairness included harsh punishment such as suspension for minor offences or after failing to check the facts; favouritism; insults and abuse of power. Young people consider any form of corporal punishment to be unfair. Frequent or severe caning in Ugandan schools has traditionally been commonplace. It was banned by government circular in 2006 but has not explicitly been made illegal under statute. The Ministry of Education launched a handbook in 2008 on alternatives to corporal punishment, recognizing that it was still being used in schools despite the ban (World Corporal Punishment Research, 2010).

> Other prefects treat people differently. Others when they are dealing with late comers they leave older students and punish the young students. (Special School focus group)

> There was a day when children were shouting in the class and a prefect entered into a class [and] started caning me instead of finding out what has happened. (Rural Primary 2 focus group)

> Some teachers here in ... like giving children corporal punishment which is being abolished in schools within Uganda. (Urban Primary 2 focus group)

Participants were asked for positive examples of fair treatment in terms of offences and disputes. These are statements of 'ought', not necessarily of 'is'. It is quite possible for a prefect who suffered injustice when young, who knows how they ought to behave now, still to act unfairly as a result of one kind of pressure or another.

> Investigating the root causes of problem before giving punishment to students. (Urban Secondary focus group)

> I should not be biased on students' side or teachers' side when making decision. (Urban Secondary focus group)

> [A good prefect] ... avoids corporal punishment. R(ural Primary 1 focus group)

> They should propose appropriate punishment for a particular offence. (Special School focus group)

Equal dignity. Just over half the groups referred to equality, dignity and mutual respect between people. However, the total number of references was fairly low in relation to the two other categories. It seems that the value of equal dignity is not firmly established in young people's minds. References to girls' education, tribalism and disability came from only two groups in each case. Surprisingly, although teachers in all schools described the integration of returnees, there were no unprompted references to 'returnees' or 'abductees'. This may indicate that they have been successfully integrated into schools and do not suffer stigmatization or bullying, but the drop-out rate of returnees is known to be high (see Murphy et al, in this volume), and they may now be invisible to young people in school. Even when religion was not mentioned specifically, the influence of religious values is apparent through the use of expressions like 'All human beings are created in God's image' (Urban secondary focus group).

Both these comments come from a 'Girls' Education Movement' club set up specifically to address issues of girls' educational inequalities:

> To encourage girls who have dropped out of school to return back. (Rural Primary 1 focus group)

> Encouraging child mothers to go back to school. (Rural Primary 1 focus group)

The following responses each come from schools which have special reason to know about disabled people; the urban primary includes an annexe for the visually disabled:

> Giving equal respect to a disabled person. (Urban Primary 1 focus group)

> Equal treatment. Helping the disabled. (Special School focus group)

Implications. Through their daily practice, schools may foster peacebuilding values. The relationship between the schools, local traditional culture and religion has created a strong basis for the value of forgiveness – which is an essential element of reconciliation. As a result of congruence between community and religious traditions, this value has been well integrated into school culture: most teachers are aware of the trauma suffered by young people and many have been trained in psycho-social support by local NGOs.

Schools expect young people to keep good order through the prefect system. NGOs have had some impact on the fairness of school systems, through training on day-to-day conflict resolution and non-punitive approaches. However, superficial teaching about rights without their reciprocal elements of responsibility has led to tensions. Fairness is aimed for by schools but evidence from the young people shows it is not reliably achieved. For a more effective educational contribution to peace, corporal punishment must be finally and completely abolished, prefects better trained, and teachers' levels of professionalism and attendance raised.

The value of equal dignity does not seem well developed and may be rather dependent on religious teaching rather than anything specifically fostered in most schools. Disabled children are integrated in several schools, and in two schools there is action to reduce the barriers to girls' education. During the war there was clearly considerable stigmatization of returnees, which led to high drop-out. Teachers claim that returnees have been integrated, but the proportion is not known. There is almost no evidence of inter-ethnic tension in this district, which is composed very largely of one ethnic group. Levels of ethnic tension would merit further investigation, especially in more ethnically mixed areas.

NGOs have made a contribution to values development. The involvement of NGOs is likely to decline now that the war in Uganda appears to be over [9], and therefore these advances will have to be maintained by building values and methods to teach them into the teacher training system. There is some evidence that this is understood by officials and educationalists in Northern Uganda.

Actions for Skills

Responsibility for good order through 'legitimate' authority. Some young people are gaining practical experience of leadership and authority through their contribution to the good order of the school, and they are learning about conflicts of loyalty. This contributes to their skill development, as they have to learn to balance competing demands.

The prefect system works similarly in all the schools in the study, whether primary, secondary or special. Prefects' duties include monitoring cleaning, organizing assemblies and food queues, and preventing vandalism and trespassing in the teachers' quarters. Prefects are important for peaceful school order since teachers are overloaded, with classes of up to 90 students, and they spend any spare moment marking in the staffroom. By referring matters upwards, but also trying to hold teachers to account, the prefects are at an important interface in the school.

Both secondary schools have formal students' disciplinary committees linked to the staff disciplinary committee, following national policy. Due process is also seen in the appointment of prefects. First, there are written applications vetted by staff. The candidates then campaign and are elected by fellow students. Most schools appear to give their prefects some basic training, but references to prefects' meetings were rare, implying that once appointed, prefects are left to get on with it. It is clear that being a prefect is not easy, as it leads to conflicts of loyalty.

> My experience as head boy is that arranging students to line up for meals is very difficult. Most students don't want to follow lines and in case if I advise them, they turn against me. On several occasion I have [been] threatened and disturbed during the night by those student. (Urban Secondary focus group)
>
> As a health prefect I am in charge of sanitation and at most cases the community around the school use the latrine badly such that I feel I should resign but I feel also that is my work to make sure that it is clean. (Rural Primary 2 focus group)

Fair problem solving in the school. Some young people are developing skills of problem solving and negotiation. Prefects have a role in caring for younger children, monitoring health conditions and settling disputes, in boarding dormitories or in classes unattended by teachers. Prefects' manners towards fellow students were courteous and relaxed, in my presence at least. Interviews with teachers revealed that many prefects take a proactive role in counselling and problem solving, but it is clear that some prefects are unjust or biased some of the time. The prefects and club groups give quite convincing accounts of their actions to build a peaceful cooperative culture in school.

> Being kind and humble, respectful and exemplary, courageous and confident. (Rural Secondary focus group)

When issues are reported upwards, students generally trust their teachers to be fair and to sort out the problem peacefully. The references are more often to 'talk' or 'counsel' than to punishment. Where punishment is used, it is usually cleaning or 'slashing' (grass cutting). There is one account of a situation where the students decided not to report some serious matter. The use of the terms 'counselling' and 'guidance' was general; 'trauma' was also used several times. This is further evidence of the students' peaceful values and their confidence to sort out some problems without recourse to teachers.

> it happened last year when the head boy come together with the head girl and they play sex ...we did not tell the teachers because we knew they would be suspended or it would spoil their name or spoil the name of the school. (Upper Primary 1 focus group)

> Giving advice to people with loggerheads and discouraging stereotyping and hatred along tribal lines. (Urban Primary 1 focus group)

> it is quarrelling between two people in the dormitory, then we try to stop them quarrelling ... discuss with them what have made them quarrel ... giving amnesty to children when they have fought or when they have done something wrong. (Urban Primary 2 focus group)

Sensitization. There is a culture of 'sensitization' in the district, which has been fostered by a wide variety of NGOs. Every school has several clubs whose purpose is to raise consciousness of important issues such as HIV/AIDS, domestic violence and girls' education. The traditional dances of the area are combined with songs composed by the groups themselves, and performed at assemblies, or in villages. The clubs provide a context for discussion, teamwork and the building of self-esteem. However, the amount of activity is variable, and several clubs referred to me had not met for some time or had been wound up.

> We are promoting team spirits through playing football and participating in debating. (Urban Secondary focus group)

> To organize drama or role plays that show those things, which are against children's rights. (Urban Primary 1 focus group)

Girls' Education Movement groups in two rural primary schools are using music, dance and drama to give assemblies, and to go into villages to teach parents the importance of girls' education. Boys are members of these groups as well as girls. In one school the whole group was making sanitary pads from local materials so that girls did not need to miss school – especially in the all-important exam period – and were requesting supplies from UNICEF. The group also encourages child mothers to return to school after giving birth.

Democratic participation for school improvement. There is little evidence of a structured, institutional approach to democratic participation in the development of the school. Although I saw a number of examples of class rules that had been negotiated in discussions between the teacher and students, this seemed to be the initiative of individual teachers rather than whole-school policy. In one case it was claimed that the prefects were consulted about revisions to school rules, but it was not possible to see exactly what they had contributed.

Teachers' attendance, time-keeping, and adherence to the code of conduct is a serious problem in Gulu district. Most students put up with this and prefects appear to feel bound to discourage student protests, but there are signs of assertiveness in some schools.

> Trying to hold teachers to account. (Urban Secondary focus group)
>
> Telling the teachers that corporal punishment is against the right of a child. (Urban Primary 1 focus group)

An interesting meeting observed between a music, dance and drama group and their teacher 'patrons' dealt with a series of problems and complaints. The group displayed assertiveness with good manners and the warm relationship between teachers and young people was obvious (Urban Secondary). Many schools have a regular slot for 'debate', which is handled competitively with local and national competitions. While undoubtedly this can develop rhetorical skills and confidence, it does little for reasoned discussion and compromise. The one class debate I observed had a less than helpful title: 'War is better than Aids', and the competitive approach to debate led to a chaotic and disorderly conclusion.

Implications. School students are used to putting themselves forward for school authority, using hustings and manifestos. They participate in elections of their peers. Senior students serve on disciplinary committees. However, schools are still very hierarchical, and especially at primary level, pupils have few avenues for expression and no formal processes for being listened to or heard. Indeed many teachers feel that young people have been superficially taught about their rights, and are keen to push for what they want, without enough awareness of the reciprocal nature of rights or a notion of rights and responsibilities. This links back to the lack of proper in-school structured teaching about rights, and is impeding opportunities for students to express themselves. Those with grievances, such as poor food, often strike and demonstrate, sometimes violently; however, the more demanding skills of advocacy, such as engaging with local government and power holders, seem to be outside their experience.

The local teacher training college has developed a process of institutional discussion and participation in which the students can have a positive impact on college improvement. When these trainees become primary school teachers, they may be more disposed to encourage real student participation. Some school clubs are providing a context for peacebuilding skills development: in the form of discussion and action planning. They are involved in sensitization of issues like girls' education using music, dance and drama. They go into local communities with messages of anti-stigmatization. However, these groups need constant refreshment by NGOs to prevent their gradual decline.

Peacebuilding education aimed at 'positive peace' requires people to be educated to take their future into their own hands, through an understanding of the possibilities and constraints of local and national politics. The 'active citizen' is not simply the recipient of orders and controls. Participation skills can be developed at an early age, and school is the public arena for such development. A valuable step for all schools in post-conflict areas would be to establish methods for listening to young people's considered views, both in formal settings such as school councils, and through informal groups. Most teachers in the schools I visited have a good relationship with their students, and are used to listening to them, so the conditions are ripe for further development.

Conclusion

In the aftermath of this long and destructive war, the people of Northern Uganda need a sense of dignity and hope that they are part of a national project to create an open and fair society, in other words 'positive peace' (Galtung, 1969, 1985). Education has an important part to play in this, first of all through basic provision and access. Until now a major challenge has been the return of displaced schools to their home sites, the building of classrooms and latrines, and achieving adequate staffing levels. These goals have not yet been achieved, and they place significant obstacles in the path of peacebuilding education.

I have argued that schools could contribute to positive peace through their formal and non-formal curriculum and school culture. Young people can become active citizens through a synthesis of knowledge, values and skills. In the schools studied, children have learned about a limited range of rights but largely indirectly from NGOs and not from the formal school curriculum. When the NGOs reduce their activities in the region this learning may be lost to a new generation. Schools are fostering the value of forgiveness but are less effective in inculcating fairness and equal dignity. They are providing opportunities for action in keeping peaceful order, in problem solving and sensitization about girls' education, but they give little chance for organized democratic participation in school.

Education for positive peace in this region would be improved by:

1. A coherent curriculum that teaches all pupils at upper primary level the essentials of the local and national law and politics, the global human rights system, and the relationship between rights and responsibilities.
2. Greater teacher adherence to the code of conduct, a commitment to fairness and equality at every level, and the final formal abolition of corporal punishment.
3. Thorough training of prefects who help keep order in schools so that everyday disputes are handled fairly, with due process.
4. A concerted effort to adapt the authoritarian school culture so that the learners can have a voice that is really listened to, and can learn democratic participation from an early age.
5. Revision of the teacher training curriculum to incorporate the knowledge, values and skills that have thus far been fostered through a high level of NGO involvement in the district.

Unless young people are educated better in how to be active citizens with a stake in the future, there will always be a risk of, at worst, a future outbreak of rebellion against central government, and, at best, a region that will be unable to reduce structural violence.

Notes

[1] For example, Convention on Civil and Political Rights, Convention on Economic and Social Rights, Convention on the Rights of the Child.

[2] See also Article 29(b) of the Convention on the Rights of the Child, which commits states to direct education towards respect for human rights and fundamental freedoms.

[3] Lee (1985) describes an 'Asian attitude to human rights': 'Different civilizations or societies have different conceptions of human well-being, hence they have a different attitude to human rights issues' (p. 131). The Iranian representative to the UN in 1981 described the United Nations Human Development Report as a secular understanding of the Judeo-Christian tradition, which could not be followed without a direct contradiction with Islam (Littman, 1999).

[4] I took verbatim notes of a speech by a presidential official to secondary school leavers offering free military training in the gap between school and university, in which he promised them they would be able to shoot a rifle with live ammunition. He also implied that such training might become compulsory.

[5] For an evaluation report of this programme see: http://www.stsinternational.org/Research_reports_instl_mats/STS_report_REPLICA-Uganda_evaluation_Creative_Associates_final.pdf

[6] Interview with David Okidi, the station manager.

[7] This subject is being withdrawn, ostensibly to simplify the curriculum in preparation for 'universal secondary education', which leaves the secondary curriculum with even less content relating to politics and participation.

[8] The one group which did not refer to unfairness was from the teachers' training college.

[9] Evidence from interviews with NGO officers.

References

Ali, T. & Matthews, R. (Eds) (2004) *Durable Peace: challenges for peacebuilding in Africa.* Toronto: University of Toronto Press.

Arthur, J. & Wright, D. (2001) *Teaching Citizenship in the Secondary School.* London: David Fulton.

Baines, E. (2007) The Haunting of Alice: local approaches to justice and reconciliation in Northern Uganda, *International Journal of Transitional Justice*, 1(1), 91-114.

Baxter, P. (2000) *Teacher Activity Book – peace education programme.* Geneva: United Nations High Commission for Refugees.

Behrend, H. (1999) *Alice Lakwena and the Holy Spirits: war in Northern Uganda 1986-97.* Oxford: James Currey.

Benn, R. (2000) The Genesis of Active Citizenship in the Learning Society, *Studies in the Education of Adults*, 32(2), 242-256.

Blau, J. & Moncada, A. (2005) *Human Rights: beyond the liberal vision.* Oxford: Rowman & Littlefield.

Borer, T. (Ed.) (2006) *Telling the Truths: truth telling and peace building in post-conflict societies.* Notre Dame: University of Notre Dame Press.

Boulding, E. (2000) *Cultures of Peace: the hidden side of history.* Syracuse: Syracuse University Press.

Buckland, P. (2005) *Reshaping the Future: education and postconflict reconstruction.* Washington, DC: World Bank.

Bush, K. & Saltarelli, D. (Eds) (2000) *The Two Faces of Education in Ethnic Conflict: towards a peacebuilding education for children.* Florence: Innocenti Research Centre.

Carlton, E. (1995) *Values and the Social Sciences.* London: Duckworth.

Civil Society Organizations for Peace in Northern Uganda (CSOPNU) (2006) *Counting the Cost: twenty years of war in Northern Uganda.* http://www.oxfam.org/sites/www.oxfam.org/files/uganda.pdf (accessed 16 April 2010).

Crick, B. (2000) Introduction to the New Curriculum, in D. Lawton, J. Cairns & R. Gardner (Eds) *Education for Citizenship.* London: Continuum.

Cunningham, J. (1991) The Human Rights Secondary School, in H. Starkey (Ed.) *The Challenge of Human Rights Education.* London: Cassell.

Cunningham, J. (2000) Democratic Practice in a Secondary School, in A. Osler (Ed.) *Citizenship and Democracy in Schools: diversity, identity, equality.* London: Trentham Books.

David, C. (2002) Does Peacebuilding Build Peace? in H.-W. Jeong (Ed.) *Approaches to Peacebuilding.* New York: Palgrave Macmillan.

Davies, L. (2004) *Education and Conflict: complexity and chaos*. London: Routledge.

Duerr, K., Spajic-Vrka, V. & Martins, I (2000) *Strategies for Learning Democratic Citizenship*. Strasbourg: Council of Europe.

Frost, M. (1996) *Ethics in International Relations: a constitutive theory*. Cambridge: Cambridge University Press.

Galtung, J. (1969) Violence, Peace and Peace Research, *Journal of Peace Research*, 6, 167-191.

Galtung, J. (1985) Twenty-Five Years of Peace Research, *Journal of Peace Research*, 22, 141-158.

Gamarnikov, E. & Green, A. (2000) Citizenship, Education and Social Capital, in D. Lawton, J. Cairns & R. Gardner (Eds) *Education for Citizenship*. London: Continuum.

Gibney, M.J. (Ed.) (2003) *Globalizing Rights: the Oxford Amnesty Lectures 1999*. Oxford: Oxford University Press.

Government of Uganda (2007) *Peace Recovery and Development Plan for Northern Uganda*. Kampala: Government of Uganda. http://www.ugandaclusters.ug/dwnlds/0502Programs/PRDP/PRDPSept2007.pdf (accessed 19 May 2010).

Griffiths, R. (1998) *Educational Citizenship and Independent Learning*. London: Jessica Kingsley.

Gurr, T. (2000) *People versus States: minorities at risk in the new century*. Washington, DC: US Institute of Peace Press.

Halpern, D. (1998) Teaching Critical Thinking for Transfer across Domains, *American Psychologist*, 53(4), 449-455.

Hanlon, J. (2006) 200 Wars and the Humanitarian Response, in H. Yanacopulos & J. Hanlon (Eds) *Civil War, Civil Peace*. Oxford: James Currey.

Harber, C. (1998) Political Culture, Education and Democratic Citizenship in Africa, in O. Ichilov (Ed.) *Citizenship and Citizenship Education in a Changing World*. London: Woburn Press.

Harber, C. (2004) *Schooling as Violence: how schools harm pupils and societies*. London: Routledge.

Hofstede, G. (2001) *Culture's Consequences*. Thousand Oaks: Sage.

Inglehart, R. & Welzel, C. (2005) *Modernization, Cultural Change and Democracy*. Cambridge: Cambridge University Press.

International Network for Education in Emergencies (INEE) (2007) *Peace Education Programme*. http://www.ineesite.org/page.asp?pid=1062 (accessed 19 February 2009).

Jeong, H.-W. (2005) *Peacebuilding in Postconflict Societies*. London: Lynne Rienner.

Jones, T. (2005) Implementing Community Peace and Safety Networks in South Africa, *Theory into Practice*, 44(4), 345-354.

Kerr, D. (2000) Citizenship: an international comparison, in D. Lawton, J. Cairns & R. Gardner (Eds) *Education for Citizenship*. London: Continuum.

Kostelny, K. (2008) *Psychosocial and Protection Outcomes of Child Centred Spaces: research on young children in Northern Uganda*. Richmond: Christian Children's Fund.

Lederach, J. (1997) *Building Peace: sustainable reconciliation in divided societies.* Washington, DC: US Institute of Peace Press.

Lederach, J. (2005) *The Moral Imagination: the art and soul of building peace.* Oxford: Oxford University Press.

Lee, M. (1985) North Korea and the Western Notion of Human Rights, in J. Hsiung (Ed.) *Human Rights in East Asia: a cultural perspective.* New York: Paragon House.

Littman, D. (1999) Universal Human Rights and Human Rights in Islam, *Midstream Magazine*, 2, 2-7.

Lockyer, A., Crick, B. & Annette, J. (Eds) (2003) *Education for Democratic Citizenship: issues of theory and practice.* Aldershot: Ashgate.

Lord, J. & Flowers, N. (2006) Human Rights Education and Grassroots Peacebuilding, in J. Mertus & J. Helsing (Eds) *Human Rights and Conflict: exploring the links between rights, law and peacebuilding.* Washington, DC: US Institute of Peace Press.

Mamdani, M. (2001) *When Victims Become Killers: colonialism, nativism and the genocide in Rwanda.* Princeton: Princeton University Press.

Motani, Y. (2007) The Emergence of Global Citizenship in Japan, in B. Levinson & D. Stevick (Eds) *Re-imagining Civic Education.* Lanham: Rowman & Littlefield.

Oberschall, A. (2007) *Conflict and Peace Building in Divided Societies: responses to ethnic violence.* London: Routledge.

Obura, A. (2002) *Peace Education Programme in Dadaab and Kakuma, Kenya: evaluation summary.* Geneva: United Nations High Commission for Refugees.

Osler, A. & Starkey, H. (1996) *Teacher Education and Human Rights.* London: David Fulton.

Osler, A. & Starkey, H. (2005) *Changing Citizenship: democracy and inclusion in education.* Buckingham: Open University Press.

Osler, A., Rathenau, H-R. & Starkey, H. (Eds) (1995) *Teaching for Citizenship in Europe.* London: Trentham Books.

Reardon, B. (2000) Peace Education: a review and a projection, in R. Moon, M. Ben-Peretz & S. Brown (Eds) *Routledge International Companion to Education.* London: Routledge.

Robinson, J. (2007) *Listening to Youth: the experiences of young people in Northern Uganda.* New York: Women's Commission for Refugee Women and Children.

Schwartz, S. (1992) Universals in the Content and Structure of Values: theoretical advances and empirical tests in 20 countries, *Advances in Experimental Social Psychology*, 25, 1-65.

Sen, A. (2009) *The Idea of Justice.* London: Allen Lane.

Tomlinson, K. & Benefield, P. (2005) *Education and Conflict: research and research possibilities.* Slough: National Foundation for Educational Research.

United Nations (UN) (1945) *Universal Declaration of Human Rights.* http://www.un.org/events/humanrights/udhr60/index.shtml (accessed 14 March 2009).

United Nations (UN) (2005) *World Programme for Human Rights Education.* http://www2.ohchr.org.english/issues/education/training/programme.htm (accessed 6 October 2008).

United Nations Children's Fund (UNICEF) (2010) *United Nations Convention on the Rights of the Child.* http://www.unicef.org.uk/tz/rights/convention.asp (accessed 15 April 2010).

Wessells, M. (2005) Child Soldiers, Peace Education and Postconflict Reconstruction for Peace, *Theory into Practice*, 44, 363-369.

World Corporal Punishment Research (2010) http://www.corpun.com/rules3.htm#uganda (accessed 15 April 2010).

Notes on Contributors

Alastair Ager, PhD, is Professor of Clinical Population and Family Health in the Mailman School of Public Health, Columbia University, New York, USA. He has worked in the field of global health and development for over twenty years, after originally training in psychology at the universities of Keele, Wales and Birmingham in the United Kingdom. He was head of the Department of Psychology at the University of Malawi from 1989 until 1992, and subsequently served as Foundation Director of the Institute of International Health and Development at Queen Margaret University College, Edinburgh. Immediately before joining Columbia he was Senior Research Manager for the UK Department for International Development. He has wide international experience as a lecturer, researcher and consultant across sub-Saharan Africa, South Asia, Europe and North America, working with a range of intergovernmental, non-governmental and governmental agencies. In 2009 he was appointed as Executive Director of the Global Health Initiative based at the Mailman School of Public Health. He is author of over one hundred scholarly publications. He served as Research Director of the Care and Protection of Children in Crisis initiative through which the research reported in this volume was conducted.

Stephanie E.L. Bengtsson is a doctoral candidate in International Educational Development at Teachers College, Columbia University, New York, USA. Her research interests include inclusive education, humanitarian aid and development, the relationship between global and local forces in educational settings, and educational policy discourse within the field of development. She has worked as an education consultant and researcher for UNICEF and the Inter-Agency Network for Education in Emergencies (INEE). She has also served as the coordinator of the Center for African Education at Teachers College. She holds an AB in English Literature from Harvard University, and an MPhil in International Perspectives on Special and Inclusive Education from the University of Cambridge, United Kingdom.

Neil Boothby, EdD, is the Allan Rosenfield Professor of Clinical Forced Migration and Health at Columbia University's Mailman School of Public Health, New York, USA. His research has focused on the effects of armed conflict and violence on children in Cambodia (1980-82), Mozambique (1988-2005), Guatemala (1983-86), former Yugoslavia (1992-93), Rwanda (1994-96), Darfur (2005-present), Palestine (2001-present), Sri Lanka, (2002-present), and Indonesia (1999-present). Boothby is also Director of the Program on Forced Migration and Health at the Mailman School of Public Health, and is the Principal Investigator of several research projects. One of these projects – the Care and Protection of Children (CPC) Interagency Learning Network – is a constellation of more than 75 agencies working worldwide on the development of an evidence base for efficacious child protection programming in war, disaster and post-crises settings. Boothby has published extensive on children and war concerns, and also has received a number of awards for his fieldwork, including the Red Cross Humanitarian of the Year Award and the UN's Global Achievement Award for Excellence in the Social Sector.

Colin Brock is UNESCO Chair in Education as a Humanitarian Response and Senior Research Fellow at the Department of Education, University of Oxford, United Kingdom. A graduate in geography and anthropology, he taught in high schools for 10 years before becoming a lecturer in geography at the University of Reading. An unexpected secondment to the Overseas Development Agency (now the Department for International Development) found him as Education Adviser in the Caribbean Development Division of the Foreign and Commonwealth Office. On his return to the United Kingdom he moved into the world of international educational development through appointments at the universities of Leeds, Hull and Oxford. He has been fortunate to work in most major areas of the developing world for multilateral and bilateral agencies and has published widely in this field.

Jeremy Cunningham is a former UK state secondary school head teacher, and a doctoral student at the Open University. His practical experience in the development of citizenship education and student participation, and the establishment of school links with African schools, led to an awareness of the huge challenges facing African students, teachers and heads in the aftermath of violent conflict. He has published chapters on democracy in school, developed curriculum materials for Amnesty International, and is a former editor of the *World Studies Journal*.

Betty Akullu Ezati is a lecturer in the Department of Educational Foundations and Management, School of Education, Makerere University, Uganda. She teaches history of education, research methodology and gender and education. She holds a Higher Diploma in educational policy analysis from the University of Alberta, Canada, a Master of Education focusing on teacher education and a PhD focusing on gender and education from Makerere University. She also participated in a project that designed online courses to assist secondary school teachers in resources limited areas. She trains academic staff at the university level in pedagogy and andragogy skills. For the last three years she had spearheaded a collaborative research project on education in post-conflict areas with a focus on Northern Uganda. The collaboration with the partners (Queen's University Belfast, Northern Ireland, Kigali Institute of Education, Rwanda, and Fourah Bay College, Sierra Leone) has enabled her to gain more insights into possible strategies teachers can adopt in post-conflict teaching and learning situations. Her research interest includes gender and education (education of minorities), indigenous knowledge education and conflict, teacher education and children's rights and higher education.

Mitsuko Matsumoto is a doctoral candidate at the Department of Education, University of Oxford, United Kingdom. Her doctoral project explores the relationship between education and conflict, based on an empirical case of Sierra Leone where she has conducted seven months of fieldwork. In addition, her research interests range to peace education and research capacity development in developing countries, in particular West and Central Africa, in which she has received Master's degrees at the University of Oxford and Teachers College, Columbia University, New York, USA. She had previously worked for the UN Liaison Office of Soka Gakkai International (SGI), a Buddhist association that promotes peace, culture and education. Besides working with UN agencies, other organizations and individuals, she had led workshops, titled 'Victory over Violence', promoting values and behaviours based on the philosophy of non-violence to pupils at various schools in New York city.

Maureen Murphy, MPH, is the Coordinator for the Care and Protection of Children in Crisis-Affected Countries Learning Network (CPC Learning Network) based at Columbia University's Program on Forced Migration and Health in New York, USA. Previously she worked with the American Refugee Committee International as a member of their International Programs Team and, most recently, was the Head of Office for their Eastern Equatorial Office in Southern Sudan. Maureen has also worked with the Agency for Technical Cooperation and Development in Tajikistan and International Planned Parenthood's East, Southeast Asia and Oceanic Regional Office in Kuala Lumpur, Malaysia. She holds a Master's degree in Public Health from Columbia University and has a professional interest in improving monitoring and evaluation of humanitarian relief programmes, particularly in the realm of reproductive health and gender-based violence programming.

Tomoe Otsuki is a PhD candidate at the Ontario Institute for Studies in Education of the University of Toronto. Her doctoral studies pursue how historical remembrance serves as pedagogical praxis for a more democratic society and future possibilities. Her research areas are the pedagogy of commemoration practices, of testimonies of the survivors of atrocities, East Asia's history textbooks controversy, and the politics of collective memory and national identity in East Asia. Otsuki's doctoral dissertation traces the genealogy of the dominant discourse, 'Hiroshima rages, Nagasaki prays' and investigates how this atomic bomb discourse was produced and established through a process of exclusion of other voices, erasure of the remnants of the bomb, and the imposition of the act of praying upon the body of Nagasaki's atomic bomb victims and citizens.

Christine Pagen has engaged in the theories and practices of education and development in and after conflict through academic and practical work with organizations such as the Inter-Agency Network for Education in Emergencies, USAID, UNICEF, the United Nations Office for the Coordination of Humanitarian Affairs, and Search for Common Ground. Her field experience includes the countries of Afghanistan, Sudan, Kazakhstan, and Pakistan. Christine holds a PhD in Comparative International Education and Political Science from Columbia University, New York, USA and an MA in International Educational Development from Teachers College, Columbia University.

Julia Paulson is a doctoral researcher at the University of Oxford and a part-time lecturer at Bath Spa University. Her research focuses on post-conflict educational policy making, transitional justice and reconciliation. She is editor of *Education and Reconciliation: exploring conflict and post-conflict situations* to be published by Continuum in 2011, and General Editor of the Oxford Transitional Justice Research Working Papers Series. Julia has worked as a consultant with the Inter-Agency Network for Education in Emergencies, the International Center for Transitional Justice, UNICEF and UNESCO.

Jeremy Rappleye recently completed his doctoral studies at the University of Oxford, United Kingdom and is now a JSPS Special Research Fellow at the University of Tokyo, Japan. He has written extensively on the themes of transfer and external influence on domestic education policy formation in an era of globalization. His recent work on Nepal includes co-editing a Special Issue of the journal *Globalisation, Societies, and Education* entitled 'Education Reform in Nepal: from modernity to conflict' (2010). He is currently undertaking research for a full-length book on Nepal along similar lines. That volume will be published in early 2012 and is co-authored with Professor Stephen Carney.

Cornelius Ssempala is a lecturer at the School of Education, Makerere University, Uganda. He lectures in Sociology and Philosophy of Education. He holds a PhD in education from the United Kingdom. His research area covers education and conflict, teacher professional ethics and child rights (education of minorities). For the last three years he has participated in a collaborative research project on education in post-conflict areas with a focus on Northern Uganda. He has undertaken research in teacher education, especially professional ethics. The collaboration with the partners (Queen's University Belfast, Northern Ireland, Kigali Institute of Education, Rwanda, and Fourah Bay College, Sierra Leone) has enabled him to gain more insights into education in post-conflict areas.

Peter Ssenkusu is a lecturer in the Department of Foundations and Management, School of Education, Makerere University, Uganda. He is currently undertaking a PhD focusing on civil violence and primary school leadership in Northern Uganda (1986-2007). He also has an International Advanced Diploma in child rights, classroom and school management from Lund University, Sweden. His areas of interest are education and civil violence, child rights, and school management.

Lindsay Stark, MPH, DrPH is Professor at Columbia University, New York, USA in the Program on Forced Migration and Health. Her work focuses on developing and piloting new methodologies to measure protection concerns and program response. She has helped pioneer the development of instruments such as the Neighborhood Method to assess incidence of human rights violations and a Participatory Ranking Method that has been included as part of both the World Health Organization Assessment Tool Kit and the Inter-agency Child Protection Assessment Resource Kit. Dr Stark has led assessment and evaluation projects in Africa, Asia and the Middle East with a range of UN, government and NGO partners. She is currently Director of Research and Curriculum for the newly established Center on Child Protection in Indonesia – a collaboration between Columbia University, the University of Indonesia and UNICEF.

Michael Wessells, PhD, is Professor at Columbia University, New York, USA in the Program on Forced Migration and Health and Professor Emeritus at Randolph-Macon College. He has served as President of the Division of Peace Psychology of the American Psychological Association and of Psychologists for Social Responsibility and as Co-Chair of the InterAction Protection Working Group. He is former Co-Chair of the Inter-Agency Standing Committee (UN-NGO) Task Force on Mental Health and Psychosocial Support in Emergency Settings which developed the first inter-agency, consensus guidelines for the field of mental health and psychosocial support in humanitarian crises. Currently, he is co-focal point on mental health and psychosocial support for the revision of the Sphere humanitarian standards. He has conducted extensive research on the holistic impacts of war and political violence on children, and he is author of *Child Soldiers: from violence to protection* (Harvard University Press, 2006). He regularly advises UN agencies, governments, and donors on issues of psychosocial support. Throughout Africa and Asia, he helps to develop community-based, culturally grounded programs that assist people affected by armed conflict.